excellence in

Global Supply Chain Management

Understanding and Improving Global Supply Chains

excellence in
Global Supply Chain Management

Understanding and Improving Global Supply Chains

Stuart Emmett & Barry Crocker

ISBN 1-903-499-55-0
978-1-903499-55-9

Printed and bound in the United Kingdom by
4edge Ltd, 7a Eldon Way Industrial Estate, Hockley, Essex, SS5 4AD.

Contents

About this book

This book complements the other **Excellence in...** titles, for example, in Procurement, in Supplier Management, in Supply Chain Management, in Inventory, in Freight Transport, Services Procurement, and Warehouse Management.

The real fact today is that we do actually live "in a global village" where many countries' former self-sufficiency has now moved onto a global stage. We can now find that distance impacts from local sources can soon grow into global problems. Witness for example, the increased price of steel around 2005 and the economic recession that started in the USA in 2008, which by early 2009 had adversely affected most global trade.

Managing supply, demand and consumer markets from global perspectives therefore involves dealing with constant change and increased volatility. It also requires a new understanding of culture and different ways of doing things. No longer are organisations able to assume their national values; new processes can be enforced, or are going to be automatically adapted globally.

We practically explore, in this book, how to manage such differences; this book is not about the debate on whether going global is good/bad from a green and sustainability aspect. Other books, including "Green Supply Chains" (2010) by Emmett and Sood cover this topic.

In writing this book, we have endeavoured not to include anything that if used, would be injurious or cause financial loss to the user. The user is however strongly recommended before applying or using any of the contents, to check and verify their own organisation policy/requirements. No liability will be accepted by the authors for the use of any of the contents.

It can also happen in a lifetime of learning and meeting people, that the original source of an idea or information has been forgotten. If we have actually omitted in this book to give anyone credit they are due, we apologise and hope they will make contact so we can correct the omission in future editions.

About the authors

Barry Crocker
I am a lecturer in the Salford Business School at the University of Salford and am currently the Programme Leader for the MSc Procurement, Logistics and MSc Supply Chain Management. Previously, I had many years industrial experience in various management positions in the field of transport, warehousing and physical distribution.

I have also been an assistant chief examiner for the professional stage of the CIPS Diploma; an external examiner for several universities, and am currently external examiner for Leeds Metropolitan University.

My previous publications include, as co-author with Stuart, The Relationship Driven Supply Chain (2006), Excellence in Procurement (2008), Excellence in Supplier Management (2009) and Excellence in Services Procurement (2009) and with Bailey, Farmer, Jessop and Jones Procurement Principles and Management (2008). I have conducted many training sessions for multinationals in Africa, the Middle East, the Far East and Russia in the field of Procurement, Logistics and Supply Chain Management. Many of these were undertaken with co-authors, David and Stuart.

I would like to give special thanks to my lady, the lovely Rosalind, without whom this book would not have been possible.

Stuart Emmett

After spending over 30 years in commercial private sector service industries, working in the UK and in Nigeria, I then moved in Training. This was associated with the, then, Institute of Logistics and Distribution Management (now the Chartered Institute of Logistics and Transport).

After being a Director of Training for nine years, I then choose to become a freelance independent mentor/coach, trainer and consultant. This built on my past operational and strategic experience and my particular interest in the "people issues" of management processes.

Trading under the name of Learn and Change Limited, I now enjoy working all over the UK and on five other continents, principally in Africa and the Middle East, but also in the Far East and North and South America.

Additional to undertaking training, I also am involved with one to one coaching/ mentoring, consulting, writing, assessing and examining for professional institutes' qualifications. This has included being Chief Examiner on the Graduate Diploma of the Chartered Institute of Procurement and Supply and as an external university examiner for an MSc in Procurement and Logistics.

My previous publications include, as co-author with Barry, The Relationship Driven Supply Chain (2006), Excellence in Procurement (2008), Excellence in Services Procurement (2009) and Excellence in Supplier Management (2009).

Other titles include Improving Learning & for Individuals & Organisations (2002), Supply Chain in 90 minutes (2005), Excellence in Warehouse Management (2005), Excellence in Inventory Management (2007, co-written with David Granville), Excellence in Supply Chain Management (2008), Excellence in Freight Transport (2009), Green Supply Chains (2010, co-written with Vivek Sood) and a series of seven Business Improvement Toolkits (2008) with individual titles on motivation, learning, personal development, customer service, communications, systems thinking and teams. Whilst these toolkits are written for a general audience, the case studies and examples have many supply chain applications.

I am married to the lovely Christine and with two adult cute children, Jill and James; James is married to Mairead, who is also cute. We are additionally the proud grandparents of three girls (the totally gorgeous twins Megan and Molly and their younger sister, Niamh).

I can be contacted at stuart@learnandchange.com or by visiting www.learnandchange. com. I do welcome any comments.

1: Introduction to Supply Chain Management

The Supply Chain: an introduction

The term Supply Chain refers to the process which integrates, co-ordinates and controls the movement of goods, materials and information from a supplier through a series of customers to the final consumer. The essential point with a supply chain is that it links all the activities between suppliers and customers to the consumer in a timely manner. Supply chains therefore involve the activities of buying/sourcing, making, moving, and selling.

The supply chain "takes care of organisation" following on from the initial customer/ consumer demand. Nothing happens with supply until there is an order; it is the order that drives the whole process. Indeed, some people logically argue that the term supply chain could be called the demand chain.

So the Supply Chain bridges the gap between the core aspects of Supply & Demand, as shown below:

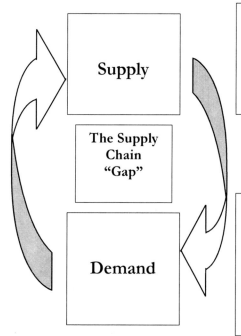

Supply

The Supply Chain "Gap"

Demand

For example: When is the product made?

Where is it made? Which suppliers?

How much and how many are required?

How and when is it delivered?

For example: When is the product required?

Where is it needed?

How many and when are needed?

What is the mix required? How is it required?

What distribution network to use?

The philosophy of Supply Chain Management is to view all these processes as being related holistically so that they:

- Integrate, co-ordinate and control,
- the movement of materials, inventory and information,
- from suppliers through a organisation to meet all the customer's and the ultimate consumer's requirements,
- in a timely manner

A diagrammatic view follows, where it will be seen that the flows of products and the flows of information are represented by ideas, order creation, and cash/orders:

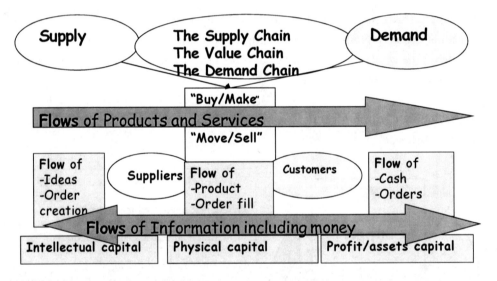

In the above diagram:

- The demand chain represents the creation of demand, for example, marketing and selling with product development.
- The supply chain represents fulfilment, for example, procurement and buying, production and making, with distribution and moving.
- The value chain represents performance, for example, financial measures and capital.

The activities of Buying-Making-Moving and Selling take place in the operational functions of Purchasing, Production, Distribution and Marketing. If each of these functions were to work independently, then inventory stock levels will increase not only internally, but also across the supply chains that feed in and out from an organisation.

It is also important to realise that each organisation has not one supply chain, but many, as it deals with different suppliers and has different customers. For each individual finished product or line item, whilst some of the buying, making, moving and selling processes will be identical or very similar, the total supply chain for each product will be different and will involve often a complex network. This also goes, for example, far beyond the first supplier and includes the supplier's supplier, then that supplier's supplier and so on.

Many organisations in their supply chain management do not work on the supply chain in this way and often stop with the first level supplier; they seem to forget that the supply chain is effectively a large network of supplier/customer players.

Multiple and Globalised Supply Chains

As supply chains vary, the term "multiple supply chain management" perhaps becomes a better description – but it is a cumbersome one. At a simple level, consider the following globally-reaching supply chain (part only) for Lee Cooper jeans:

Customers: Worldwide, who buy from agents, wholesalers and retailers who have received finished products from a factory in Tunisia that gets supplies of:
- Denim cloth from Italy, which uses dye from West Germany and cotton from Benin, West Africa and Pakistan.
- Zips from West Germany, which use wire for the teeth from Japan and polyester tape from France.
- Thread from Northern Ireland, which uses dye from Spain and fibre from Japan.
- Rivets and Buttons from USA, which use zinc from Australia and copper from Namibia.
- Pumice (used in stonewashing) from Turkey.

The example above shows that, with supply chain management, therefore, there are many different supply chains to manage. These supply chain networks will contain organisations from all the main following sectors; many of these will be globally located:
- **Primary sector:** Raw materials from farming/fishing (food, beverages, and forestry), quarrying/mining (minerals, coals, metals) or drilling (oil, gas, water).

- **Secondary sector:** Conversion of raw materials into products: milling, smelting, extracting, refining into oils/chemicals/products; and machining, fabricating, moulding, assembly, mixing, processing, constructing into components, sub-assemblies, building construction/structures and furniture/electronic/food/paper/metal/chemicals and plastic products.
- **Service or tertiary sector:** organisations, personal and entertainment services, which involve the channels of distribution from suppliers to customers, via direct, wholesale or retail channels. Services include packaging, physical distribution, hotels, catering, banking, insurance, finance, education, public sector, post, telecoms, retail, repairs etc.

Organisations will thus have many supply chains, both internally and externally, that interact through a series of simple and/to complex networks.

Of course, these networks can be domestic, international or global in reach – as Ronald Reagan once famously said, "We now live in a global village."

Flows of Materials, Information and Money

In organising the material flows from any national, international or global locations, the following is required:
- Forecasting of the demand requirements.
- Sourcing and buying from vendors/suppliers. At some stage, in this "supply cycle", there will be a manufacturer/producer involved. These may possibly be well down the supply chain when the supplier is an agent, a "trader" or a wholesaler or some other kind of "middle person".
- Transport.
- Receiving, handling, warehousing, and possibly storage.

The material flows are triggered by information, as information is needed for decision-making. Information is also used to:
- Implement other activities.
- Plan.
- Organise.
- Direct and co-ordinate.
- Control.

Information flows therefore link internal organisation activities, and also link external suppliers and customers. Effective information, communication technology (ICT) will process orders, track and trace progress and provide timely and real-time visibility. The supply cycle information loop covers:

- Forecasts.
- Buying.
- Purchase order and transactions.
- Stock information.
- The demand or customer cycle information loop covering:
  o stock information
  o replenishment and picking/order assembly
  o transport and delivery
  o invoicing
  o payment

The integration of the supply and demand information loops leads to an integrated system.

It can also be seen that money flows are involved, as information integrates materials and money flows. The design of the supply chain will determine the following monetary aspects:

- Asset investment, for example, this is minimised by outsourcing.
- Inventory holding and carrying costs, for example, from decisions on stock holding policy.
- Debtors balances, for example, the customer order cycle times.
- Creditor balance, for example, from holding lower stock levels.
- Exchange rate variations from non-domestic trade, for example by balancing the material flows.

It is in the planning, organising and controlling of these "total/whole/holistic" materials, information and money flows, in which supply chain management will provide competitive advantage.

This is why Professor Martin Christopher noted that 'the future is one of competing interdependent supply chains, and not one of individual organisations operating independently'. Individual organisations therefore need to work together to manage the flows. These flows are determined by demand; therefore demand "pulls" the product, in turn meaning flexible responses are needed "upstream" to satisfy the "downstream" information flow demand. Supplier bases may therefore have to be rationalised, as not all will be able to provide any new requirements for flexible, on time, in full deliveries; this is a requirement for demand driven supply chains.

Start at "home"

The starting point however, must firstly be to examine the internal supply chain. Too many organisations start with Supply Chain Management (with much time and effort), by working only with the closest suppliers and customers. They should, however, first ensure that all their internal operations and activities are integrated, co-ordinated and controlled. Organisations should ask their suppliers and customers whether their internal supply chain is working well; they may be surprised by the answer.

Reorganising internally means ensuring that, for example, production, procurement, logistics, marketing or whatever are the functions involved do not operate as shown below:

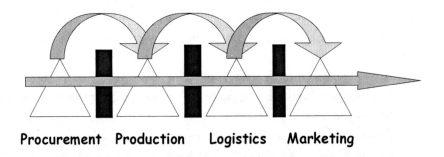

Procurement   Production   Logistics   Marketing

Here, we see that there are effectively walls between each function, creating a barrier to the flows of goods and information. Instead of these flowing smoothly and horizontally across the functions, they are actually being "thrown over the wall", not only taking longer, but also increasing the chance of damage.

We therefore need to ensure that all internal operations and activities are integrated, co-ordinated and controlled, so that we have them working together and joined up, as shown opposite:

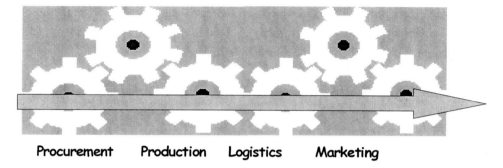

Procurement   Production   Logistics   Marketing

We will look later at how to get effective internal organisational structures.

Manage the inventory

In the supply chain, the flows of goods and information will need co-ordinating to minimise inventory levels. Levels of inventory that are too high can be viewed as the main negative symptom of a supply chain, and a root cause that needs treatment. Additionally, and as noted above, in supply chain management there are many different supply chains to manage, and these supply chains will usually contain organisations in many different sectors; all of these organisations in the network could have badly managed inventory.

As has been said, holding stock is an admission of defeat in supply chain management. Stockholding is anti-flow and can be analogous to water flowing. Water does not always flow evenly at the same pace along a stream. It sometimes gets trapped in deep pools, is blocked by rocks and other obstacles hidden below the surface. These rock and obstacles impede the smooth swift flows of the stream.

Here the stream represents the flow of goods and information in the supply chain. The pools of water are the inventory holdings, and the rocks/obstacles represent the waste in the process from poor quality, re-ordered goods, returned goods etc. If a stream is to flow fast and clear, then the rocks and obstacles have to be removed. To do this, the water (and inventory) level has to be lowered so that the rocks are exposed. Inventory can, in this sense, be seen to be hiding more fundamental problems, and as such can be seen as the "root of all evil" in the supply chain.

Inventory is, therefore, the common component that needs addressing throughout the Total Supply Chain. The format of inventory can include raw material, sub-assemblies, work in progress or finished goods (which are often held at multiple places in the supply chain). The format of inventory and where it is held is of common interest to all supply chain players and must therefore be jointly investigated and examined.

Case Study: Demand Solutions Helps Heineken USA Serve a Cold One

Heineken USA (HUSA) imports, markets, sells and distributes Heineken along with other premium beers in its expanding portfolio through a network of nearly 650 beer distributors throughout the USA. Easier said than done, this supply chain requires precise forecasts and meticulous planning.

Even with breweries on the other side of the Atlantic, long brewing lead-times and seasonal market demands, the organisation operates one of the best-performing supply chains in the industry. Forecast accuracy is a key enabler for HUSA in operating the supply chain that makes them the biggest container shipper on the trans-Atlantic.

As with most packaged consumer goods organisations, forecasting demand for a new product, big or small, is always a challenging process.

The Heineken supply chain management department faces an interesting challenge. Its physical supply network structure is optimized for logistics and does not align 1:1 with its sales-force organization as each of its six demand centres feed into several different sales zones.

Prior to implementing Demand Solutions, the HUSA supply chain staff had to manually map the forecasts built for the demand centres onto the sales zones in order to have a basis for discussions with the sales force.

"Now we map the sales region to the demand centres automatically, and we can view the data from the point of view of the network structure or the sales organization," says Setnes at Heineken.

"That is a huge advantage, especially in rolling out new products or supporting promotional programs. We are able to have conversations with the individual sales regions about expectations in a transparent way and track and report against progress and targets."

Managing a Forecast-Driven Supply Chain

The forecast from Demand Solutions provides the starting point for HUSA's conversations that make up the sales and operations planning. Through monthly meetings with the sales force in the field, the regional demand planners collect numbers, discuss trends and solicit information regarding upcoming programs and competitor activities.

"We ask sales what they think will happen, not what algorithms we should use," says Setnes. "If our competitors run promotions with large displays at retail - that will impact our sales. So we need to have these conversations and gather intelligence on what is happening in the field."

Working off their monthly sales forecasts, the regional demand planners update and tweak their forecast each week. Demand Solutions automatically maps the regional sales forecasts into a network forecast.

Every Thursday, Setnes and his team then send the consolidated demand-centre forecasts to the brewery in Amsterdam so it can update its planning for several months out.

Forward Thinking

With Demand Solutions operating smoothly, the team is improving methods of incorporating the forecasts into sales and supply chain planning. "Before, when our forecasts were tied to the demand centres, all the responsibility for their accuracy fell on the supply chain group," says Setnes.

"Now that we have the forecasts integrated into the sales-organization structure, we can achieve a much more collaborative approach and engage in good discussions on how we perform as a team."

"Our supply chain team has moved their forecasting process from the desk to a collaborative process; improving the information sharing and communication across operational, financial, marketing and sales departments," says Dan Sullivan, Chief Financial and Operating Officer at HUSA.

Local Knowledge

Heineken values local-level detail in traditional brewing recipes and in data collection. The organisation can now include and measure the performance of local detail all the way to the demand centres with Demand Solutions. That's important in an organisation where demand can change rapidly because of weather, pricing and media.

"Demand Solutions keeps a separate copy of your history, so you can remove items such as new product launches, one-off promotions and unseasonable weather to provide a clean history for predicting forward," says Setnes.

"This is especially helpful when you have introduced new products in the previous year. New product launches produce very noisy data because there is so much loading in at the distributors and retail level. We plan to take full advantage of Demand Solutions' separate historical records in our future planning."

Heineken's forecasts are in the thousands of pallets, but demand often occurs as a salesperson closes a deal for a few pallets a month. The organisation can now adapt to the multiple measurement units and has achieved a level of communication that did not exist prior to Demand Solutions.

"When we share numbers that are meaningful to sales, we have better conversations. They can see that the information they provide us helps keep the demand centres at the right level of stock to support their programs," says Setnes.

The numbers and facts that make Heineken USA the biggest containerized importer on the trans-Atlantic are as follows:

16: percent of the world's beer industry the U.S. represents
233: million hectolitres of beer U.S. citizens drink in an average year
1,501: million hectolitres of beer consumed globally each year
55 000: containers Holland ships to Heineken USA per year
40: the size in feet of the containers
1 000: the weekly average number of containers Heineken USA receives from Holland

8 to 14: the lead-time in days for beer to ship from the Netherlands to the East Coast

5: the lead-time in weeks for beer to ship from the Netherlands to the West Coast

Source: www.demandsolutions.com

Supply Chain History

In the UK, the history of the supply chain can be viewed as passing through three phases. With any such formalisation, there is overlap, but at least an ideal-typical view is provided below that enables key areas to be viewed more clearly.

Attribute	Functional Supply Chains	Responsive Supply Chains	Adaptive Supply Chains
	To the 1980s	**The 1990s**	**The Noughties**
Integration focus	Over the wall	Transactional	Collaboration
	Reactive/Quick fixes	Responsive	Decision/Proactive
	Monopoly suppliers	Competition in suppliers	Joined up networks of enterprises
Customer focus	Customer can wait	Customers wants it soon	Customer wants it now
	"You will get it when we can send it	"You will have it when you want it"	"You will get it"
Organisation focus	Departmental and ring fencing.	Intra-enterprise. "Internal" involvement.	Extended enterprise involvement.
Product positioning	Make to stock	Assemble to order	Make to order
	Decentralised stock holding	Centralised stock holding	Minimal stock holding
	Store then deliver	Collect and cross dock	Whatever is needed
Management approach	Hierarchical	Command and control	Collaborative

Technology focus	Point solution	ERP	Web connected
Time focus for the organisations	Weeks to months	Days to weeks	Real time
Performance focus	Cost	Cost and service	Revenue and profit
Collaboration	Low	Medium	High levels
Response times	Static	Medium	Dynamic

Meanwhile on a more general basis, IBM has the following Supply Chain Maturity Model that also shows developments and differences in using the supply chain philosophy.

	Static SC	Functional excellence SC	Horizontal integrated SC	External collaboration SC	On demand SC
Processes and products	Ad hoc processes. "Over the wall". Production is focussed on standard products.	Formalised processes. Limited market research.	Formal processes. Internal integration. Cross-functional teams.	Joint product designs with suppliers and customers. Co-ordinated product launches.	Formal integrated process with suppliers and customers
Customer Demand	Quarterly and manually produced plans. Frequent over and under stocks.	Some system generated planning. High inventory levels.	Forecast sharing with some suppliers. Internally integrated planning.	Customer "pull". Supplier partnerships. Daily planning.	Automatic adjustments to buying, making, and moving processes.
Buying	Unknown spend by commodity. No formal supplier relationships. All buying is done in house.	Master contracts with key suppliers. Central managed supply management.	Cross-functional leveraged buying. SLAs with key suppliers.	Integrated supply network. Several procurement functions are outsourced. Central sourcing organisation.	Virtual outsourced network. Visibility of orders, inventory, forecasts and shipments.

Customer fulfilment and logistics	Many logistics networks.	Some outsourcing of logistics.	Enterprise integration.	Integrated distribution network with customers.	Open network with rapid reconfiguration. Variable cost structures.
	No logistics outsourcing.	Different services to key customers.	Common use of outsourcing logistics and contract manufacturing.	Common outsourced partners.	All non-cores are outsourced.
		Some online customer ordering.	Cross-functional visibility. Differentiated services with customer segmentation.	Visibility on total order-to-order cash cycle. Demand driven with managed replenishment	End to end performance monitoring with alert exceptions.

The Benefits of a Supply Chain Management Approach

As has already been noted, competition in organisations can come not just from organisations competing against each other, but increasingly also from competing supply chains, where competitive advantage is to found by doing things better or by doing things more cheaply.

Looking for these advantages extends from within an organisation, towards the supply chains. This will mean looking to remove sub-functional conflicts from all the interdependent processes, whether these processes are internal or external to an organisation. Accordingly, it is the supply chain that now provides the competitive advantage for organisations.

This will in turn mean taking a total supply chain approach to examine and total the costs of all the functions, then matched to the service levels. If this is done, and by continuing to minimise the costs for each sub-function, then this could mean:

- Buying in bulk from multiple sources (only Purchasing is being optimised); but for example, this will lead to high storage costs.
- Making fewer products with long production runs (here only Production is being optimised); which means limited ranges, poor availability etc.
- Moving in bulk (only Transport being optimised); but gives infrequent delivery etc.

- Selling what is produced (only Marketing being optimised); but it may not be needed.

Supply chain structure and benefits

The way the supply chain is structured and managed is therefore critical - some reported benefits of adopting a supply chain approach follow. Significantly, it will be noted that different approaches give different results:

	No Supply Chain: Functional Silos	Internal Integrated Supply Chain	Plus, External Integration to the first level only
Inventory days of supply Indexed	100	78	62
Inventory carrying cost % sales	3.2%	2.1%	1.5%
On-time, in-full deliveries	80%	91%	95%
Profit % Sales	8%	11%	14%

It can be seen that, with a supply chain approach, inventory costs fall, as profit and the service fulfilment increases: the "best of both worlds" for the organisation undertaking the approach. This, however, must start internally ("win the home games first").

Working together internally within organisational structure

We noted earlier that there is a need to ensure that all internal operations and activities are "integrated, co-ordinated and controlled" so that we have them working together and joined up, as shown below:

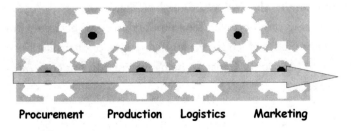

Procurement   Production   Logistics   Marketing

An organisation must therefore be appropriately structured towards, for example, a Cross-Functional Model (CFM) so that it is able to practice supply chain management effectively. There will be a need to remember peoples' career paths, and guard against having a matrix structure with potential for unclear accountability and in-fighting over responsibilities.

There is never an easy way to construct a CFM and it will need careful compromise on all of the following:

1) Organise around processes and not tasks

- Separate management from operational supervision. Management is generalised and at senior levels. Supervision is about the people actually doing the work.
- Operations may remain hierarchical and functional, reporting to (several) process-based managers.
- Operational supervisors will need training in Cross-Functional appreciation.

2) Flatten the hierarchy

- Organise the hierarchy according to the level and type of work and responsibility; and not the number of people. For example, warehouse operatives and courier vehicle drivers at ratios to management of 10 plus to 1 and 30 plus to 1 respectively.

3) Keep a team focus

- This encourages self-management.
- Ensure there are clear SMART objectives with the reward mechanism being the team performance.
- Develop multiple competencies.

4) More suppliers/customers contact

- Remember these are the next links in the process, irrespective of whether they are internal and external suppliers/customers.
- The customer is the only one who can give relevant feedback on how we do the job.

From some most useful approach research undertaken by R. I. van Hoek and A. J. Mitchell (2006), we have a summary of some action items needed to ensure internal alignment in organisations:

Peers
- Support exchange programmes and job rotations across functions.
- Invest and understand each other's problems and build relationships: capture the voice of other functions and be able to articulate plans in their language, not our jargon.
- Develop appropriate KPIs across functions; ensure that KPIs are linked or at least co-ordinated and are not driving conflicting behaviour.
- Joint problem solving teams to tackle common issues.

Individuals
- Trace and learn from the cause of lost orders — delivery time, price, specification.
- Encourage open communication.
- Avoid pointing blame.
- Visit & "see, smell, understand customers — get under their skin".
- Create regular dialogue between sales and supplying units.

Bosses
- Join sales on key customer visits to ensure you are close enough to the customer in driving the supply chain agenda and focusing efforts and service and be credible with sales when discussing service.
- Align goals between functions and link these to incentives.
- Encourage the use of the same language; avoid functional jargon and promote the use of organisation's language (profit, customers, service etc.).
- Support appropriate forecasting tools.
- Ensure that operations/supply chain people are seen to take action on old issues and communicates the results to other functions (don't forget to tell others what has been done, there is no way that others know when you don't tell them).

Teams
- Collaborate on common issues not functional pet-projects.
- Reach consensus on priorities; do not set a functional agenda but an organisation-wide focus that will engage peers.
- Work on improving accuracy of performance information and tell peers upfront when shipments are going to be late, do not surprise peers with bad events when they happen.

- Awareness training in supply chain and sales.
- Improve the initiative planning process to focus on essentials peers care most for mostly (service, execution, price etc.) and articulate initiatives in those terms.

Internal alignment is critical for effective supply chain management. However it is often external people, like suppliers and customers, who are the first to realise when this alignment is non-existent.

Working together externally

The additional benefits of supply chain management will only come when there is an examination of all costs/service levels together with all the external players with an aim to obtain reduced lead-times and improved total costs/service for all the parties in the network. This means, therefore, going beyond the first tier of suppliers and looking also at the supplier's supplier and so on. It represents more than data and process; it includes mutual interest, open relationships and sharing. The optimum and the "ideal" cost/service balance will only ever be found by working and collaborating with all players in the supply chain. This is an important topic and we shall come back to it later.

A key area here is to balance the service aspects with the costs. A significant part of organisation's cost will be found in the Supply Chain, and managing all of the flows of goods and information across the supply chain networks is therefore essential in bringing about the required cost/service balance: a big promise and often never an easy approach, but one that can result in the perfect ideals of:
- Increased/improved service, reaction times, product availability etc.
- Reduced/improved total cost, total stock levels, time to market etc.

Doing things differently can improve performance and where costs rise and market prices are unable to be increased, then a new style of supply chain management can be beneficial.

Lead-time

Lead-time is perhaps the critical component in supply chain management. However it is usually viewed incrementally and sub-optimally.

Just as time is cash, and cash flow is important to organisations, equally important are the associated flows of goods and information that have generated the cash flow in the first place. The cash-to-cash cycle time (C2C) is at the root of cash flow, and reducing the time from buying to the receipt of payment for sales is therefore critical.

What follows is a basic view of lead-time covering all the elements involved; first, by looking at the eight types of lead-time which is then followed by an analysis of the component parts of these eight types:

Lead-time	Action	By
Pre-order Planning	User	Customer
Procurement	Order placing	Customer to supplier
Supplier	Order despatching	Supplier
Production	Making to order	Supplier
Warehouse	Supplying from stock	Supplier
Transit	Transporting	Supplier
Receivers	Receiving	Customer
Payment	Paying	Customer to supplier

Component parts of Lead-times

Lead-time	Lead-time Stage	Steps, by date
Pre-order Planning	User Need	Analysing status to determining need to order
	User Requisition	Need to order to date of order requisition
Procurement	Order preparation	Order requisition to order release date
	Order confirmation	Order release to date of confirmation
Supplier * see also the production and warehouse lead-times	All the stages here are in the production and warehouse lead-times	Confirmation to order despatched date

Production (e.g. made to order)	Order processing	Date of order receipt to date order accepted/confirmed
	Preparation	Order accepted to date manufacture starts
	Manufacture (Queue time, set up, machine/operator time/inspect/put away times)	Start of manufacture to date it finishes
	Pack/Load (to the Warehouse or to Transit LT)	Finished manufacture to date order despatched
Warehouse (e.g. available ex stock)	In stock	Date goods arrived to date of order receipt
	Order Processing	Order receipt to date order is accepted or confirmed
	Picking	Date order accepted to date order is available/picked
	Pack/Load (to Warehouse or to Transit LT)	Order available to date order despatched
Transit		Date despatched to date order received
Receiving		Date order received to date available for issue/use
Payment	Credit	Date invoice received or of other "trigger," to date payment received
	Payment processing	Date payment received to date cash available for use

Supply lead-time

The supply lead-time (SLT) should not be confused with the above mentioned supplier lead-time. The supply lead-time is actually the total of all the above lead-times, excluding the payment lead-times. Supply lead-time is the total time from the "start" of determining the "need", to the "end" of the product being available for use. This is shown below.

Supply and Supplier Lead-time

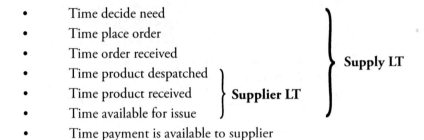

- Time decide need
- Time place order
- Time order received
- Time product despatched
- Time product received
- Time available for issue
- Time payment is available to supplier

Supply lead-time therefore involves many processes such as:
- Internal processes of the pre-order planning lead-time, from analysing the order status/determining when to order, requisitions and authority "signing off" up to, the placing of an order.
- The external supplier lead-time from order receipt, to the delivering of the goods.
- The internal process of the receiving lead-time (date order received to checking and placing into store and notifying the system and users that the product is available for issue).

The supply lead-time involves many different parties internally in an organisation and also externally, including both the supplier and the customer.

Lead-time examination

Lead-times must be examined using real examples, whilst ensuring that all appropriate stages and steps are included. There may also be additional lead-times for some players, for example, the customs clearance lead-time with imports.

After each lead-time stage has been quantified, analysis will show if there is a way to do things better. It can be expected that many reductions in lead-times will come from information flows and not from the goods flows.

Lead-time variability

A crucial aspect when examining lead-time is variability as when lead-times are realistically looked at, then a range of times will be found; for example from 20 to 50 days. This range represents the variability of lead-time where average calculations are of little practical assistance and can be dangerous if used for planning and decision-making.

It is this variability that so often represents the uncertainty found in the Supply Chain and which is traditionally dealt with by holding safety stocks to cover against the uncertainty.

The variability must, however, be examined by all those involved, before finally working together to agree that lead-times becomes a fixed item. Then the variability and the uncertainty are removed by having fixed known reliable lead-times; the length of the lead-time being of secondary importance.

The problem of lead variability can be illustrated as follows:

If: lead-time (LT) is halved from 12 to 6 weeks and lead-time variability (LTV) stays the same at ± 4 weeks, then:

Current LT			New LT		
LTV	LT	LTV	LTV	LT	LTV
-4	12	+ 4	-4	6	+4

Total LT

8 to 16 weeks	2 to 10 weeks
(Index 100 to 200)	(Index 100 to 500)

So, if LTV stays the same, then there is higher disruption/costs and reduced speed (index of 1 to 2 from 1 to 5).

Reducing lead-time variability

The following are some ways to consider in reducing lead-time variability:

Demand LTV

- Predictable known orders/size/make up.
- Predictable order times.
- Data accuracy on what customers want/when/price.
- Is it "end" demand or is "institutionalised" through inefficient "not talking" supply chain players (internal and or external).

Supply LTV

- Predictable known LT.
- Get correct quantity first time.
- Get correct quality first time.
- Data accuracy on what is supplied/price.

The importance of lead-time in inventory can be seen in the expression, "uncertainty is the mother of inventory". The length of lead-time is of secondary importance to the variability and uncertainties in the lead-time. It is the variability that causes disruptions and results in stock-outs, which in future are then covered by holding more stock, that then results in stock overages.

Time is cash, cash flow is critical and so are the goods and information flows; fixed reliable lead-times are therefore more important than the length of the lead-time.
The following case study illustrates the importance of lead-times to one major organisation:

Case Study: Lead-times Crunch at B&Q

Steve Willett, director of supply chain at B&Q, came to the firm last July from the US, where he worked for aerospace and engineering firm Allied Signal There, he was on the other side of the fence feeling the pressure that Wal-Mart puts on its suppliers. But he has come away with a profound admiration for the quality of supply chain management in the US and a burning ambition to mimic it in the UK. "We want to be a world-class supply chain that is talked about as a leader in the field," he says.

"Effective delivery performance by the supplier has to become a minimum requirement for doing organisations with B&Q. The norm of delivery is far better in the US than in the UK, but the supermarkets here have effectively driven up the performance of their suppliers and we are going to do the same for the DIY industry."

B&Q's wider strategy of slashing the retail prices of goods through savings has led to growth of between 25 per cent and 30 per cent a year for the past few years. However, it has also meant that savings are being constantly sought from the supply chain. Since September, Willett has put different supply chain projects in place, with Easter at the front of his mind.

"The Easter trading pattern is very significant because it is so concentrated and there is no time to recover," he says. On some seasonal lines, such as garden furniture, there is a 15-month lead-time, but on others, such as peat, the constraint is how many lorries the organisation can get on the ferries from Ireland.

At Easter, the line between store and warehouse often becomes a little blurred, with 40-foot containers sometimes sitting in the car parks to maximise the selling space inside the stores.

Project work
The supply chain projects, which have examined almost every aspect of the firm's supply process, have looked at:
*   How handling can be minimised, so that stock can be taken from the delivery lorries to be stored on pallets in the 300 stores;
*   Ensuring that space is given to the best-selling lines, so that they maintain a constant presence on the shelves;
*   E-replenishment mechanisms;
*   Ensuring that the five regional consolidation centres that handle stock from abroad are incorporated into the delivery from the four distribution centres;
*   Ensuring that new procedures are put into place, with 30 implementation managers working in the stores;

Supplier development
Willett says this last one is not as sinister as it sounds. "We are not expecting overnight revolutions and saying to suppliers, 'perform or else'. It's a matter of working with them to set targets and help them to get there. Supply chain

management is one of the organisation's biggest internal costs and, if we are to deliver savings to the customer, we have to become more efficient.

There will be suppliers that will be too slow and unable to get there as we ratchet the bar down, and I have no doubt we will lose some along the way. But, with that said, we want to achieve a fairly stable supplier base and work with suppliers in partnerships."

Mark-Paul Homberger, B&Q's vendor performance manager, predicts that some household names will be de-listed from the firm's supplier base.

B&Q has instituted a system of green, amber and red status for suppliers, where green signifies a fine relationship, amber that there will be no new organisations and red that they should sort themselves out or face being de-listed. "We have to ensure availability to the customer and if suppliers can't get their act together on lead-times, we are absolutely serious that we will source elsewhere," explains Homberger.

B&Q is going the same way as supermarket giants Tesco and Sainsbury's (owner of rival DIY chain Home base), he suggests. "Our vendor-buying agreements will include agreed service levels and, crucially, lead-times," he says.

"When things fall apart at the seams, we need to know what the action plan is to recover. Often with domestic suppliers, poor performance can be attributed to the fact that they won't invest the capital, but we want to emphasise that it is really in the supplier's interest to give us a better deal."

Source: Supply Management 20 April 2000

Customer Service

This is commonly measured by the following On-time, In-full (OTIF) measurements:
- Cycle Lead-time (On time delivery or OT): e.g. Daily delivery service, order day 1 for day 2 delivery.
- Stock Availability (In full delivery or IF): e.g. 95% orders met from stock.

- Consistency/Reliability: e.g. 95% orders are delivered within 3 days.

Actual achievement in organisations varies; the following may be helpful for comparison purposes:

Key Performance Indicators - average figures from UK manufacturers
(Source: Best Factory Awards 2001)

Industry sector	On time delivery reliability	In full ex-stock availability	Stock-turns per annum
Process	91.0%	97.5%	14
Engineering	92.0%	96.0%	13
Electrical	96.0%	98.2%	9
Consumer household	98.1%	99.0%	21

(These stock turns figures can be misleading. These are calculated from financial annual accounts by dividing the sales turnover, by the value of the stock assets on hand, to give an average yearly figure of stock asset value turn. This would not be the same as the physical stock turns).

Customer importance

It is only the order from the customer that triggers all the activity in the supply chain. Without a customer order, no supply chain activity is required. The customer is only interested in buying delivered products.

Customer service levels are a variable and each customer service variable has a cost associated with it. The relationship between cost and service is rarely linear, but more of an exponential curve. So for example, a 10 per cent increase in service may mean a cost increase of 15 or even over 50 per cent. Other examples from transport include that we pay more for first class mail than for second class mail; we pay more for a service offering an overnight parcel delivery than for a three day or a deferred delivery.

Customer Value

Customers will place a value on many aspects of the total service offering. Value is placed by customers primarily against delivery/availability but also against quality, the cycle lead-time and the cost and the service levels. Perception is reality: different customers can see these as being inter-related or may view them independently. It is therefore important for organisations to understand the specific reality as seen by the customer. The following are the aspects of criteria that customer's value:

Quality is "performing right first time every time" and involves:
- Meeting requirements.
- Fitness for purpose.
- Minimum variance.
- Elimination of waste.
- Continuous improvement culture.

Service is about "continually meeting customer needs as the market changes", and involves:
- Support available.
- Product availability.
- Flexibility.
- Reliability.
- Consistency.

Cost is about knowing what the costs really are and then looking at how to reduce them.

This involves the:
- Design of product.
- Manufacturing process.
- Distribution process.
- Administration process.
- Stock levels.

Cycle lead-time is about knowing what the lead-times really are and then looking for ways to reduce them. This involves considering:
- Time to market.

- Time from order placement to time available for issue.
- Response to market forces.

Quality, cost, service and time are all inter-linked and customer value can therefore be seen as:

Increasing Quality * Service
Reducing Cost * Lead-time

An organisation will ideally try to improve the quality and the service, whilst, reducing the cost and lead-times. All of the aspects are inter-related and connected and for example, it matters not to the majority of customers where the goods come from or whether the goods are transported by road, rail, sea, air etc. After all, customers are interested in buying available or delivered goods.

The customer is the reason for the organisation's existence, so continually working to serve the customer better is critical. But who is the customer? The traditional view is perhaps the one that pays the invoices, but by seeing the next person/process/ operation in the chain as the customer, this way of thinking means there may well be hundreds of supplier/customer relationships in a single supply chain. If all these "single" relationships were being viewed as supplier/customer relationships, the "whole" becomes very different.

The Customer is the key; it is their demand that drives the whole supply chain; finding out what Customer values and then delivering it, is critical. The view of one major organisation on customer service in the supply chain, is illustrated below:

Case study: Wal-Mart: The Supply Chain and Customer Service
(Wal-Mart is the U.S. organisation that owns the UK organisation Asda).

Sam Walton and the Wal-Mart retail chain revolutionised the role of Logistics.

Walton explains the Wal-Mart philosophy (Walton 1992):

"Here's the point. The bigger Wal-Mart gets, the more essential it is that we think small...If we ever forget that looking a customer in the eye, greeting him or her, and asking politely if we can be of help is just as important in every Wal-Mart store today as it was in [first little store], then we just ought to go into a different organisations because we'll never survive in this one."

Wal-Mart supply chain supports that vision by "thinking small" and observes the following points:

- Serve one store at a time.

The objective of the supply chain — serving customers — is achieved store by store, department by department, customer by customer.

- Communicate, communicate, and communicate.

Keep a constant flow of communication through meetings, phone calls, information system reports, pep talks, and seminars.

- Keep your ear to the ground.

Managers need to get out of their offices and into their facilities for a real "hands-on, get-down-in-the-store" perspective.

- Push responsibility—and authority—down.

Allow operations-level staff to be "managers of their own organisations," and to identify and implement improvements.

- Force ideas to bubble up.

Encourage managers to propose ideas for new ways to work.

- Stay lean, fight bureaucracy.

As organisations grow, duplication can build up. "If you're not serving the customer, or serving the folks who do, we don't need you."

Problems in integrating Supply Chains

As will have been seen already, the "theory" of effective and efficient supply chain management is relatively clear; it is the application and the management practices that are difficult. Supply Chain management is classic common sense; but then, whilst it may be sense, it is not necessarily very common.

Some of the reasons for this and the problems found in supply chain management are due to the following factors:

- Inaccurate forecasting of demand.
- Volatile markets and demand patterns.
- Unwillingness to share information.
- Power "forcing" by large dominant customers/buyers.

- Resistant "monopoly" suppliers.
- Poor ICT.
- Management styles and approaches.
- Poor and unreliable delivery performance.
- No control of supply or supplier lead-time.
- Global/long distance suppliers and or markets.
- Resistance to change.
- Lack of knowledge/resources.
- Misunderstanding of how independently managed processes interact.

To add to these problems and difficulties, the following case study reflects wide ranging views of what was needed to re-structure UK manufacturing. The links to supply chain management principles are very clear.

Case Study: Restructuring UK Manufacturing Supply Chains

1) Restructure capital:
Emphasise has been on short-term growth which is "fashionable" to the city. However, long-term investment is needed

2) Examine and invest in processes:
Examine waste in capital, process standardisation, product portfolio rationalisation, and work across the supply chain by:
- getting the internal supply chain correct: styles, culture, trust, communication.
- developing a clear way forward: tangible deliverables, aligned accountabilities, adequate resources.
- transparency: forecast and performance information with consistent actions.
- driving time performance: lengths of time for each process,: total time, lead-time excesses.
- adding value with the process, not cost.
- developing reliability for what is out of tolerance.

3) Segment the portfolio:
- view each product as a separate supply chain with varied demands, product characteristics, operational capability, distribution channels,

supplier profiles, and market dynamics.
- install effective KPIs: to give visibility and to drive action.
- install internal/customer/supplier relationships at each interface.

4) Invest in product leadership:
Labour intensive, low value products are not the way forward, understand costs and trim lower margin products. Value add products are needed.

5) Develops skills base:
Relying on others to train is not acceptable; this has been the problem from the last 20 years.

6) Know the market:
Market research is needed.

7) Consolidate:
Critical mass is needed, as in automotive and electronics.

Source: Based on a report in SHD December 2002

Type I and Type II Supply chains: A contrast

As stated earlier, supply chains differ and the following model for two types of supply chain presents an "extremes" view to stimulate debate and discussion about the changes that may be needed. This is not intended to be a "good" or "bad" comparison.

The reality and the practice will be found in the "grey" between the "black/white" extremes; also, some aspects can be mixed between the two types. For example Type I on the main drivers and products; but Type II on inventory and buying etc.

Attribute	Type I Supply Chain	Type II Supply Chain
	Production led **Push** **More about supply**	**Market led** **Pull** **More about demand**
Main driver	Forecast driven. Growth from volume output and ROI. Financial performance profit driven. "Pump" push. From Supply to demand. Mass production.	Order driven. Growth from customer satisfaction. Customer focus, value driven. "Turn on the Tap" pull. From demand to supply. Mass market.
Products	Launched. Functional, standard, commodities. Low variety. Long product life cycle.	Transition. Innovative, design and build, fashion goods. High variety. Short product life cycles.
Inventory	"Turns." Stock holding. Just in case. Hold safety stock. Seen as an asset/protection.	"Spins." Little stock holding. Just in time. No safety stock. Seen as a liability.
"Buying"	Buy goods for anticipated and projected demand/needs. Instructed suppliers. Arms length, played off on a short-term basis. Confrontation. Adversarial. Narrow range of suppliers. Low cost buying. Inspection on receipt.	Assign capacity on a daily basis. Involved suppliers. Committed suppliers, long term. Cooperation. Alliances. Ordered supplier base of specialists. Total Acquisition Cost buying. Quality assured.

"Making"	"Build."	"Supply."
	Proactive with orders.	React to orders.
	Economy of scale.	Reduce waste.
	Continuous flow and mass production.	Batch, job shop, project methods of production, "customising".
	Long runs.	Short runs.
	Low production costs.	Higher production costs.
	High work in progress inventory.	Low work in progress inventory.
	High plant efficiency e.g. 24/7.	High effectiveness but with lower plant efficiencies.
	Labour is an extension of the machine.	Labour brings the continuous improvements.
	Ordered "push" schedules and reliable demand forecasts/make to stock.	Flexible "pull" Kanban schedules with make/assemble to order.
"Moving"	Move slower in bulk.	Move faster in smaller quantities.
	Large/less frequent deliveries.	Smaller, frequent deliveries.
	Storage is high cost.	Storage is low cost.
	Transport is a low cost.	Transport costs are higher.
	Fewer but larger RDC type deliveries.	Many varied and dispersed destinations.
Customers	Predictive demand.	Un-predictive demand.
	Cost driven.	Availability driven.
	Are only handled at the top or by the "customer service" department.	Everybody is customer focussed.
Information	Demand information is sometimes passed back.	Demand information is mandatory.
	Used mainly for "executing".	Used also for planning purposes.

Handling of Customers orders	10% forecast error and algorithmetic based forecasts.	40-100% error with forecasts more consultative based.
	Continuous scheduled replenishment.	Real-time visibility throughout the supply chain.
	More "push".	More "pull."
	Stock outs rarer (1-2%) and are dealt with contractually.	Stock outs are immediate and frequent (10-40% p.a.) and volatile.
	Stable and consistent orders, some predictable weekly type ordering.	Cyclical demand, many unpredictable orders.
	Clear cut ordering.	EDI/Visibility ordering.
	Service levels are more rigid.	Service levels are more flexible to actual forecasts.
Deliver from stock lead-times	Immediate, fast in one or two days.	Immediate to long; slower and from days to weeks.
Make to order lead-times	1-6 months as mainly making "standard" products for stock.	1-14 days.
Costs	Mainly in physical conversion/movements.	Mainly in marketing.
	Inventory costs in finished goods.	Inventory costs in raw materials/WIP.
	Cost control very strong and any gained savings are retained.	Revenue generation and any gained savings are shared.
Producer selling price	Low selling price.	Higher selling price.
	Few markdowns.	Many end of season markdowns.
	5-20% profits.	20-60% profits.
	Low risk.	Higher risk levels.

Organisation methods	Silo/hierarchical management with some "cells".	Flatter structures with Cross-functional teams.
	"Top down" to staff gives orders and responsibility.	Top down and bottom up giving assistance; everyone is responsible.
	Professional managers who are more driven by power.	Leaders/educators who are people driven.
	Transactional/ownership.	Partnership/collaborative.
	Self interest.	Customer interest.
	Protective interfacing links.	Visible integrated links.
	Slow to change, change is mainly resisted, and maintenance of the "status quo".	Quicker response with continuous improvement and more embracive of change.
	Internal fragmentation with instructed employees.	"Joined up" structures with involved employees.
	Tendency for "blame" cultures.	More "gain" structure.
	"Fire-fighting."	"Fire-fighting."
	Little trust.	Extensive trust.
	People a liability and numbers are to be reduced wherever possible.	People are an asset to be invested in.
	Narrow skill base.	Multiple skill bases.
	Outside recruitment.	Internal recruitment also.
	"Do what you are told"	"Do what you think is best"

The Supply Chain Rules

In summary, the following Supply Chain "Rules" have been noted in "The Supply Chain in 90 minutes" (Emmett, 2005).

Supply Chain Rule number one: "Win the home games first": Many organisations start into Supply Chain Management by working only with the closest suppliers and customers. They should however first ensure that all of their internal operations and activities are "integrated, co-ordinated and controlled."

Supply Chain Rule number two: The format of inventory and where it is held is of common interest to all supply chain players and must be jointly investigated and examined.

Examples of the format of inventory include raw material, sub-assemblies/work in progress or finished goods. This is often held at multiple places in the supply chain, and is controlled (in theory) by many different players who usually work independently of each other. This results in too much inventory being held throughout the supply chain.

Supply Chain Rule number three: The optimum and the "ideal" cost/service balance will only ever be found by working and collaborating fully with all players in the Supply Chain.

Full benefits of supply chain management will only come when there is an examination of all costs/service levels together with all the players. This will result in reduced lead-times and improved total costs/service for all parties in the network.

This means, therefore, going beyond the first tier of suppliers and looking also at the supplier's supplier and so on. It represents more than data and process, it includes mutual interest, open relationships and sharing.

Supply Chain Rule number four: Time is cash, cash flow is critical and so are the goods and information flows; fixed reliable lead-times are more important than the length of the lead-time.

The importance of lead-time in inventory is seen in the expression "uncertainty is the mother of inventory." The length of lead-time is of secondary importance to the variability and uncertainness in the lead-time. Again, an examination of lead-time throughout the supply chain, involving different players and interests, is critically needed.

Supply Chain Rule number five: The Customer is the organisation's; it is their demand that drives the whole supply chain; finding out what Customers value and then delivering it is critical.

The customer is the reason for the organisation's existence, so continually working to serve the customer better is critical. But who is the customer? The traditional view is perhaps the person that has placed the order/pays the supplier's invoice; but by seeing the next person/process/operation in the chain as the customer, this way of thinking means that there are many supplier/customer relationships in a single supply chain. If all of these "single" relationships were being viewed as supplier/customer relationships, then the "whole" would be very different.

Supply Chain Rule number six: It is only the movement to the customer that adds the ultimate value; smooth continuous flow movements are preferable.

The movement to the customer, undertaken as quickly as possible whilst accounting for the associated cost levels, is really all that counts in adding value.

Supply Chain Rule number seven: Trade Off by looking holistically with all the supply chain players.

There are many possibilities and opportunities available to Integrate/Co-ordinate/Control across the supply chain(s) networks, starting by "winning the home games first", in and between the internal functions; followed by all of the external connections to the supply chain networks.

Supply Chain Rule number eight: Information flows lubricate the supply chain; using appropriate ICT is critical.

Information is required at every stage of the supply chain and for all of the levels of supply chain planning. All parts of the supply chain rely on ICT in the planning, operational, administrative and management processes.

2: Understanding the Difference with Global Supply Chain Management

Global Supply Chains

People have always been willing to trade for goods they did not have or otherwise produce.

However in the old model of production there was a local supply chain. Here the local market enjoyed the advantage of locally produced goods and paid a premium for goods produced elsewhere that were then transported to the consuming market. This gave rise to traditional manufacturing areas and traditional agricultural areas which was also a function of the use of local natural resources, labour availability, local infrastructure and of transport services and low cost.

The Industrial Revolution then next increased trade and the range of transport services with its wide scale mechanization of production, whereby production and consumption were no longer required to be local, thus creating a need to transport raw materials (in) and finished goods (out). This in turn gave rise to cheaper mass produced goods being available for more widely located consumers. Using economies of scale this led to a situation for organisations where the more goods that were made available, the greater the market size became.

In the current Global Supply Chain, we now find that production and manufacturing is not dependent on local natural resources; neither is food availability dependent on local production. Additionally, the location of production is not dependent on location of the intended market, as now low production and transportation costs are the driving factor. This in turn has given rise to greater economies of scale where the decentralization of production is enabled by both reliable transportation service and also by the easy reach of global media and communications with organizations and consumers.

We can also see some of the more recent reasons to globalise as follows:
*   1960s = resource availability, such as cheaper labour.
*   1970s = low production costs.
*   1980s = financial opportunities.
*   1990s = political considerations.

- 2000s = makes for good organisations (for example with, brands, "worldly" cultures, skilled labour, "the global village") and ICT will more readily enabled.

A growing trend, therefore, in many industries, is the extent and reach of supply chains with global trading strategies and operations. Consequently world trade (the organisation of buying and selling for money or credit, or exchanging commodities by barter) has gown dramatically in a very short time; for example, as consumers we are all involved in the global reach of supply chains.

Consider the traditional English Sunday roast. The beef may be from Australia, the green beans from Thailand, the carrots from East Africa, the broccoli from Guatemala, the potatoes from Italy, the fruit from Chile; overall this represents a global travel well in excess of 40,000 miles.

Trading Globally

Organisations that produce goods can find it advantageous to trade globally for the following reasons:
- They have underused production capacity, so can sell the excess.
- They have underused selling capacity, so need to import more products to sell.
- Wish to diversify, and not be exposed to only one place or market.
- They have cyclical peaks and troughs, for example, when it is quiet they can turn to selling overseas.
- The lower prices of imports (from cheap labour, favourable exchange rates and economies of scale) can give overall cheaper prices than found with domestic/national/regional buying.
- The price for exports is better (exchange rates, market based pricing).
- Quality is only available from imported products.

Global economies also change and can also sponsor global trading; reasons here may be as follows:
- The growth of world brands, for example, Coca Cola, MacDonald's.
- The switching of production, for example, textile production from the UK to Morocco/Turkey/East Europe and to India/China.

Features of Global Trade

Global location requirements

When a multinational organisation looks for a global location, the following requirements have featured, in order of top 5 importance as follows:

1. Availability of labour.
2. ICT(Information Communication Technology).
3. Local logistics service providers.
4. Physical infrastructure.
5. Local and qualified suppliers.

It is interesting to note that the nearness to customers comes much later than the above top five, and is found at number 9.

Balance of payments

Overseas trade has critical effects on a country's Balance of Payments, that is, the difference between what is exported (where currency is received inwards from overseas) and what is imported (where payment is outwards and is made overseas).

The aim for any National Economy is to export more, so that imports can then be self funded. The UK, however, has a growing trade imbalance as we import more that we export, therefore, in the national economy, this difference has to be made up elsewhere.

The Balance of Payments is also affected by the following:
*   Visible trade e.g. products.
*   Invisible trade e.g. services.
*   Capital items e.g. money transfers.
*   Payments are influenced by gold standards, fixed exchange rates and floating exchange rates.

Global Trade Differences

There are many differences between domestic and global trade:

- Greater distances.
- Less face/face communication.
- Different languages and cultures.
- Varied documentation requirements.
- Longer credit periods/cash flow problems.
- Varied options to transfer ownership.
- More risks from unannounced changes to local politics, customs regulations, and documentation requirements.
- Different currencies and foreign currency risks.
- Longer lead-times.
- Complicated movements and costs.
- People need to have wider and broader skills sets and expertise.
- Honouring contractual terms after any default.
- Involved legal processes.

Checklist: Challenges and Barriers to Building Global Supply Chains

- Uncertain political stability.
- Self-serving governments.
- Currency fluctuations.
- Lack of infrastructure in some countries (roads, port facilities, trained labour, utilities, communications).
- Lack of critical mass of purchasing activity causes inadequate supplier inventories or supply arrangements and results in much "buyout" activity for purchased items.
- High transaction costs.
- Requirements to use in-country agents or partners.
- Lack of potential for repeat purchases.
- Instability of technology applications (What is the shelf life of these applications?) Long term? Will the buyer get a return on its investment by the time the system is fully implemented?
- Slow adoption of e-organisations be even some best in class organisations.
- Local content requirements and issues (requirements to use in-country contractors, agents, distributors, materials and manufacturers).
- No or limited free trade zone availability.
- Partner/contract limitations requiring bidding for all procurement activities and inhibiting alliance-building.

- High logistics and transportation costs.
- Different time zones makes communication difficult.
- Financial risks are higher in overseas organisations activity overall due to more uncertainties, e.g. projects can he stopped or stalled abruptly for a variety of reasons, e.g. change of government, civil war, terrorism.
- The nature of global/overseas purchasing activity (may be fragmented and/ or scattered, is such that there is usually a poorly developed mechanism for materials planning and scheduling.
- Long/unpredictable supplier lead-times due to lack of local manufacturers.
- Irregular cycle times.
- Protectionism.
- Limited number of qualified global suppliers.
- Insufficient supplier process technology.
- Project work, especially overseas, tends to be independent and not easily linked to "run and maintain" global activities.
- Limited availability of trained personnel for purchasing or supply management positions.

Source: Building Global Supply Chains: A New Mosaic Comes of Age. Ralph G. Kauffman and Thomas A. Crimi, ISM 87th Annual International Conference Proceedings 2002.

A driver for many UK organisations is the perceived customer expectation for more product complexity/variation, coupled with "I want it now" urgency. This will often result in revisions to the organisation objectives for the product value/service offering. The following wider and potentially global issues may be involved:

- Do we need to work more closely with suppliers?
- Do we move manufacturing to offshore or outsource the whole or part of the operation?
- What are the effects of product complexity? For example, shorter product life cycles and increasing product customising of products, may mean assemble to order manufacturing instead of make to stock methods of manufacturing.
- What are the effects of transport and Customs complexity? For example, increasing distances travelled between manufacturing sites and markets; parts may be made in Mexico and Brazil for assembly in Taiwan with the finished products supplied to a world market.

Likely consequences of these wider issues could be:

- Distances change in the supply chain; meaning examination of the total process and associated lead-times.
- Improving the visibility; meaning co-ordinating functions by a proactive real-time monitoring of goods and information flows.
- Managing the whole supply chain; meaning integrating the processes whilst effecting trade off analysis and Total Acquisition Cost (TAC) examinations.
- As is normal for global supply chain management this involves both imports and exports in the overall trade between countries; meaning attendant threats and opportunities for organisations, such as cheap imports of substituting products that are manufactured locally and/or, more export opportunities.

Checklist: Global Supply Chain Objectives

While, in general, the objectives of global supply chains are the same as domestic supply chains, particular sets of objectives vary according to the situation and organisations strategies and objectives that exist.

Some of the objectives of global supply chain management that are frequently encountered include:

- Leverage spend (across organisations units and geographic boundaries).
- Align incentives for integration of activities (buyers, suppliers, end-users).
- Enhance timeliness and speed of information flows.
- Optimize supply chain operation (members, capabilities, costs).
- Reduce inventories across the chain.
- Use synergy from the supply chain to capture and diffuse best practices across the chain.
- Satisfy all host country requirements (within limitations).
- Establish and promote world class benchmarking activities.
- Identify supply chain cost drivers and reduce costs across the supply chain (structural streamlining).
- Reduce non-value adding activities.
- Promote total cost of ownership and economic value added perspectives and score-keeping (scorecards).
- Identify total supply chain costs.
- Achieve the ability to secure materials and services of the right quality worldwide in a cost-effective manner.

- Dramatically increase coordination within your organization and throughout the supply chain.
- Produce shorter cycle times in all organisations processes.
- Drive improvements in customer services resulting in greater customer satisfaction.
- Increase information sharing.
- Promote "just in time" data.
- Supply base rationalization.

Source: Building Global Supply Chains: A New Mosaic Comes of Age. Ralph G. Kauffman and Thomas A. Crimi. ISM 87th Annual International Conference Proceedings 2002.

Global trends

The following global trends can be observed:

- Emerging economies are increasingly becoming the worldwide production centres for consumer and intermediary goods and services.
- Increasing dependence on international trade means more variable supply chains.
- Port congestion, container shortages & infrastructure imbalances may impact on transportation costs and service levels, offsetting the lower sourcing costs.
- Lean manufacturing and zero inventory goals shift the burden of working capital backwards in the supply chain.
- Increased exposure to energy and currency exchange fluctuations.
- Increased security measures on terrorism and theft.
- Environmental regulations.
- Concerns over ethical labour practices and Intellectual Property Rights (IPR).

Case Study: Global Supply Chain Trends

Executive Summary

While the survey reveals numerous strategies used by organisations to manage their supply chains on a global basis, we have identified ten major trends that are driving innovative supply chain design and configuration across all industries:

1) Globalization is accelerating, leading to large structural shifts for global supply chain organizations and new challenges to successfully manage supply chain performance.

While past globalization initiatives focused on manufacturing and assembly, future globalization will also target product and technology development.

2) Pressures to reduce cost and penetrate local markets are the two key drivers of accelerated globalization.

3) Despite average cost reductions of 17% per globalization initiative, many organisations have difficulty realizing savings in management costs. The gap between planned and actual benefits is caused by internal barriers that prevent full support of globalization efforts, and external network partners that fail to achieve expected performance.

4) China and India continue to emerge as major targets for globalization, while Eastern Europe is catching up as a top off-shoring destination. Investments in North America and Western Europe also remain strong as organisations look to secure access to local markets and key resources.

5) Product quality and safety, as well as supply chain delivery and security, are the most critical concerns when expanding the supply chain globally. Four major risk mitigation strategies, including the deployment of organisation resources at supplier locations, are employed.

6) Major barriers to globalization include limited supply chain flexibility and the lack of internal competency to manage partners. Better visibility and management across the supply chain are important keys to overcome these barriers.

7) Environmental sustainability is a key consideration in the development of future globalization strategies. Today, sustainability is mainly driven by the need for regulatory compliance and satisfaction of customer demand. It is not yet considered a strategic differentiator.

8)   Acceleration of supply chain maturity, enabled by advanced supply chain practices, appears to have reached a plateau. Among those surveyed, supply chain maturity differs significantly across geographic regions and industries.

9)   By 2010, the need for greater supply chain flexibility will overtake product quality and customer service as the major driver for improving supply chain strategy. Many supply chain leaders have developed effective strategies to improve global flexibility.

10)   The COO agenda across industries and geographic regions is converging on improving supply chain flexibility and performance. Organisations around the globe face similar challenges in building effective international operations and supply chain networks.

Source: PTRM 2007; Global Supply Chain Trends 2008-2010

3: Managing Supply Chain Risk

Views on risk

There are many views of risk and for example, a report by Price Waterhouse Coopers (2007) notes the following views:

"Don't be afraid to take a big step. You can't cross a chasm in two small jumps."
David Lloyd George

"There are costs and risks to a program of action, but they are far less than the long-range risks and costs of comfortable inaction."
John F. Kennedy

"If we listened to our intellect, we'd never have a love affair. We'd never have a friendship. We'd never go into organisations, because we'd be too cynical. Well, that's nonsense. You've got to jump off cliffs all the time and build your wings on the way down".
Annie Dillard

"There came a time when the risk to remain tight in the bud was more painful than the risk it took to blossom".
Anais Nin

Global instabilities and risk

Having high degrees of certainty will eliminate risk, however global trade has many levels of risks that actually work towards creating uncertainty. Most organisations therefore have to continually find ways to manage uncertainty and variability; the following gives an overview of some of the many causes of variability found in global supply chains:

Economics risks
- Rates of growth (boom to bust).
- Balance of payments.
- Fiscal policy.
- Dollar/euro/sterling influence.

- Inflation levels.
- Variable prices.

Political risks
- New systems and polices.
- Dictatorships.
- Elections bringing changes.

Legal risks
- IPR and copyright control and enforcement.
- Trade barriers.
- Product liability.
- Monopolies controls.

Inventory/Financial Risks
- Obsolescence.
- Markdowns.
- Stock outs.
- Excessive.
- Mismatched.
- Networked stock.
- Penalises for non-delivery.

Chaos Risks
- Over-reactions.
- Unneeded interventions.
- Mistrust.
- Distorted information (Bullwhip effect).
- Nervousness, leading to higher costs, over-ordering and inventory squirreling.

Disruption and Decision risks
- Terrorism.
- Strikes.
- Weather.
- Hijacking.
- Decisions are as good as the information on which they are based, therefore poor information can mean making poor decisions.

Such variables are risks that can easily create instability, and from an organisation's perspective, there is more turbulence, uncertainty and volatile supply/demand. With product manufacturing and volatile supply and demand, we can see that two distinctly different types of products are made, for example:

Functional products with the following characteristics:
- Long product life cycles.
- Low profits (10%).
- Low variety (for example, 15 variants).
- Low forecast errors (10%).
- Low stock outs (2%).
- Use a make to stock method of production (as if use make to order, then the lead-times are too long).

Examples: FMCG products like pet food, tinned soup, nappies

Innovative products with the following characteristics:
- Short life cycles (6 months).
- High profits (50%).
- High variety(100s with clothing sizes, colours).
- High forecast error (100%).
- High stock outs (30%).
- Make to order with short lead-times (for example, 2 weeks).

Examples: clothing fashions, computers.

The wide ranges of vulnerability in global supply chains therefore require changes to organisations strategy and a need to improve visibility to overcome the lack of confidence in the following:
- Order cycle times.
- Order status.
- Demand forecasts.
- Supplier's ability to deliver.
- Manufacturing capacity.
- Quality of the products.
- Transport reliability.
- Services delivered.

Vulnerability therefore creates a lack of confidence, and as an example, the potential reaction from the customer-facing end of an organisation can be where:

- The sales team believes that order cycle and order fulfilment times are not reliable.
- They now devise their own means of addressing this.
- Stock is ordered so as to have supplies to support their key customers.
- They may also place phantom orders to secure supply (i.e. they now hold their own private buffer stock).
- Causes inefficiencies and creates a risk spiral.

This resulting so-called risk spiral has many examples:

- Sales start over ordering since they do not have the timely visibility of the correct demand signals, or they know from experience that supplies may be late or insufficient to fill the complete orders.
- Production plans are based on inflated production lead-times, due to having a similar lack of visibility and control. "Safety lead-times" are commonly used for example, in standard MRP, since production planners do not want to be blamed for production delays.
- Lack of means to expedite or having little flexibility in manufacturing will also mean that any yield shortfalls or production downtimes have to be made up by additional production, and as a result, the lead-times are stretched out in production plans.

Visibility

Having visibility is a key to risk management and with global supply chains we can see a problem of weak confidence with the long end-to-end pipeline time, i.e., the time it takes for material to flow from one end of supply chain to the other. This can also be affected by the overseas subcontracting of manufacturing and by offshore sourcing, which can then contribute to the length of time.

Associated with this pipeline length is the lack of visibility within the pipeline and, therefore, any player in a supply chain will have little detailed knowledge of their order status and of what goes on in other parts of the supply chain.

Ways of improving visibility are to share information among supply chain members, which means overcoming the traditional view and belief that 'information is power', and the view that this power will be diminished when information is shared. Significantly, in supply chains the reverse is true: when information between supply chain members is shared, its power increases significantly, as shared information reduces uncertainty and for example, reduces the need for safety stock.

As a result, the system becomes more responsive and, ultimately, could even become demand-driven rather than forecast-driven; thereby bringing in make-to-order supplier production options.

(An excerpt from "Mitigating Supply Chain Risk through Improved Confidence", IJof PD&LM, Vol 34, No 5, 2004, Christopher & Lee).

Supply chain visibility is the number one challenge for chief supply chain officers according to an IBM report. Their study, "The smarter supply chain of the future" (2008), is based on detailed conversations with some 400 chief supply chain officers in 29 industries around the world.

The top challenges found in this report were:
*   70 per cent said visibility impacted their supply chains to a significant extent.
*   Risk also scored highly (60 per cent) and was an escalating concern. "A crisis in one country or region can now ripple very quickly across the world economy creating tremendous turbulence. As supply chains have become more complex, global and stressed, the executives we spoke with believe they must drive far more intelligence throughout their supply chains if they are going to anticipate rather than react."

Other aspects that were reported are as follows:
*   Increasing customer demands (56 per cent).
*   Cost containment (55 per cent).
*   More globalisation (43 per cent).
*   Many organisations went on to report issues with global sourcing including unreliable delivery (65 per cent), longer lead-times (61 per cent), and poor quality (61 per cent).

The study also suggested that globalisation had contributed more to revenue growth rather than to efficiency and found that executives were actually more focused towards the following top priorities:

- Strategy alignment.
- Continuous process improvement.
- Cost reduction.
- Organisational silos were also identified as a major problem.

Clearly visibility whilst being the top challenge was actually not the top priority.

This may be because the reporting organisation's supply chains, does not have a great deal of control after the order has been placed. For example, even if information is obtained on demand, changes may lead to the supply chain or procurement manager to be helpless for the following reasons:

- The suppliers may not be flexible enough to respond to late changes.
- There are actually no alternative freighting options available.
- The production line is inflexible and production schedule changes are not feasible.

In turn, IBM sees that this creates a loss of confidence in the supply chain processes and structures.

Confidence

The impacts of this loss of confidence can then "knock on" and mean that supply chain managers have to hedge against supply chain uncertainties and risks. This then creates supply chains that have the following features:

- Without visibility and control, the supply chain has safety stock buffer inventories in more than one place with more than one player; buffering being used as a hedge against the uncertainties and risks in the supply chain. Such excessive inventory, then leads to higher financial risks.
- Investing in excessive capacity.
- Logistics providers build slack into their operations and quoted transport lead-times often will have built in safety times; ultimately, extra shipping capacity may need to be purchased.
- With the lack of visibility of shipment and requirement schedules, this creates unnecessary expediting of shipments, or leads to using the wrong mode of transport.
- Difficulties in being responsive to customers, reacting to changes in market conditions and in being competitive in providing customer service.
- Lead-times quoted to customers will now tend to be longer, since added

protection is needed as sales departments do not have confidence in the supply chain.

- Similarly, contracts may be constructed in ways that do not give much flexibility to customers, and special requests by customers are turned down.
- The supply chain is no longer competitive and is liable to market risks.

Restoring supply chain confidence

The number one aspect here is information accuracy, visibility and accessibility. Throughout the supply chain, the key operational metrics and status reports do need to be accessible easily by key members of the supply chain and also there is the need to ensure the information should be:

- accurate and timely, therefore rendering it useful for all parties for planning and re-planning purposes.
- tightly managed and updated as timely as possible, therefore enabling confidence to the parties using the data who know it is reliable and accurate.

When deviations from the plan have occurred, alerts are needed for the appropriate parties in the supply chain. Here, intelligent controls are needed to determine if the deviations are normal, random events, or if they represented some systematic or unexpected changes that warrant attention.

A parallel to statistical process control can be drawn here, as a process control chart should be sensitive enough to detect out of control conditions, but not overly sensitive so as to cause the system to be overly nervous, with a lot of unnecessary changes and corrections.

Responsive corrective actions are then needed to provide all supply chain players with contingency plans and the tools to make corrective actions when out of control conditions have been detected. For example, if the shipment schedules have deviated from plan, then there should be clearly defined contingency plans to take appropriate actions, such as using alternative supply sources.

Agile/synchronous supply chains

These require transparency of supply/demand and pipeline inventory as close to real-time as possible. It also requires a willingness on the part of all the members of the supply chain to work to a single supply chain plan that will capture and share information across a supply chain and who will put aside the traditional arms length relationship and moves towards closer, collaborative arrangements.

The benefits according to IBM are much more than cost reduction, but also, the reduction of market risk; this in turn will:
- Increase sales and market share.
- Penetrate new markets.
- Enable speedy new product introduction.

Clearly, whilst not all supply chain risk is created through a lack of confidence amongst supply chain members, the contention by IBM is that improvements in confidence can have a significant effect on mitigating supply chain risk.

Procurement Risk

In a Price Waterhouse Coopers (PWC) report of 2007, some of the past organisational challenges for procurement were detailed as per below:
- Maverick buying.
- The reduction of manual processes.
- The lack of data.

This in turn has created a response of more supplier consolidation, outsourcing, consortium buying and the use of procurement cards. Moving forward, PWC sees that the future procurement and organisational challenges are as follows:

- Procurement integration, for example, in the internal supply chain, with external supplier/customers.
- Reduction of transaction costs.
- Policy compliance, for example CSR, ethical practices, sustainability.

PWC notes that we have already seen some responses to such challenges from using more total solutions, for example, the use of total cost of ownership (TCO), supplier optimisation and, as in the above mentioned IBM report, better linkages in the supply chain using real-time information.

The traditional focus of procurement has been on reducing internal costs, for example by downsizing, automating and organisational process reengineering, however, PWC see that there is an under focus on external purchased goods and services costs, which they see can be improved by supply chain integration, and by strategic procurement, especially where external supplier spending is high.

As on average, this spend is at 55% of revenue then any reduction in spend goes straight to the bottom line, e.g. a 5% reduction in costs can result in 50% increase in profit; however to get this could mean increasing sales by 50% or by reducing overheads by 20%.

Most organisations however concentrate on reactively managing current "issues" or "crises" - but by investing time in a correct risk management process, this is an effective way of stopping those future risks from turning into crises. Essentially this involves a move from being "reactive" to being "proactive", as is more fully detailed in the diagram below:

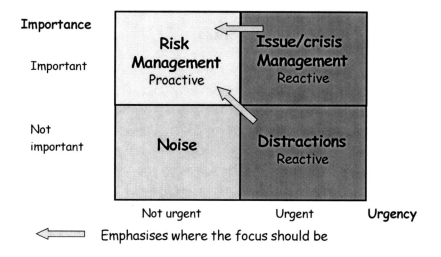

Source derived from: Covey, "7 habits of Highly Effective People"

Risk Management

This needs a risk management culture that involves:
1)   Procurement strategy.
2)   Managing procurement risks.
3)   Evaluation and prioritisation of risks.

1) Procurement Strategy

The starting point is to categorise/segment what is bought so that we can focus resources where we can concentrate on the important few, and not the trivial many, for example, using the Kraljic model:

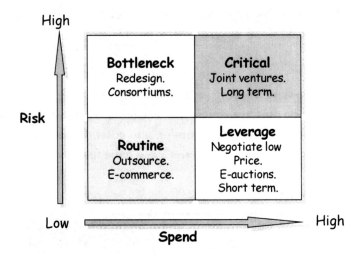

- Routine items: Routine buying of commodities, needing efficiency. Relationships may be conducted at "arms length" for those low value items required irregularly; e.g. stationery.
- Leverage items are those where a high volume is purchased from a competitive market with many suppliers. Here therefore the need is to continually buy at the lowest cost; e.g. standard commodity items.
- Bottleneck items: Need here is to ensure the supply and reduce the risk on non-supply and disruption to the organisations, often difficult as there are often only a few monopoly suppliers; e.g. OEM spare parts.
- Critical items require closer relationships to ensure competitive advantage is maintained. These will involve longer term relationships and partnering approaches with suppliers.

An example of such a categorisation is as follows:

Strategic items
- Critical items are 5 % of suppliers and known as strategic suppliers.
- Bottleneck items are 10% of suppliers and known as key suppliers.

Tactical items
- Leverage items, are 35% of suppliers and known as preferred suppliers.
- Routine items are 50 % of suppliers and known as other suppliers.

2) Managing procurement risks

This will involve an examination of the following:

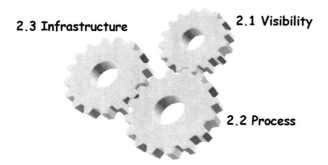

2.3 Infrastructure   **2.1 Visibility**

2.2 Process

2.1. Visibility
- Is all the information needed available?
- Who has the data/accessibility?
- Are the categories correct/reviewed when?
- Is the category data clean/out of date?

2.2. Process
Do all of the processes, shown on the procurement cycle diagram below, from need to review, actually support us?

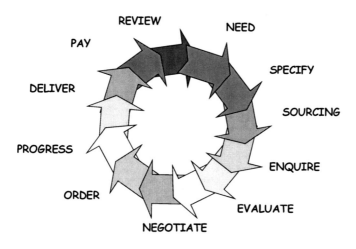

REVIEW   NEED
PAY
SPECIFY
DELIVER
SOURCING
PROGRESS
ENQUIRE
ORDER
EVALUATE
NEGOTIATE

Other key questions to be answered here are as follows:

- How do you determine your customers' needs?
- How do you determine areas of risk?
- How do you measure your customer satisfaction levels?

2.3. Infrastructure

Are we comfortable with our:

- Organisation structure, for example should it be cross-functional?
- Technology, for example are we using the right ICT?
- Facilities, for example, do we have the right infrastructures?
- People, for example, have we got T-shaped people, those that have depth in procurement skills but also have cross-functional supply chain skills?

3) Evaluate and prioritise the 6 risks

1) Strategic vulnerability:

- Public boycott.
- Negative media coverage.
- Merger and acquisition activities.
- Ethics violations.
- Product issues.
- Union climate.
- Ineffective planning.

2) Hazard vulnerability:

- Product liability.
- Major disruption in DC.
- Loss of key facilities.
- Lighting strikes.
- Earthquake.
- Flood.

3) Financial vulnerability

- Changes in regulations.
- Exchange rates.
- Recession.
- Commodity price increases.
- Energy prices.

4) Operations vulnerability
- ICT failures.
- Theft.
- Key suppliers fail.
- Accidents.

5) Reputation risks
- "Guilt by association" as use suppliers deemed irresponsible by others.
- Judged as buying non environmental goods/services.
- Ethical standards.

6) Stakeholder pressures
- NGOs.
- HMG.
- Investors.
- Peer pressure.

All of these 6 risks need evaluating, then assessing and categorising, as follows:

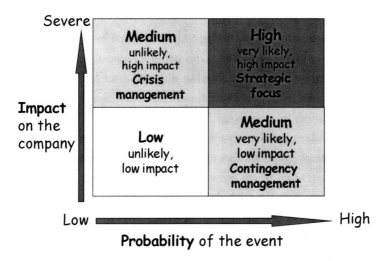

Risk Management is then used, ensuring a proactive and not a reactive view, as follows (overleaf):

Importance	Not urgent	Urgent	
Important	Risk Management Proactive	Crisis Management Reactive	
Not important	Noise	Distractions Reactive	
	Not urgent	Urgent	Urgency

Case Study: Risk assessment in purchasing

Specific issues and questions to be addressed include:

• Whether or not a **supply strategy** is in place in the organisation and is widely known and understood. If not, one needs to be devised and agreed with everyone and all agree to abide by it.

• Addressing the **financial implications**/risk involved, including the level of investment in stock.

• Critically reviewing the **planning estimates** given by each function within the organisation to guard against demand being inflated at each stage.

• How **dependent is the organisation on particular key suppliers**; are they single sourced/dual sourced/multi-sourced? This should be critically reviewed and changes implemented as necessary.

• How **dependent are the suppliers on the organisation's organisations?** While it might be of some comfort to learn that the buyers organisation is their biggest customer, this is not necessarily an ideal position to be in. The buyers' organisations with them, while profitable to them, may not provide a sufficient margin to fund new technology or organisations re-engineering. Also, if they have other customers, they may obtain new ideas from them which could be of general benefit.

• Have the **supplier's capacity** and development plans been reviewed? What are their production facilities like? Are their quality control procedures satisfactory? Is their production facility flexible enough to meet both anticipated and unforeseen requirements? Do they have efficient transport delivery arrangements?

- What **contingency plans** do the suppliers (as well as their trading partners) have in the event that they have a problem, for example, labour difficulties?
- The **supplier suppliers**, and the supply chain as a whole, should be kept under constant review to ensure that there are no weak links.
- **Contracts** with suppliers should be kept under review, ensuring that the buyer's interests are clearly represented. All contractual clauses need to be examined; for example is there a service level agreement with consequences for non-performance. Can quantities be varied and by how much, how often and is there a cost for doing so? Can the buyer suspend or cancel the agreement and in such cases does a penalty apply?
- **How are suppliers selected?** Specifically, is there a formal procedure and, equally important, is there a set procedure for regular reviews? Has their financial position been reviewed? Is their environmental and ethical policy acceptable, and does it align with that of the buyers organisation? Is their management team easy to work with and are there cross relationships at senior levels in the two organisations to resolve problems should they arise?
- What steps can the buyer's organisations take **to compensate** for 'lumpy/irregular demand' such as seasonal fluctuations?

The purchasing professional should remember they are the link between their own organisation and the supplier. Demand planning should have been done at a corporate level with input from purchasing. Changes or fluctuations in the suppliers' capability levels should also be monitored as these can assume key significance.

4: Understanding Global Trade Terminology

UK: Her Majesty's Revenue and Customs (HMRC)

When considering the movement of goods and products in and out of the UK, the influences of HMRC must be taken into account; HMRC being the result of the 2005 merger between HM Customs & Excise and the Inland Revenue. In the UK, a strong influence on Customs practices is the European Community Single Market European Act. The single market is defined as: *"An area without internal frontiers in which the free movement of goods, persons, services and capital is ensured in accordance with the treaty of Rome"*.

An historic watershed was reached in the history of the EU on the 1st May 2004 with the full membership of Cyprus, Czech Republic, Estonia, Hungary, Latvia, Lithuania, Malta, Poland, Slovakia and Slovenia; this brought in a single market of over 500 million consumers in 27 countries.

This enlargement effectively means that supply chain management is now influenced by Tax planning such as duty and tax deferrals and tax reductions. Some responses and impacts for EU and global organisations can therefore be as follows:

- Centralised purchasing.
- Contract or consignment manufacturing.
- Regional sales trading organisations.
- Centralised imports.
- Centralised warehousing.

HMRC Controls

All goods that leave or are brought into the UK are subject to controls from HMRC who are responsible for protecting "Revenue" and secondly to protect the "State". These responsibilities can be summarised as "State" protection by stopping illegal movements of drugs, arms, pornography and people and "Revenue" protection by collecting duty and taxes.

To carry out these responsibilities, HMRC effectively control and enforce the following:

- Value Added Tax.
- All customs duties collected on goods from non-EC countries. The basis for duty being a calculation on the value of the goods.

- All excise duties on principally tobacco, alcohol and mineral oils. The basis for duty being not value but on some measure of volume, weight or unit.

Customs law is not static and is continually evolving. Additionally Customs regulations are complex and often very specific. Therefore, up-to-date knowledge of customs law for specific organisations is critical, and also needs to be checked out fully for specific countries to verify what may be applied to individual requirements. Further information is available from:

- EU Regimes: www. hmrc.gov.uk; www.berr.gov.uk (this is the former Department of Trade and Industry (DTI));
  www.export.org.uk; www. businesslink.gov.uk; www.europe.eu.
- Non-EU regimes: your local UK chamber of commerce; appropriate UK-based embassy/commercial attaches; export agent in the appropriate country.

The Customs Tariff

This comprises of the following three volumes:

1. Volume 1 contains essential background information for importers and exporters. It covers duty relief schemes and the contact addresses for organisations such as Department for Organisations, Enterprise & Regulatory Reform (the former Department of Trade and Industry (DTI)), Department of Environment, Food and Rural Affairs (formerly MAFF, Ministry of Agriculture and Fish) and Forestry Commission. It also contains an explanation of Excise duty, Tariff Quotas and many similar topics.

2. Volume 2 contains the 16,000 or so Commodity Codes set out on a chapter-by-chapter basis. It lists duty rates and other directions such as import licensing and preferential duty rates. These are explored further below

3. Volume 3 contains a box-by-box completion guide for import and export entries (the C88 form), the complete list of Customs Procedure Codes (CPCs) for importing and exporting, the Country Codes for the world and lists of UK docks and airports both alphabetically and by their Entry Processing Unit (EPU) numbers, along with further general information about importing or exporting.

The Tariff is the "bible" which covers every type of goods by nomenclature commodity coding. This coding has worldwide recognition so it is important to know exactly what the coding(s) is/are that cover one's own goods. The classification used is as follows:

- Digits 1-6 is the nomenclature e.g. 530101.
- Digits 7/8 are for EC statistics.
- Digit 9 is for export statistics to non-EC countries.
- Digit 10/11 cover non-EC imports.
- Digits 12-15 cover special imports from non-EC countries.

Preferential Duties

In addition to the permitted duty free movement between EC member states, other preferential duties are found. In outline these are as follows:

- EC Preferences: these allow duty free or lower duty for goods originating in certain non-EC countries.
- Inward Processing Relief: this allows relief from duty and VAT on non-EC origin goods which are to be exported outside of the EC.
- End Use Relief: this allows for certain non-EC origin goods to be imported at preferential rates for a specific use. VAT is still paid.
- Customs Warehousing: this allows for goods of non-EC origin to be stored without the payment of duty or VAT.
- Free Zones: these are areas which allow goods to be exempt from all customs control.

Further information is available from the sources shown above.

Single Administration Document (SAD)

This combines export, import and transit documentation within the EU with an eight copy documentation set; where copies 1-3 remain at export and copies 4-8 travel with the goods.

Basic Export Procedures

Export declarations are only needed for goods that are:
- sent within the EU that are not in free circulation in the EU.
- sent outside the EU.

There are two basic ways of making entry:

1) When all details are known at the time of export then Pre-entry is used with SAD and pre-entry is mandatory for restricted or dutiable goods. Special procedures however apply for:

- goods exported from bonded warehouse.
- goods in transit through the UK.
- licensed goods, such as arms.
- some common agricultural policy (CAP) goods.
- goods exported for process, repair or exhibition purposes.

2) When all details are not known at the time of export then a Simplified Clearance Procedure (SCP) can be used, and goods cannot be loaded onto the exporting vessel, without customs having been notified. The documents to be used here can be one from:

- copy 2 of SAD.
- standard shipping note.
- CMR consignment note.
- Dangerous goods note.
- Own document.

The important qualifier here is that the export trader has a customs registered number (CRN) with an export identifier (ECI) entered on the above document. After export, 14 days is allowed to match the SCP with the complete post shipment documentation (i.e. as required for pre-entry).

As will be seen with basic import procedures (following), various schemes allow local export clearance and period entries to be made, subject to certain terms and conditions.

Basic Import Procedures

Every consignment imported must be cleared through customs. Arrangements must be made to pay any duty or tax before they are released. There are variations in the basic procedures, for example, goods being imported on inward processing relief, goods for customs warehousing.

Customs clearance and entry documentation is often left with freight forwarders/forwarding agents, who will give advice and undertake the appropriate procedures as agents to the importer. Care needs to be taken as any incorrect procedures by freight forwarders will be undertaken as agents to the importer; therefore any "buck" stays with the importer and any incorrect procedures could not only result in wrong rates being paid, but also in fines.

Any delays in customs clearance will most certainly result in rent and/or demurrage/ detention charges being levied on the goods. These can be very expensive as port and clearance areas are designed mainly for transit and not for storage. So, in the event of there being any "undue storage", the charges are often set deliberately high to discourage such storage usage.

Basic documentation import requirements are as follows:
- A clear commercial invoice.
- A packing list or details of individual items in each package.
- Clear instructions on delivery address.
- Transport document such as the document of title bill of lading.
- Documents related to any specialised customs requirements such as certificate of origin, import licence etc.
- Preparation of customs import entry. This involves; determining the correct tariff heading; availability of any appropriate supporting documentation (such as those above); establishing the value for customs purposes (this is principally the transaction value adjusted to give the price at the first point of entry into the EC); preparing the customs entry; accounting for VAT payment (for example, either this will be due immediately, or for approved importers, it can be deferred using a bank guaranteed facility): and checking to ensure insurance covers the delivered value including VAT and duty.

As stated above, preparation of customs entries is a specialist task. A high percentage of error is found in prepared entries. This not only adds to the administration workload of all involved but also contributes to delay and extra costs.

Checklist: 7 mistakes with Customs Entries

Incorrect Classification
The customs classification of import is often difficult, especially with mixed or new products because the customs tariff struggles to keep abreast of technological

developments. Average duty rate on import to the EU is 4% of the landed costs of the imports, but rates vary from 0 - 217%. Therefore any error can have significant implications to an organisation's margins with adjustments upwards and downwards.

Failing to make all the necessary adjustments to the purchase invoice price
The customs regulations provide for a number of items that must be added, or may be deducted to the invoice price for customs duty purposes. Each adjustment is subject to various conditions.

Typical additions you may need to make to your customs value include royalties, selling commissions, insurance and freight costs to the EU, tooling and materials supplied to the seller by the buyer free of charge or at a reduced cost.

Typical deductions include buying commissions, finance charges, post import support, certain warranty costs. Importers often fail to make the necessary adjustments and your agents may be unaware of their existence.

A clear understanding of your contract and the Incoterms agreed is needed to meet your valuation obligations. Unfortunately, any agents used to submit customs declarations are unlikely to know these key details.

Using an inappropriate method of valuing the goods
The customs regulations set out various methods for determining an acceptable customs value, which must be applied in a prescribed order. However, most of your imports are likely to be valued under method one, using the export sale price.

There are a number of instances where it is not possible to use this method, including transfers to branch organisations or agents, sub-contract work where the materials are provided free of charge etc. In these circumstances you will need to determine an alternative method of valuation in accordance with the methods set out in the customs regulations.

Incorrect origin on imports
The EU has entered into various trade agreements with overseas countries which allow your qualifying goods can be imported at a reduced or nil rate of duty.

Unfortunately, the system is prone to incorrect application by overseas suppliers' authorities. Where errors come to light, the customs authorities in the EU will always look to recover the full rate of duty from you.

Incorrect origin on exports

You may be asked to complete origin certificates by your customers in non-EU countries to enable them to import your goods free from duty. This helps make your goods more competitive or improve your margins.

You may be providing these documents without a clear understanding of the appropriate conditions or the evidence needed to support the legal declaration been made. If your goods are found not to qualify you may be subject to penalties. Furthermore, your customer will also be subject to penalties and additional duty demands, which they will seek to recover from you.

Incorrect application of a duty relief scheme

There are a number of customs duty relief schemes available to you to reduce or even remove the customs duty costs. However, all of these schemes require you to take on additional responsibilities. If you fail to comply with all of these obligations, forgetting to submit returns or gather appropriate evidence then any benefits you enjoy can be removed with retrospective effect.

For example, HM Revenue & Customs are currently seeking to recover duties saved by people using Inward Processing Relief (IPR) where their freight agents have not entered the correct information in one of the 54 boxes of the customs export declaration. This error usually results from your failure to instruct the agents properly.

Inconsistent treatment

The customs authorities will have a schedule of all the information you submitted at import and export when they come to carry out an audit. This schedule will often highlight different classifications applied to the same goods imported across various consignments, the entry of your goods in to duty relief procedures but no matching discharges etc. These errors are usually the result of poor communication between you and your agent or through lack of co-ordination between various different organisations functions within your organisations or group. These errors are easily identified by HM Customs and indicate a poor level of control of your customs function, making you more susceptible to lengthy and time consuming investigations. If you are not comfortable with the control of the customs function you should consider carrying out a review to highlight any potential errors, which can then be addressed going forward.

Source: www.internationaltrade.co.uk

The Documentation Chain

Accuracy in documentation for global trade is vital as mistakes are expensive and difficult/timely to correct. The following guidelines need to be followed:

Sender documents
- Invoice to include shipping marks, terms of sale, terms of payment, unit price and invoice total, with the basic consignment details (gross, net weight, dimensions).
- Packing list, if not included on the invoice.
- Certificate of origin, only for some goods/destinations.
- Inspection certificate, only for some importers countries.
- Dangerous goods note, if applicable.
- Shipping note.
- Shipping instruction.
- Export licence for some goods (some drugs, chemicals, arms/ammunition).
- Insurance policy and/or certificate.

Movement Documents
- Carriage document which acts as receipt and evidence of contract of carriage. With sea transport a full "ocean" bill of lading is a legal document of title meaning that the goods at destination will only be released to the holder of the original bill of lading.
- Customs, for example, to non-EC destinations, SAD for post entry, for example, movement certificates to EC trade agreement areas.

Documents (optional) that maybe needed by Receivers:
- Certificate of origin, only required for some goods/destinations.

- Inspection certificate, required only for some importers countries.
- Consular only required for some goods/destinations, for example, the UK based consul of the overseas country has to stamp/authenticate senders invoices.

Receivers will have to arrange for customs clearance in their own country and may require an Import Licence. Clearly, to undertake trouble free import customs clearance, all documents must match and be accurate.

Electronic Customs/Trading

UK Customs (www.hmrc.gov.uk) were pioneers in electronics that enable customs control to be moved away from the ports, keeping port-based procedures to a minimum. Import entries for non-EC goods have used the Customs Handling of Import and Export Freight (CHIEF) system for many years and export entries also have moved to a total electronic submission. Intrastate entries also exist electronically for EC goods/movements.

ElecTra is a toolkit to transmit trade documentation and replace paper documents. It is based on TOPFORM, which followed the 1960s JLCD system for aligned documents and is managed by SITPRO (www.sitpro.org.uk). In turn, ElecTra has been the basis for the United Nations electronic Trade Documents (UNeDocs), a project sponsored by the United Nations Centre for Trade Facilitation and Electronic Organisations (UN/CEFACT).

Insurance

Adequate insurance will protect the interest of those who have goods in transit. This can be especially important when buying on ex-works terms. Here not only are the freight costs to be added to the product ex-works value, but also all duties and taxes that may be payable on the goods until they arrive at the buyers final place of delivery.Insurance will provide cover beyond the liabilities of the freight handlers, as transporters, carriers and freight handler's levels of liability are limited, varied and minimal.

Most Cargo insurance policies include the globally accepted 'Institute Cargo Clauses' (ICC). There are three basic sets of clauses covering transits by sea and there are similar clauses applying for transit by air:

- ICC (A) covers "all risks" of loss or damage to the subject matter insured, subject to specific exclusions as below.
- ICC (B) Provides more limited cover on a 'named' perils basis.
- ICC (C) Provides a similar cover to the B Clauses above, but restricted to fewer catastrophe type perils.

The risks covered are as follows:

a) For loss or damage that is reasonably attributable.

Reasonably attributable risk	A clause	B clause	C clause
Accidental damage	yes	no	no
Fire or explosion	yes	yes	yes
Vessel stranding etc.	yes	yes	yes
Overturn/derailment	yes	yes	yes
Earthquake, volcano, lightning	yes	yes	yes
Theft	yes	no	no

b) Loss or damage caused by:

Loss or damage caused by:	A clause	B clause	C clause
General Average/Sacrifice *	yes	yes	yes
Jettison	yes	yes	yes
Washing overboard	yes	yes	no
Water	yes	yes	no
Total loss during loading or unloading	yes	yes	no

*General average sacrifice refers to the loss arising as a result of sacrifices that had to be made for the common safety of a ship and its cargo; for example, damage incurred to cargo during fire fighting operations or the jettisoning of some cargo to re-float a stranded vessel.

The Institute Cargo Clauses A, B and C contain a list of exclusions which are common to all three. In general terms they relate to:

- Wilful misconduct of the assured.
- Ordinary leakage or loss in weight or volume, and ordinary wear and tear.
- Insufficient or unsuitable packing.
- Inherent vice.
- Delay.
- Insolvency of Ship owners or Charterers.
- Nuclear or radioactive weapons.
- Un-seaworthiness of vessels or containers.
- War and Strikes risks. Traditionally, the Cargo insurance market has charged separately for War and Strikes risks. Rates for War and Strikes are set by a market body, the War Risks Rating Committee, whose membership comprises underwriters from both Lloyds and the Institute of London Underwriters. The committee sets basic Scale rates for War and Strikes, which are adhered to throughout the market. Occasionally, the War Risks Rating Committee will take account of potential or actual trouble spots in the world and will either decree a war rate which is higher than the standard or will refer to the more volatile trouble spots as held covered at rates, terms and conditions to be agreed by the underwriter.

In addition to the above exclusions the Institute Cargo Clauses Band C also contain an exclusion relating to malicious damage.

Cargo Open Cover

Policies can be used that will provide automatic cover for all defined shipments for twelve months, at agreed rates and conditions. Then you calculate the premiums and include insurance costs in the contract price quoted to customers. A declaration of sending is then made, and the premium adjusted accordingly.

The scope of cover available is negotiable, but typically this will include: All Risks cover from warehouse to warehouse, and/or Catastrophe cover from port to port.

The advantages are that the open cover policy covers all shipments which fall within the scope of the policy. There is therefore no risk of there being any goods uninsured. Because of the expectation of continued shipments through the 12-month period, the rates are usually lower than for a single voyage. For high volume 'Open Covers' insurance brokers are able to provide a supply of Certificates of Insurance, which you can issue yourself.

Incoterms

In trading overseas a major decision is to be taken on who pays freight charges and when the liability transfers between senders/receivers, shippers/consignees and suppliers/customers. There are many options available that have different separation points. For example, in UK national trade the carriage paid home is a standard accepted term of delivery; in international trade this is, however, not the norm and it may be that the ex-works term is used, which means the buyer is responsible from "ex-works" for example from the sender's/supplier's premises.

It is interesting that in the early 2000s in the UK trade, the major FMCG retailers have rediscovered the ex-works terms with their "factory gate pricing" (FGP) concept, whereas "ex-works" within the standard international commercial terms (Incoterms) have been in existence since 1936.

Incoterms are currently grouped as follows:
- E Terms: Goods available at sellers own premises (named).
- F Terms : Goods delivered to a named place/carrier appointed by buyer.
- C Terms: Goods carried to named destination, but with no risk to the seller after shipment or despatch.
- D Terms: Goods carried to named destination, with all risks to the seller.

Looking at these in more detail, the following terms apply to any transport mode:
- EXW = Ex Works
- FCA = Free Carrier
- CPT = Carriage Paid
- CIP = Carriage Insurance Paid
- DAF = Delivered Frontier
- DDU = Delivered Duty Unpaid
- DDP = Delivered Duty Paid

The following terms only apply to sea or inland waterway transport:
- FAS = Free Alongside Ship

- FOB = Free On Board
- CFR = Cost and Freight
- CIF = Cost, Insurance, Freight
- DES = Delivered Ex Ship
- DEQ = Delivered Ex Quay

As mentioned above, the place must be named, e.g. EXW Manchester, CIF Hong Kong.

The current version is Incoterms 2000, with the next version expected as Incoterms 2010, but at the time of writing, this was scheduled to be released late in 2010 and if then released, would take effect on January 1, 2011.

It is expected for example that there will be a new term, DAP (Delivered At Place), that merges the former less popular DAF, DDU, DES and DEQ terms, which contain areas of overlap.

When using Incoterms, the version must be shown, for example, FOB Felixstowe (Incoterms 2000).

By looking at what is involved when costing international trade, the following costing sheet shows more fully the appropriate break points on freight charges and the liability transfers involved when using Incoterms.

Incoterms Costing Sheet

Customer: Terms of delivery:
Enquiry for: Terms and methods at payment:
Enquiry dated: Transport by:

UNIT COST
Percentage profit...
Overseas agents commission...
Export turnover, levies..
Other costs...
TOTAL EXW

Packing ....

Marking...

Strapping or bundling...

Transport to Docks/Depot/

Airport...

Loading charges..

Demurrage/Storage...

Heavy lift charges...

Customs clearance (export)...

Other charges..

TOTAL FOB/FCA

FREIGHT

Weight...

Volume..

Ad valorem...

Surcharges..

Rebates..

Other charges..

TOTAL CFR/CPT

MARINE INSURANCE

Insurance premium..

TOTAL CIF/CIP

UNLOADING...

TOTAL DEQ/DAF

Transport to buyer..

Import duties/taxes...

Customs clearance (import)..

TOTAL DDP

FINANCING CHARGES
Banking...

ECGD premium...

Other Charges..

TOTAL

The chosen Incoterm is a term for the contract of sale and is not the contract of carriage, as Incoterms tell the parties what to do with respect to:
- The division of costs and risks between the parties.
- Export and import clearance.
- Who is to organise the transport of the goods.

The choice of Incoterms is central to conducting global and international organisations; it also relates to pricing and to control decisions. For example, an organisation exporting may need to know what the prices of their products are in the destination market; but if for example, ex-works pricing is being used then this will not enable a full view to be taken.

If they were to use DDP terms then this could mean selling in a market at different prices with a better profit; as they are now able to price at what the "market will stand", rather than using an ex-works or FOB pricing with a only "standard" profit margin.

Another example is where an organisation is importing from say the Far East and may wish to control the movements more closely, so they have the visibility of arrival times. When they buy CIF UK Port or DDP, then this control can be lost. If they were to change to buying on ex-works or FOB Far East Port terms, then this will give them the full control of the routing and shipment to the UK.

However, switching existing suppliers/customers over to different terms may not be easy, as they may be reluctant to abandon existing transport arrangements and also reluctant to revealing their pricing structures.

Normal commercial rules of negotiation will therefore often need to apply to bring in this change. In the demise of Marks and Spencer in the late 1990s, changing terms to FOB supply severely strained supplier relationships due to this being imposed without real discussion but with an automatic expectation from Marks and Spencer that the change would be made.

The following Case Study emphasises changing Incoterms:

Case Study: Changing to buying EXW

A substantial amount of goods are imported into the UK every year. With more organisations deciding to outsource manufacturing, then this trend continues to grow. Indeed importing is already the norm for many organisations, especially those involved in handling FMCG.

Importing involves a more distant supplier with extended transit lead-times. As lead-times are one the critical components when deciding how much to order from suppliers, then knowledge and control of this lead-time is necessary. Indeed, fixed reliable lead-times are a "mandatory" component for effective inventory management.

However, what often happens is that many UK buyers decide to import on CIF or C&F Incoterms and therefore, they leave the organisation of the transit with the supplier. Effectively therefore, the associated supplier lead-time is also externalised. Importing organisations will then often spend and waste time expediting and checking where the goods are, when they will arrive etc.

Delays in transit times can also cause potential product shortages, impact on customer service levels and to not satisfying customer requirements. With regular repeat orders, then any delayed transit times will also inevitably lead to increased stock levels, as the buying organisation will then be holding additional stock as a protection against the uncertainty of the suppliers lead-time.

Benefits of changing to EXW/FOB terms

It is however possible to better control imports by switching to Ex-works (EXW) or Free on Board (FOB) Incoterms and the following benefits will then be realised:

- Control and knowledge of exactly what is happening; (management needs to recall here that the management cycle not only involves planning, organising, directing but also controlling).
- Visibility and knowledge of exactly where the products are during the transit; as simply, the transit it is now in your direct control.
- Cheaper freight costs as you are now directly paying them. Importers and buyers need to appreciate that suppliers have a margin on the freight costs they have paid; after all, they are not over time, going to be loosing money.

2 steps on how to change

1) Starting out
A useful place to start is to understand some of the aspects of total supply chain management, for example:

- What are your costs of holding inventory?
- What supply lead-time is required?
- What part of the supply lead-time, is the transit lead-time?
- What would be the effects of reliable and consistent on time in full receipts for your organisations?
- How does the above compare to your current situation?

Answers to these questions are always revealing and also often show, how the internal structure is fragmented and unorganised to undertake effective importing.

Answers will also provide the basis for accessing the benefits of changing.

2) The next steps
- Ask for the suppliers EXW price.
- Negotiate freight terms, possibly by going out to tender for a global or regional freight forwarder.

• Check on the track/trace system to be used. This can be a simple key point reporting with spreadsheet recording, or, an instant on demand access to a carriers system.

• Assess the risk of changing, for example, any extra management costs, the insurance costs and the risks of direct exposure to regular variations in freight rates.

• Compare and contrast the current CIF price against the new EXW price plus the freight, insurance and risk costs. It is important to ensure a like for like comparison with the current methods as many of the current costs may well be hidden.

• If deciding to change, and effectively changing the procurement and buying strategy, then ensure that the internal structure will support the changes.

What others have done

There is much evidence to support that the changes detailed above are worthwhile as shown by the following three case studies.

1) A major food retailer had spending of £1200 million on imports via third party wholesalers and £500 million on direct imports. For example, home and leisure products were ordered through UK agents who arranged everything to DDP.

Meanwhile, beers, wines and spirits were bought EXW works or FOB with freight arranged through various forwarders. A change in management identified that they had:
• no systems.
• no cost visibility.
• no economy of scale.
• poor product availability.
• an internal fragmented structure; for example,
• Trading on product selection, negotiations, selection of suppliers, and ordering
• Finance on letters of credit, payments; Logistics on order quantity and phasing into supply chain.

The organisation tendered and then outsourced to one forwarder but maintained and determined carrier selection when appropriate. The reported results were:
- Freight costs fell by 8 per cent.
- Duty charges reduced by 10 per cent.
- Fuller visibility of supply chain.
- Reduced stock levels.
- Centralised the previous fragmented internal control as a new structure followed the new strategy.

2) A major clothes retailer with nearly 200 stores had 70% of products imported, mainly from Far East. They identified that they had the following problems:
- No accurate data therefore no visibility.
- Orders arrive "unexpectedly".
- 40% time spent of phoning/checking.
- Paid high demurrage/rent port costs.
- Restricted on buying currency forward.
- Poor QC.

The solution was to:
- Change from C&F to FOB and use one UK forwarder.
- Set up a simple database tracking on transfer points. PO, confirmed, tariff heading, cargo booked, authorise shipment, confirm shipment, documents banked, documents received, arrival time, clearance time, arrival at DC., QC checked, released/available.
- Integrated all their internal systems.

The benefits reported were:
- Lower demurrage costs.
- Improved warehouse efficiency due to scheduled arrivals.
- Improved finance due to forward currency buying.
- Quicker customs clearances.
- Better product availability.

3) A supplier of branded and own label cleaning products to major retailers:
Cost-cutting initiatives had become a way of life in the face of major supply

chain challenges. The organisation's supply chain manager noted that: "In the past four or five years we have had to work hard at controlling our costs at a time when there have been no price increases from our customers".

The operation therefore changed to buying products ex-works. The challenge of bringing in consignments cost effectively is made more difficult by the low value nature of the products, many of which are very light and use up large quantities of space. The organisation's continued success is seen as directly related to its freight cost management and arrangements.

Payments

An invoice is needed to record of goods despatched and the terms under which they have been supplied. Invoices are also used for customs purposes and it is important that it's correctly prepared (including any needed certification or consular endorsements if required).

There are various terms of payment:
*   Open Account. This is the least secure and used where both parties know and trust each other; it is also the most common form of payment.
*   Bills of exchange. This is more secure and is a promise to pay via a bank. It is a written order by a seller to the buyer to pay on demand (at sight or at a future term or date, e.g. 60 days from the date of the invoice). Documents are exchanged when the bank has received the "promise."
*   Letter of Credit (irrevocable and confirmed). This is the most secure as payment is made/maybe guaranteed by a bank, once specified conditions are met. It is an undertaking in writing by a bank to pay for goods provided there is compliance with the conditions laid down. Letters of credit accounts for around 20 per cent of world trade. However over 60 per cent are initially rejected because of errors/omissions.
*   Cash in advance is the most secure where payment is made against an invoice and before/in advance of goods being despatched.
*   Factoring is where you "sell" your debtors receivables for a charge of 2-4 percent of the invoiced amount. The factor manages the collection. Effectively the seller then is using open account terms.

- Counter Purchase is where goods are sold and exchanged for goods supplied, which equals the value sold.

5: Understanding Cultural Issues

Definitions and Cultural Awareness

There are many definitions of culture:

"Culture is the pool of rules, beliefs, and values by which a group's members conceptually order the objects and events in their lives in order to operate in a manner acceptable to its members."

"The values, traditions, worldview, and social and political relationships that are created, shared, and transformed by a group of people bound together by a common history, geographic location, language, social class, and/or religion."

"Culture is a dynamic, constantly changing process that is shaped by political, social and economic conditions."

"An integrated system of learned behaviour patterns that is characteristic of any given society. It refers to the total way of life, including how people think, feel and behave."

"The world in which you were born is just one model of reality. Other cultures are not failed attempts at being like you. They are unique manifestations of the human spirit."

"The concepts, habits, skills, arts, instruments, and institutions of a given people in a given place."

"Culture is the way we do things around here."

Culture is therefore:
*   Dynamic, and is neither fixed nor static.
*   A continuous and cumulative process.
*   Learned and shared by a people.
*   The behaviour and values exhibited by a people.
*   Symbolically represented through language and interactions.
*   Guides people in their thinking, feeling and acting.

The Cultural Web

Culture is comprised of the following set of interlinked aspects:

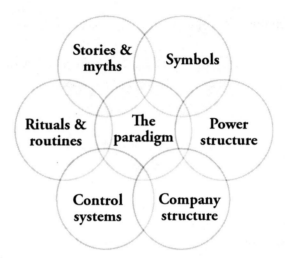

All of these are experienced in different ways by different people, as culture is a learned set of shared interpretations and is about beliefs, values, and norms. Culture affects the behaviour of large groups of people, yet every individual and nation has a set of distinctive values. However, individuals and nations have certain expectations regarding the way people think, behave, and believe.

It gets complicated, as just as in England: a Yorkshireman and a Lancastrian see themselves as being different, and there can be differences, but they also share much in common, although in certain circumstances they will choose not to!

Culture helps us and others to define who we are and creates a sense of belonging for those who understand and are familiar with it. However, culture can also be a barrier as people unfamiliar with the rules and rituals can feel like outsiders.

Consequently, cultural differences need to be seen as an asset, not a liability and managers need to be culturally aware and flexible in their leadership styles.

Culture will have varied impacts on global organisations, for example in:
- Negotiations; such as differences between western confrontation styles versus the eastern, relationship-style of negotiating.

- Human resources management; such as in different motivation sources, and in leadership styles such as individualistic versus collective/social.
- Design of organizations, such as the degrees of autonomy.
- Marketing, such as cultural differences (tastes), income differences (demographics).

This also means that working globally has some uniqueness, for example, a view that international managers have it tough as they must operate on a number of different premises at any one time.

These premises arise from:
- Their culture of origin.
- The culture in which they are working.
- The culture of the organisation which employs them.

(Source: Fons Trompenaars)

Besides the cultural problems, MNCs can also have issues with:
- The diversity of worldwide industry standards, e.g. television sets must be manufactured on a country-by-country basis.
- A continual demand by local customers for differentiated products, e.g. consumer goods that must meet local tastes.
- The importance of being an insider, e.g. customers who prefer to "buy local".
- The difficulty of managing global organizations, e.g. local subsidiaries that want more decentralization and others that want less.
- The need to allow subsidiaries to use their own abilities and talents and not be restrained by headquarters, e.g. local units that know how to customize products for their market and generate high returns on investment with limited production output.

Examining Culture

Culture is found and experienced at different layers (like in an onion), where the whole is made up of different layers but with each layer being only one part of the whole. The outer layer is the visible one and with culture, this comprises of things like artefacts and products with their own language, food styles, fashions and types of buildings and markets.

The middle invisible layer comprises of attitudes (our opinions and is what is felt or thought about) plus our values (for example what we see are good or bad influences, our aspirations and desires).

The inner layer and at the core are our beliefs, which are those things that represent the truth for us.

Culture is therefore going to be shaped by the way we:
- Think (Cognition).
- Interact (Behaviour).
- Communicate (Language).
- Transmit knowledge to the next generation (Education).

Culture has a normal distribution, and has ranges, as not all people in a culture have identical sets of artefacts, norms, values and assumptions; however, whilst there is usually a normal distribution spread, this does not mean that we can stereotype everyone in a culture. It only takes one individual (perhaps the one we are dealing with) to be different; therefore one individual's personality can mediate a culture.

So stereotyping with a generalized belief about a group of people is dangerous as is cultural discrimination (negative actions based on prejudice that lead to loss of opportunity for a certain group) and cultural prejudice (negative attitudes and emotions about a group, e.g. fear and hatred, about a group).

Prejudice can be defined as a premature judgment or an opinion that is formed without examination of the facts. Often these prejudgments are prejudices as they are based on primary or secondary dimensions and attitudes in favour of or against people that are based on these traits.

Prejudiced people tend to think in terms of stereotypes, which are generalizations made about all members of a particular group. Stereotypes exist because they provide easy and convenient ways to deal with people and are often based on one or several real experiences in dealing with others. Stereotypes then become resistant to change because people will more readily believe information that confirms their previous experience, than believe the evidence that challenges it. In this sense, stereotypes and prejudices are fixed; a potentially dangerous position when dealing with individuals who always have their "unique glory."

Models and Views of Culture

At the risk of the above mentioned dangers of stereotyping, in this section we present some different models of culture.

Broad Model of Culture

The following is a broad model of culture:

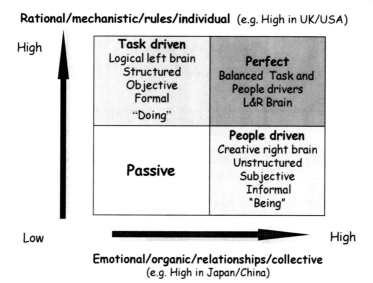

Rational/mechanistic/rules/individual (e.g. High in UK/USA)

High

Task driven Logical left brain Structured Objective Formal "Doing"	Perfect Balanced Task and People drivers L&R Brain
Passive	People driven Creative right brain Unstructured Subjective Informal "Being"

Low → High

Emotional/organic/relationships/collective
(e.g. High in Japan/China)

The above shows the predominant western view of being rational and "self" against the predominant eastern view of being more emotional and collective; many other views on west/east follow.

Cultures: Western and Eastern

Aspects	More Western	More Eastern
Culture generally	Diverse	Homogenous
Preferences	- Fight for beliefs and "positions" - Clear cut - Specific - The Facts	- Need harmony - Ambiguous - General - Unspoken agreements
"I"/"We" balance	Individualistic	Group is more important
Emotions	Displayed in public	Held back in public
Orientation	Towards results	Process orientation

Communication	Verbal preferences	Non-verbal preferences (eye contact, body language)
Verbal communication	What is spoken	Who is speaking
View of Time	Follow times strictly	More relaxed view
Objectives	Outcome orientated	Relationship and process orientated
Organisations/Respect and face	Organisations on hand and the details. Manners mildly important. Direct criticism can be acceptable	Look for respect to be shown. Good manners are important. Use "positives" e.g. if might work better if…."
Seniority	Age and rank of less importance	Counts a lot; age, rank and years of service
Personal space	Some find closeness embarrassing.	Will often "sit close." Mirror the body language.

Checklist: Western/Eastern Culture and Timeliness

Aspect	More Western "Through time"	More Eastern "In time"
Living/Life	In the future and work from now towards the future. May however, live on past memories= procrastinators who do not like the future and will do little that will take them to it. They are more focussed on the past and "what used to do".	In the present and work for "today".
View of past/future	See past on left and future on the right= "lets work towards it".	See the past as behind them, the future is "a mystery".
Focus	"What going to do".	"Here and now".
Deadlines	Deadlines important for example, good at keeping appointments.	Less sense of urgency.
Planning	Plan ahead.	Poor at planning ahead
View of time	Time is precious as once gone, it's gone and cannot be recovered.	Time is a gift to enjoy now, there will be more time coming, so relax

West	East
Individualism	Collectivism/group
Achievement	Modesty
Equality	Hierarchy
Winning	Harmony
Internal self-control	External control
Pride	Saving face
Respect for results	Respect for status
Respect competence	Respect elders
Time is money	Time is life
Action/doing	Being/acceptance
Systematic	Humanistic
Tasks	Relationship/loyalty
Informal	Formal
Assertiveness	Indirectness
Future/change	Past/tradition
Control	Fate
Specific/linear	Holistic
Verbal	Non-verbal

In the West, individualistic dominance emphasises goals, rights, attitude and needs, where:

- People see themselves as independent and autonomous.
- Identity is individual.
- In conflict, the response is individual.
- Achievement involves individual goal-setting and action.
- Everyone is capable of making their own choices.
- People are autonomous.
- People are accountable to themselves.

As a consequence there is focus on:
- First acquaintances, close friendships and intimate partnership between two individuals.
- A strong social norm of monogamy reflected in laws.
- An emphasis on voluntary choice due to high mobility.
- Easy long distance relationships therefore a greater availability of relationships.
- Rules in relationships may be less important, since if they are broken the relationships can be left and other found.

In the East there is a group emphasis: individual's attitudes needs and duties support the group, where:
- People see themselves as part of a circle of relationships.
- Identity is as a member of a group.
- In conflict, response is chosen jointly.
- Maintaining group harmony and cohesion is important.
- Choices are made in consultation.
- People are part of a hierarchy.
- People are accountable to the group.

As a consequence there is more emphasis on:
- Long-term kinship and social group relationships (more than two).
- A higher frequency of polygamous relationships.
- A lack of voluntary choices in relationships, due to more stationary lifestyles, with less long distance communication, leading to less availability.
- Obligations to family and social norms, for example, marriages arranged to take into account the wishes of others.
- There is a tendency for relationship interactions to be more governed by group need or equality based resource sharing and obligatory reciprocity.

- Concern for heritage, customs and traditions, thus change is viewed with suspicion, perhaps leading to greater stability.
- Rules are adhered to because of the need to maintain long-term commitment.

Astute readers may see some conflicts in the above views; this merely highlights the problems when giving broad generalizations, as individual people and situations will always vary widely.

Having said this, the reality is often that people simply do have generalised views that are born out of personal experience. The following case study provides a most interesting supply chain related aspect of such views.

Case Study: East and West Contracting Styles

Eastern respondents' comments:

The following phrases have been extracted from approximately a dozen respondents who identified with the Eastern contracting style:

- Relationship is important.
- Our communication is expressed implicitly.
- We are respectful to age and seniority.
- We are more straight-forward but less assertive.
- We have more bidding and tendering.
- Real organisations is conducted in a less organisations-like environment.
- We rely on relationship to resolve issues.
- Relationship is everything.
- Face to face contact is important.
- Our legal counsel sits with the organisations, their legal counsel is separate from the organisations.
- We are too soft, they (Western style) are too aggressive.
- They are legalistic.
- They have competitive negotiation.
- Their contracting process is time-consuming and slow.
- They are willing to have an argument over terms.
- They rely on protection of the law.
- They are slow to move towards approval.

- They are too procedurally rigid.
- They are too procedurally flexible. and
- They rely on email.

Western respondents' comments:

The following phrases have been extracted from a dozen respondents who identified with the Western contracting style:

- Their (Eastern style) emphasis on procedure is stifling.
- They are unwilling to argue, but will stall instead.
- They are less confrontational.
- They are lacking in urgency.
- Their organisations people focus on organisations terms.
- They are fast to make organisations decisions, and slow to respond to contractual queries.
- We have more legal involvement.
- We are more confrontational. and
- The contract is the end of negotiations. for them, the contract is the beginning of negotiations.

Trends

The following words and phrases were used to describe the trends that the respondents observed:

- Like the intermingling of two liquids.
- Global guidelines with local adaptations.
- The importance attached to relationships has evolved since the 1980s.
- Proper contracts, bidding processes and involvement of legal organisations are very much in place in the big cities to ensure interests are taken care of.
- Compromise is acceptable with "approved risks".
- We have one contract system globally.
- We use our Asian contract terms but there is little difference between those and the terms Western organisations use.
- Western organisations are more willing to allow liquidated damages clauses to remain in the agreements because they are enforced so rarely.

- Western organisations are becoming more understanding and flexible due to the importance of Asia as a marketplace and the rise of Asian organisations competing head-to-head with Western organisations.
- Standard contracts are becoming more well balanced. and
- Contracts used to be secondary, with price and delivery the only contested terms. This has changed in the last five years. Corporations are now open to discuss warranty, payment terms, change orders and many other terms, and adopting a flexible approach.
- Western partners are becoming more flexible in their contracting
- The parties are taking a "bottom-line" approach (including velocity of deal flow) to resolve issues when cultural issues make progress difficult.

Source: Contracting Excellence IACCM October 2008

Global Cultures Model

Model aspects here are where there is Dominance or Preference in the following aspects:

1. Rules or Relationships.
2. Individual or Collective Group.
3. Rational or Neutral or Emotional feelings.
4. Specific or Diffuse involvement.
5. Doing or Being.
6. Sequential time or Synchronic time.
7. Internal or External direction.

(After: Riding the waves of culture (1993) Trompenaars)

The above 7 aspects then give rise to the following overviews:

1. Rules or Relationships

Rules
- Legal contracts.
- Only one way.
- "Deal is a deal".
- Rational.

- Let's do organisations.
- Formally consistent.
- Publically will change.
- Fairness - we are all the same; rules determine.

People Relationships

- Contracts are modified.
- Several perspectives.
- Will evolve.
- "Wandering".
- Get to know you.
- Informal.
- Change in private.
- Fairness - each case on its merits; relationship determines.

2. Group/collective or Individual

Group

- "We".
- Decisions referred.
- Joint responsibility.
- Build relationships.
- Low turnover of people.

Individual

- "I".
- Immediate decisions.
- Take personal responsibility.
- Quick deal preferred.
- High turnover of people.

3. Emotional or Rational feelings

Emotional

- Wide range of voice tone.
- Non-verbal body language as shows feelings.
- Flows.

- Can be "heated".
- "Touchy/feely" is liked.
- People focus.

Rational or Neutral
- Flat voice tone.
- Hides feelings as prefers "facts".
- Can "explode" when releases bottled up feeling.
- Usually is "cool".
- No touch/contact as personal space is maintained.
- Facts focus.

4. Specific or Diffuse involvement

Specific
- Direct may appear to be "blunt".
- Principled.
- Objective.
- Quick/will take risks.
- Structured.
- Titles are not important.
- Keeps private and organisations life separate.

Diffuse
- Indirect may appear to be "evasive".
- Personal morality.
- Subjective.
- Takes time/plays it safe.
- "Flows".
- Titles and age are important.
- Private and organisations life are connected.

5. Doing or Being Status

Doing/achieving
- Achievement first.
- Knowledge and skills.

- Qualifications.
- Management by objectives, performance pay.

Being/ascribed
- People first.
- Position and seniority.
- Background.
- Management by rewards from manager or higher authority.

6. Sequential or Synchronic time

Sequential
- History is respected and "now" has no deadlines for completion.
- One by one ordered and structured steps.
- Time is measurable.
- Current performance.

Synchronic
- More from now towards the future with agreed specific deadlines.
- Multiple steps.
- Time is approximate.
- Future potential.

7. Internal or External direction

Internal
- Technical, mechanistic world.
- Dominant attitudes.
- Discomfort with external change.
- Conflict and resistance means have convictions.
- Focus on self.
- Win some, loose some.
- "I control".

External
- Natural, organic world.
- Flexible attitudes.

- Comfortable with natural change.
- Harmony and respond means has sensitivity.
- Focus on others.
- Win together, lose apart.
- "I'm Controlled".

Developing Cultural Sensitivity

The following six phases model shows the stages that people may do through when dealing with cultural differences:

1. Denial; "there is not a problem" or unaware/disinterested.
2. Defence; feels threatened and sees differences as negative.
3. Minimisation; considers others cultures "trivial".
4. Acceptance; respects and curious on differences.
5. Adaptation; changes behaviour to interact effectively.
6. Interaction: able to shift naturally.

(Source: Dr Milton Bennet Development Model of Intercultural Sensitivity)

These phases are highlighted more in the following case study:

Case Study: Embracing Cultural Differences in the Global Work Place

The Shipping Industry could lay claim to being the industry that more than any other, makes it possible for a truly global economy to work. It connects countries, markets, organisations and people, allowing them to buy and sell goods across continents despite geographical, cultural and organizational borders. The thrust towards globalization and its multi-cultural aspect has resulted in the growth of diverse workforces. Managers are increasingly concerned with scenarios consisting of many cultures, languages, markets, politics and customs.

When working among not only a diverse workforce but also a variety of suppliers and customers, culture influences every aspect of the current work place. Arguably, cultural factors rather than economic aspects make the difference between success and failure of organizations today. Hence there is an increasing need for shipping and logistics professionals to be sensitized to the value of both cultural and workplace diversity.

Careers in international or culturally diverse organizations require a positive attitude towards intercultural differences. Whether working and living domestically or as an expatriate, professional competence in both organisations and culture is essential. Nowadays, cross-cultural and linguistic competence is perceived as crucial not only for organizational competitive edge but also for the individual's strategic career development. A person who is not sensitive to cultural differences is closing the door on many career opportunities. The question that arises is:

How can shipping and logistics professionals develop cultural sensitivity to avoid cultural pitfalls in today's diverse work place?

Dr Milton Bennet who created the Developmental Model of Intercultural Sensitivity describes six phases a person goes through when developing Intercultural Sensitivity. The first three stages of denial, defence and minimization are experienced when a person undergoes 'culture shock' while working for the first time in a work place culturally different from ones own domestic environment. The last three phases are increasingly experienced by international or expatriate professionals who are required to live and work in a country culturally different from their own. The six stages are detailed providing pointers on how to behave and adapt to improve one's capacity for intercultural sensitivity.

Denial: Unaware or disinterested in the existence of cultural differences.
People at the first phase of 'denial' tend to consider their own culture as the only real one. To develop sensitivity one needs to first recognize cultural differences by becoming knowledgeable of the differences and difficulties of doing organisations and working across cultures. Take the initiative to connect with the "international" or the "foreigner" and be respectful of their language and customs.

Defence: Feels threatened by cultural diversity and perceives the differences as negative.
Culturally defensive people tend to be highly critical of other cultures because they consider their own culture to be the only good one. The challenge here is to

try and identify basic similarities with peers and friends from 'other cultures'. Be patient when communicating. Listening to understand and then be understood will help in communicating and collaborating effectively in a culturally diverse work place.

Minimization: Considers other's culture to be trivial.

People at this phase believe their own culture to be superior. They try to correct their peer's behaviours to meet their own cultural expectations. The challenge here is to be aware of ones own attitudes and their influence on interactions in the work place. Understand specific cultural issues prevalent in the work place avoid stereotypes and try to appreciate differences in language and customs.

Acceptance: Respects and is curious of cultural differences.

Ones own culture is considered to be just one among many, so people in this phase are aware of and understand the need to accept different norms and practices in a multicultural workplace. For professionals who value communication and collaboration, this stage is a reasonable goal to achieve. Establish rapport and synergy in working relationships. This helps develop sensitivity in interactions with others who are culturally different.

Adaptation: Willingly changes behaviour to interact effectively in a different culture.

This willingness to adapt to new customs and practices usually develops with increased knowledge and awareness of the other culture. Professionals networking between an organization and its clients need to be at this level of intercultural sensitivity.

Integration: Able to shift naturally into another cultures' frame of reference.

To develop this ability, people in this phase require in-depth knowledge of at least two cultures (one's own and another). Long-term expatriates who live and work in other countries experience the other cultures' customs and practices over extended periods. This develops an in-depth understanding and ability to naturally assimilate with culturally diverse environments. However, the challenge here is in dealing with issues related to cultural identity. Expatriates and professionals with experience in cross-cultural collaboration and networking usually reach this level of intercultural sensitivity.

Cultural sensitivity in the workplace leads to cultural competence in working effectively with people of different cultural backgrounds. Sensitivity to cultural diversity is:

- being aware of your own attitudes and how it is impacting interactions with others culturally different from you.
- being able to understand specific cultural issues experienced by colleagues and customers.
- the willingness to accept and adapt the organisations practices, norms and customs of different cultures.
- the ability to naturally integrate and interact effectively in a culturally diverse workplace.

Old-fashioned friendship built out of mutual respect helps build and maintain long-term relationships in a culturally diverse work place. Do not allow cultural differences or prejudices to become the basis for criticism and judgments.

Differences are neither good nor bad. What we do with them is the key.

Author: Dr. Janaky Grant, Organization Development Specialist for Rasmussen & Simonsen International Pte Ltd.

Handling different cultures

Checklist: Handling Culture, Be AWARE

- A =   ACCEPT the other person's behaviour without judging it based on what that behaviour means in your culture.
- W =   WONDER what the other person's behaviour means in their culture, rather than what it means in your culture.
- A =   ASK what it means to the person, showing a respectful interest.
- R =   RESEARCH and read about the other person's culture so you are able to place their behaviour in the context of their cultural world view. (For skilful practitioners, learning is an ongoing process. We are never "finished" with our learning.)
- E =   EXPLAIN what their behaviour means in your culture.

Demonstrate or describe the behaviours in your culture that would express similar feelings or meanings, so they can learn new behaviours that will help them function in your culture.

There is therefore a need to establish a right attitude toward cultural differences. Reading extensively for cultural information will help as will watching TV/movies and communicating with native speakers. Language can however be an obstacle as when someone speaks English, it will not be spoken nor understood in the quite same way as in England. Indeed English spoken in differ parts of England varies, as it does in Scotland, Wales or Ireland (all are part of the UK), as does English spoken by Americans; as has been said, "the British and Americans are people divided by a common language" and also, "you can buy in any language, but to sell, you have to speak their language."

Therefore people can learn the language, the culture, the organisations protocol and professional practices and show respect for the local customs and cultural sensitivity. Finally we should never assume similar values to ours, be aware of our own hidden values and take risks and try new behaviours.

6: Managing Global Sourcing

Introduction

Global sourcing is often used as a description when what is actually meant is International Procurement/Sourcing. Some text books with titles such as "Global Purchasing", "Global Procurement or "Global Sourcing" will also have subtitles which indicate that they really mean "International Procurement", which is often the majority of their content.

Many commentators are also now using the term "Low Cost Country Sourcing" (LCCS) as a euphemism for International/Global sourcing.

Global sourcing, however, is more of an approach following the globalisation of large multinational conglomerates, and from a range of industries and services. Due to such globalisation of corporations, phrases such as global purchasing or global sourcing have now become common but, as yet, are without many clear definitions.

One clear definition, however, comes from Monczka and Trent (1991):

> *"Global Sourcing is the integration and coordination of procurement requirements across the worldwide organisations units, looking at common items, process, technologies and suppliers."*

Such global sourcing will tend to be practiced only by large corporations as they have both the need and the leverage to gain competitiveness from global sourcing, and they also have the facilities around the globe to enable them to capitalise from the process. They are also often usually contractually bound with other large corporations who will have the ability to supply products to the globally located sites of the multi-national purchaser.

International Procurement

International procurement is the procurement from another country, of the products and/or services required for the organisation. It was commonly known as importing, which many organisations practice, and it requires an application of specialist skill and knowledge from individuals within the procurement function.

Later we shall look at how organisations can move along a continuum from ad hoc international procurement to more sophisticated international sourcing activities, and we shall see that many organisations will evolve into levels of activities which do not require or involve the global integration and co-ordination of the purchasing organisation's demand with the supplier's global ability to supply.

It would seem therefore that global procurement, to be totally effective, requires a globally located purchaser and a globally located supplier. There often needs to a strong element of co-location, i.e. both supplier and purchaser often need to be located in the same place or at least in the same region.

International purchasing of course does not require this co-location and often does involve a purchaser on one side of the world buying from a supplier on the other.

The following checklist covers initial questions to be asked:

Checklist: Managing Global Sourcing

- Do we have the knowledge of culture, organisations differences?
- Do we have the freight and import knowledge?
- Have we the necessary expertise?
- Should we source direct or use an agent?
- Will we get reliable supplier lead-times (SLT)?
- Will we need to "cushion" for SLT?
- What is the countries infrastructure?
- What is the countries political stability?
- What are the countries organisations methods?
- Will we be able to specify clearly what we want?
- What about fluctuating currency?
- What payments terms will be used?
- What Incoterms should be used?
- What are the impacts to varied landed costs?
- Can we fully implement our SCM methods with suppliers?
- Are there any local import requirements that apply, such as licences, quotas?

Global Sourcing Objectives

A typical overall global supply objective is to meet, or exceed the expectations of the worldwide customer and this in turn leads to more focused objectives that include:

- Creating an environment of leverage spend (across organisations units, as well as national and international boundaries).
- Optimising supply chain operations (number of members, capabilities and costs).
- Reducing inventories across the chain.
- Reducing all costs (item costs and supply chain operational costs).
- Securing assurance of supply of the right quality.

In order to achieve the above objectives, organisations must consider the following when sourcing internationally and globally:

- Counter trade (or reciprocal and compensatory trade agreements).
- Varying laws and other jurisdictional questions.
- Cultural and language differences.
- Labour and training availability, practices, laws and regulations.
- Transportation, packing, shipping, storing, import, export and customs regimes.
- Security: materials, products, personnel and intellectual property.
- Exchange rate.

These will be looked at later in this section, in rather more detail.

Evolution of Global Sourcing

Both international procurement and global sourcing have become more widely used as international trade barriers have become less restrictive. This has been occasioned through international treaties such as the European Union, North American Free Trade Agreement (NAFTA) and other trade blocs, and from the freeing of international trade through the World Trade Organisation (WTO), and former GATT Agreements (General Agreement on Tariffs and Trade).

Additionally, improved facilities for international communications, transport and logistics have all changed the commercial trading environment. The regional integration of most of Europe through the formation of the European Union, combined with the

ASEAN bloc in Southeast Asia and the subsequent development of the North American Free Trade Agreement (NAFTA), have all demonstrated that nations can gain more competitive advantages through the formation of such alliances. These groups are quite large and powerful and when combined with Japan, the areas of Europe, North American and SE Asia constitute 75 per cent of the world's GDP and 70 per cent of World Trade.

Such global trade cooperation is shown in the following diagram depicting the increases in global trade over the past decade.

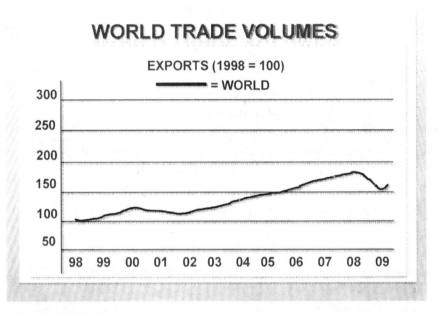

Source: FT 2009

From a procurement perspective, this has encouraged practitioners to develop ongoing relationships with suppliers and customers away from their traditional domestic marketplace.

The Strategic Global Sourcing Environment contains many issues which have to be addressed in addition to the normal issues facing domestic procurement.

Many of the factors affecting the Strategic Global Sourcing Policies of organisations can be summarised as in the diagram opposite:

Strategic Global Sourcing Environment

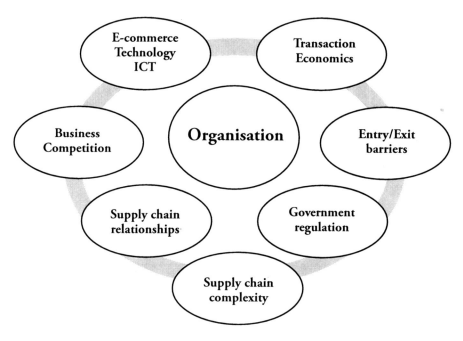

After Ritchie & Brindley (2002)

Organisations today are buying materials and components from foreign sources/low cost country sources, in order to improve their own competitive performance. International or global procurement is now therefore being viewed as a strategic weapon for improved performance and profitability, through greater product availability, enhanced technology and price advantage.

On the other hand, the increasing use of JIT and quality management in manufacturing industry, in particular in relation to sourcing, is encouraging the early participation of suppliers in the design process and in an on going development of supplier capability through the building of partnership relationships with key suppliers; this is much easier to achieve using local suppliers. Therefore there is now the challenge in global procurement of developing partnership relationships with organisations at the other side of the globe that have different values and cultural norms.

Organisations now have to face up to a series of management decisions in relation to their procurement strategy, for example:
•   Should they buy from abroad for strategic advantage rather than simple need?

- If so, what should they buy from abroad?
- From where should they buy?
- How should they buy from abroad?

Choices

When an organisation first identifies a need to obtain products from abroad, the impact of managing foreign trade can frequently be avoided. As consumers we all make purchases of items of food, clothing and other consumer items which originate from foreign countries, but we do so using domestically viewed distribution channels. Clearly such products have been obtained via a global supply chain and have, at some stage, included an importer.

Similarly, industry and commerce can purchase items originating abroad from a distributor or an importer, thus avoiding the necessity of direct dealings with a foreign vendor. Only when the volumes or values of a foreign sourced item become significant does purchasing directly from a foreign supplier normally become an issue.

A number of choices are then open:
- Buy items sourced nationally.
- Buy internationally.
- Buy internationally ad hoc as part of a strategy.

The advantages and disadvantage of international sourcing by small and medium size organisations include:
- Availability of specific items.
- Higher levels of product quality.
- Use of advanced product and process technology.
- Item price.

International sourcing may also offer additional benefits of:
- Wider range of potential items and suppliers.
- Further price improvements.
- Direct access to new technologies.
- Influence over quality.
- Improved delivery service.
- Meeting terms of offset agreements (countertrade).

- Introducing greater competitiveness to domestic markets.
- Gaining knowledge of foreign markets.

There can nevertheless still remain the problem of dealing with remote suppliers. Communications with foreign suppliers can be impaired by language, by cultural differences, by time zone differences and by the use of different systems of measurement.

Buying from abroad compared to buying domestically will also likely involve increased freight costs, import duty and customs clearance and possibly customs delays. It's also likely that you will need to pay in foreign currencies, which introduces both uncertainty of not knowing what a future cost may be and also the risk of fluctuating costs; steps can be taken to minimise this by the use of stable currencies, and by risk sharing, but such actions themselves will still incur costs.

Such added difficulties of sourcing abroad will be dealt with in further detail later in this section.

Supply market location

A number of factors affect the decision of whether and how to limit the supply market for a given item to be purchased. These include:

- Item specification and technology.
- Logistics, availability and demand.
- Item and delivery costs.
- Quality and process technology.

Let us now focus on costs.

Costs

This matrix on the next page concerns the relationship between item cost and the unit cost of delivery.

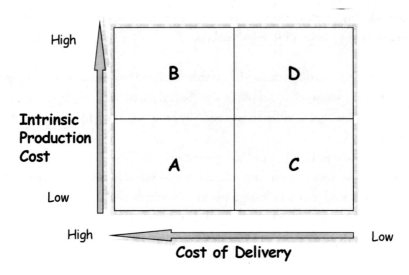

Clearly the scenarios above need to be costed in terms of total delivered domicile duty paid, total acquisition costs (TAC) and total costs of ownership (TCO), to ensure that fully informed decisions and meaningful trade-offs are made.

Obtaining items from foreign suppliers inevitably involves higher delivery costs, not only due to the increased transportation distances, but also handling charges, insurance costs and, frequently, import duty.

Buying from a foreign supplier through an extended delivery chain may incur the risk of delay and increases the risk of the product being damaged in transit. These need to be managed correctly, as it can be a serious matter if the items are of a critical nature to organisation's operations, or are subject to a significant level of demand variability as such events, will increase the TCO and may incur premium transport costs for replacement stock and other costs associated with non-availability.

However, many organisations have proved that, in many circumstances, international purchasing and global sourcing can give an organisation a competitive edge, through:
- Reduced costs.
- Better quality.
- Technological advantage.
- Improved reliability.
- Improved delivery.

All of these arise from increased leverage through enhanced volume.

The prime factor for overseas procuring will be to obtain best value for the organisation, as procuring overseas will achieve better value than with sourcing locally. Whilst the factors in favour of sourcing internationally may vary with time and be dependant on the commodity to be purchased, there are specific reasons making an overseas source a viable option, such as the following:

- Price, including labour costs, exchange rates, efficiency, economies of scale.
- Quality.
- Delivery and continuity of supply.
- Technical backup.
- Technology.
- Countertrade.

It is suggested, however, that international procurement is not, by itself, going to give the best solution to achieving the objectives, without the main strategic factors that will lead to continuing success such as the following:

- Becoming the lowest cost producer.
- Achieving world class quality.
- Maintaining constant innovation.
- Minimising time to market.

These strategic factors will only be achieved with an effect global sourcing strategy.

Richard Lamming (1991) in his paper "Global Sourcing and Lean Purchasing" put forward a number of strategies that an organisation may use to affect Global Sourcing.

These are as follows:

- Use a "local source" which is linked to a global network.
- Source through an overseas supplier who can support your overseas organisation's locations, by supplying parts direct to your site.
- Use an overseas supplier that is able to support your core organisations location, through for example, having a local development centre in your country.
- Create your own design and development support teams abroad for your various locations and source locally.

It may be possible to start by concentrating on one region, e.g. Europe or Asia then expanding from there. The steps would then be as follows:

- Choose global sites for manufacturing/support operations, in your chosen area for expansion.
- Create a supply base to match the locations, by identifying local sources capable of supporting your organisations.

Global Supply Chains have many challenges and, once integrated, can provide many trade-offs, as shown in the diagram below:

Global Supply Chains: Key Challenges

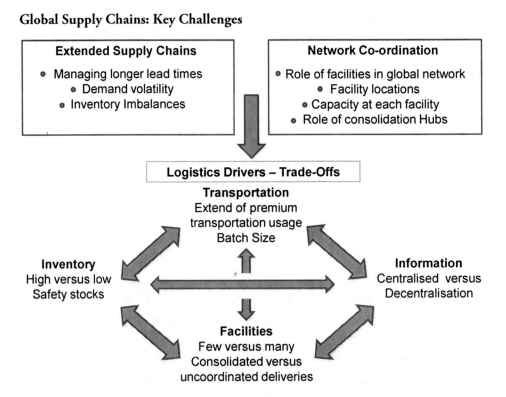

Developing Global Sourcing

Lack of knowledge of the culture, organisations practices and foreign markets, limited availability of resources for market research and foreign supplier selection will all obstruct, to a certain extent, the development, execution and implementation of Global Procurement activities.

In "Global Sourcing: A Development Approach" (1991) Monczka and Trent showed the stages than an organisation goes through as they progress from Local Procurement to a Global Sourcing strategy.

The first stage is the simple level of procurement and stage four, the most sophisticated, as a full global strategy is developed.

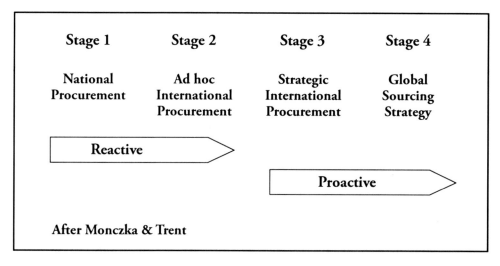

After Monczka & Trent

From this, there appear to be five steps which lead from the development of international purchasing, through to a fully integrated global strategy:

Stage 1

Domestic buyers undertake international procurement. This may require the development of new skills, which may need to be developed or are brought in, would include an understanding of other cultures, knowledge of currency and risk, and a global perspective.

Stage 2

Overseas subsidiaries or other overseas corporate units are used to help with the international procurement. They provide:

- Local knowledge.
- Close to supplier location.
- Awareness of local organisations practices.
- Good communication.

Stage 3

International procurement offices (IPOs) are set up around the world where the IPOs tasks are:

- Supplier selection.
- Progressing orders.

- Carrying out local contract negotiations.
- Clarifying communications between the supplier and corporate headquarters.
- Quality control.

Stage 4

Allocate specific responsibility to an organisation's unit for the design, source and build of certain products. This stage identifies those different units within the organisation's structure that may have a comparative achievement for the organisation. This is the first recognition of an integrated structure.

Case Study – Ford Motor Organisation

Ford Motor Organisation has moved from being an international organisation which produced different products in each of its overseas plants to satisfy local consumption, to producing continent specific products which in turn leads to the internationalisation of their suppliers, through co-location arrangements (where the supplier agrees to build a plant/supply site close to the manufacturing site) and implants (where the supplier builds a supply site within the organisation's plant).

Ford now allocates the development of a component or system to the site with the best expertise and they are also developing the suppliers in the same way. (The objective of which is to develop a common set of vehicle platforms to be built worldwide). This requires global co-ordination on a grand scale through Ford's five vehicle program centres which have worldwide sourcing responsibility for a specific class of car or truck. They identify and select the supplier against a requirement capability. Then regional locations will negotiate requirements with the worldwide supplier and perform the usual transactional buying. By this process items designed in one location will be supplied to the world.

Stage 5

The co-ordination of an integrated global sourcing strategy worldwide is the final stage and is the highest level of global integration and co-ordination. This does not mean losing sight of the other stages. It means that the organisation has evolved a system and structure able to consolidate its global network to produce the best results for the organisations as a whole, through bringing together the best suppliers who are able to give benefits in price, delivery, technology and security of supply.

The following diagram looks at the effect on performance as organisations evolve:

International/Global Sourcing – The Performance Level

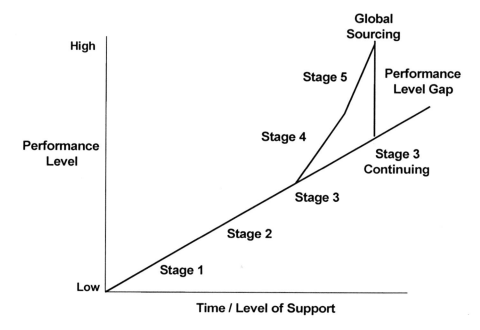

Problem areas

However, it is not all plain sailing as there is now an additional need to fully understand all the dynamics involved in a global supply chain.

There are a number of potential problem areas to consider when organisations develop their sourcing internationally and/or globally, for example:
- Delivery time.
- Political/labour problems.
- Hidden costs shipping or special export packing.
- Exchange rates.
- Payment.
- Quality/rejects.
- Tariffs/duties.
- Documentation.
- Legal problems.

- Language.
- Culture/customs.
- CSR.
- Ethics.
- Infrastructure.
- Time zones

Other aspects include the following:
- Whether there is a "critical mass" of good suppliers in the country.
- Slower adoption of e-organisations.
- Limitations in partners or contracts that demand tendering for all purchases, which inhibits building alliances.
- The potential for repeat purchasers.
- The purchasing organisation's global activity may be scattered around the world, making it difficult to co-ordinate.
- The limited number of qualified global suppliers.
- International operations of existing domestic suppliers.
- Current or potential suppliers in the target country or another country where either party already operates.
- Current or potential suppliers in third party countries.

When organisations are evaluating the standards of overseas suppliers, they need to consider the ability to trade globally and meet international standards; these factors being additional to the usual considerations that apply to pure domestic organisations.

Internationalisation of the Procurement process

Another model of the evolution of global sourcing is as follows (diagram opposite):

Stages of Evolution of Global Sourcing

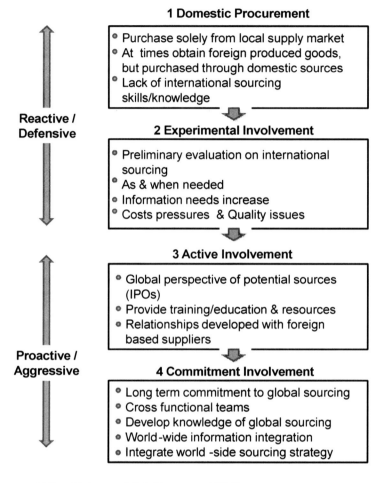

1 Domestic Procurement

- Purchase solely from local supply market
- At times obtain foreign produced goods, but purchased through domestic sources
- Lack of international sourcing skills/knowledge

Reactive / Defensive

2 Experimental Involvement

- Preliminary evaluation on international sourcing
- As & when needed
- Information needs increase
- Costs pressures & Quality issues

3 Active Involvement

- Global perspective of potential sources (IPOs)
- Provide training/education & resources
- Relationships developed with foreign based suppliers

Proactive / Aggressive

4 Commitment Involvement

- Long term commitment to global sourcing
- Cross functional teams
- Develop knowledge of global sourcing
- World-wide information integration
- Integrate world-side sourcing strategy

(After Rajagopal/McDermott 1992)

Strategic Choices for Global Sourcing

The choices of global sourcing strategies depend on the competitive advantage to be gained from global supply market, the standardisation of the purchasing processes (achieved by centralising activities in one or two countries to maximise economies of scale) and the volume of overseas buying, versus, the stages of involvement in the internationalisation of purchasing process. Four types of strategies emerge as shown as follows (diagram overleaf):

Stages of involvement in Internationalisation of the Procurement Process

	(Reactive) Low	(Proactive) High
Low		**Offensive Sourcing Strategy** • Cross functional integration • Improved information & skilled resources • Barriers overcome
Advantages of Global Supply Market, Standardisation of Purchase and Volume of overseas sourcing	**Local Sourcing Strategy**	
	Defensive Sourcing Strategy • Limited/cautious	**Global Sourcing Strategy** • Total integration of global volumes • Standardisation of parts globally • Central direction
High		

Case Study: IMI

IMI has transformed procurement into a diverse global team.

IMI has five organisations covering a wide range of areas: severe services (for example, pressure valves for use in the gas, oil and nuclear industries), fluid power (which includes braking systems), indoor climate (e.g. radiator valves), merchandise (including point-of-sale racks and equipment) and drinks dispensers.

IMI has a drive to manage cost and risk and has "pushed hard" on big initiatives around low-cost country sourcing.

Until relatively recently, IMI procurement was working on a reactive basis and almost seen as just a clerical function. "They were doing some deals, particularly on in-directs, but they weren't leveraging on direct materials; the organisations weren't talking to each other effectively. It was also very reactive, a reporting function".

"Our five organisations are quite diverse, but there are some synergies, they all buy plastics, they all buy metals. So what we have done primarily is to build a strong low-cost sourcing strategy that we didn't have".

Their Group supply chain director has 50 people who report direct to him around the world and, indirectly, a staff of about 200.

They have a decentralized, federal structure. Each purchasing director reports on a hard line to the organisations president or operations directors. But functionally, they report to the Group Supply Chain director.

All of the indirect and logistics procurement is done centrally, with each organisation having its own procurement head. The purchasing directors now meet every three months.

Global sourcing

Until recently, low cost country sourcing was about 6 per cent of spend at £800 million from the economies of Asia, Eastern Europe and South America with a combination of direct and indirect goods and services. The target is to reach 40 per cent in the next couple of years.

To achieve this aim, the organisation is setting up sourcing offices in India, Vietnam, the Czech Republic and Mexico, in addition to the existing Shanghai office in China. These offices then look after sourcing from nearby countries as well as their own.

In doing so, the function can now be much more proactive. "We manage quality and we have people in the area with market awareness, so we can give the organisations feedback on what's happening in the markets and what's being developed. We're getting to the stage where suppliers are giving us ideas on our products."

They believe that the key is to get a good sourcing office and people who know the markets, country and culture. Each of the sourcing heads is born and bred in those countries.

In China, IMI also has a quality team that ensures performance standards are met. The organisation has also run two supplier conferences to explain to suppliers IMI's plans and give suppliers the opportunity to present new ideas. In addition to this, it ran a number of education sessions covering quality management, value engineering and hedging.

Low-cost country sourcing (LCCS)

Some organisations calls LCCS "best cost country sourcing", while others refer to their favoured sourcing areas "high opportunity regions". The consensus is that the fundamentals of sourcing from foreign countries (to succeed at LCCS) are that organisations and procurement teams must overcome cultural differences and internal prejudice.

The importance of understanding the local culture has been emphasised repeatedly in literature for this subject. (E.g. even within China, there are huge differences in the political structure, legal systems and market conditions.)

Organisation like EADS favours local purchasing offices staffed by buyers with a good understanding of local culture who can deal with price issues. These offices are not limited to cost control centres. They can be used strategically, giving purchasers the opportunity to treat each contract as a "special case" and work with partners to develop a strong relationship and the vendor's skills.

Other buyers such as those employed by Bosch, champion a more direct approach, advocating hiring locals, rather than simply placing good buyers in the locality. They say it is vital to have a contact in the country that can speak the language, understand the culture and grasp the technical requirements of the product being sourced.

For many organizations, LCCS also involves a change of culture internally to manage the purchasing strategy successfully and by securing stakeholder support. Unilever for example, has said that with low-cost sourcing, buyers must be ready to overcome any preconceptions colleagues might have about what this means and the potential risks of doing so.

Procurement must first identify an opportunity and build a strong organisational case. This should involve gaining an understanding of lead-times and identifying potential risks. Getting input from other internal departments, such as those that look at finance or risk management, could help to boost their case. Creating a well-defined strategy is a good starting point for persuading stakeholders that low cost country sourcing is commercially attractive.

Case Study: KONE

Three years ago KONE's sourcing operation within the elevator and escalator manufacturer was highly decentralized, comprising around 55 country organisations, seven research and development centres and eight manufacturing operations worldwide.

It has been transformed into a unified global operating structure. At that time, less than 20 per cent of direct materials the organisation used in the manufacturing process came from low-cost countries.

KONE established local sourcing and supplier quality teams and local supplier networks to support the firm's manufacturing operations in countries such as Mexico, the Czech Republic, China and India. This increased the direct material sourced from emerging markets to more than 50 per cent of the organisation's total spend and brought substantial cost savings.

Among the challenges encountered were "difficulties obtaining complete financial records and dissimilar accounting principles undermining the financial statements 'transparency, not to mention the reluctance of many suppliers to fully open their books." To overcome the uncertainty and risk of sourcing from financially unreliable suppliers, KONE established longer-term contracts with qualified suppliers in order to build a dependable supply base.

Organisational structure can also be an impediment to progress in emerging markets such as China. KONE, like an increasing number of organisations has a highly matrixed, horizontally structured organisation; with each person often working for multiple supervisors.

In China, as in India, speed is often the critical organisations driver, so clear decision-making and direct reporting lines take on a heightened level of importance. As a result, clear identification of superiors in a hierarchical, vertical structure, is generally the preferred model because it leaves no room for ambiguity.

Bridging the gap between culture and organisations conduct with Asian suppliers can also present challenges. This has been a particular problem when using foreigners or expats with limited understanding of cultural norms and without the right connections to effectively manage the local relationships.

In order to overcome this, they have installed sourcing managers hired locally with long standing connections and contacts in the region, They manage relationships with government entities and act as key contact points for designated suppliers

KONE say that this is the key to success given contracts rarely have the same level of significance and legal stature as they do elsewhere in the world.

For example, it is important to understand the intricate personal connections and social relations network in China referred to as guanxi, the concept of social capital. Since China's organisations environment is largely relationship driven, understanding guanxi and developing long-term organisations relationships is a crucial factor of doing organisations there.

Foreign organisations attain continuous supplier commitment to intellectual property rights by building favourable guanxi, which typically involves frequent banquets and low value gift exchanges, but most importantly, transforming the transactional supplier relationships into long-term relationships.

Tight alignment and collaboration (including through joint audits) is key to delivering supplier quality. Continuous coaching and monitoring is also paramount to ensure quality systems are understood and adhered to in a methodical way and no shortcuts are taken.

To overcome these risks the organisation is planning productivity improvements, supplier development initiatives and will focus on continued recruitment and development of quality staff. As an additional back-up, it will continue its development of other emerging markets.

Case Study: Caradon

Building supplier Caradon has shifted from being an organisation that sourced predominantly in the UK, to one that has purchased from between 30 and 40 countries over the past few years.

Case Study: Cable & Wireless

Cable and Wireless Communications have seen international sourcing become an essential activity for their procurement department. Compared with a couple of years ago, a much larger chunk of their £4 billion annual spend is now placed abroad. "Concentrating on local sourcing is not an option for us anymore. If we had just gone after UK organisations, we wouldn't be the organisation we are now. We now look at a range of organisations in the US, Japan, Europe and India".

The growing trend for global sourcing has been underpinned partly by the changing role of procurement and supply chain management, especially where this has moved from being concerned with only process to one that is now focused on strategy.

For procurement professionals in larger organisations, the advantages of an international sourcing strategy are obvious; buying leverage and cost reductions. The benefits for the average small to medium sized enterprise (SME), with little buying leverage and fewer members of staff, are less apparent. But the advent of the Internet has given such organisations the opportunity to branch out. Portals, for example, can give a group of SMEs the buying power of much larger organisations.

Total Cost

While there are clear competitive advantages for SMEs and larger players alike to be gained from casting the purchasing net further afield, global sourcing also has its costs and potential pitfalls referred to earlier.

A worthwhile international sourcing strategy takes considerable management time to implement. New sources of supply have to be investigated and, during the initial stages, supplier visits are necessary.

Case Study: CGU

Director of supply chain and purchasing at insurance firm CGU says the strategy needs to be based on adding value to the organisations and must factor in the total cost, including management time, freight costs, exchange rate fluctuations and lead-times. "There is no point doing it for the sake of doing it," he insists.

"You've got to understand the firm's requirements and the marketplace and you need to source on the basis of total cost. Goods may appear to be cheaper at first, but you've got to transport them in the timeframe you want. It is not worth changing to a new supplier if there will only be a marginal benefit."

Checklist: Global Sourcing practice

• Do your homework and research any potential sources thoroughly.
• Respect cultural differences, build diversity into your team and take time to understand potential suppliers' cultures.
• Empower your managers to take risks and be innovative.
• Be aware of the risks involved, such as fluctuations in currencies, and manage them carefully.
• Ensure you have control of the freight and logistics.
• Use a Cross-functional team approach.

Supplier visits

Cultural differences can be problematic. If you don't speak the same language as the seller, then what you think they said via the interpreter and what they thought they said might be very different. Distance negotiation is not as straightforward as discussing organisations with a local supplier. Indeed as many are discovering even in purely domestic trade, building relationships via e-mail is difficult and is less rewarding than building them face-to-face; not seeing a supplier's physical reaction makes it more difficult to know when you are striking a good deal.

Legal and contractual differences from country to country must also be investigated. This is especially relevant if you are buying over the Internet, as it isn't always clear which law applies. Is it the one in force in your supplier's country, your own country, or the country in which the server is located?

For all these reasons switching from an established supplier base to a substantially new one has its hazards.

Case Study

Supplier's view: China's textile trade shrugs off quota.

Manufacturers keep expanding despite US and European efforts to stem the flow.

With 6,000 employees, 400,000 square meters of factory floor that throb with 1,600 knitting machines, dyeing vats and dryers and its own power station, the Fuan Textile Complex stands out even in the outsize industrial landscape of southern China.

Fuan was the second-largest Chinese exporter of fabrics last year, shipping $390 million of knitted material, two- thirds of it destined for clothing stores in the United States. Even as competition intensifies, organisations based in China are becoming increasingly nimble and versatile.

Hundreds of the workers at Fuan are not machine minders but lab technicians. They test fibres on computerized monitors, try new fabrics in sweat simulators and dozens of different washing machines, and assemble strips of sample fabric, all apparently identical in colour to the casual observer, that are despatched to the United States and Europe so that designers there can choose between faintly different shades of dye.

This combination of cheap labour, productivity and logistical savvy is considered likely to ensure that Chinese- made fabrics and textiles will be an increasing presence in garment stores across Europe and North America, even with quotas in the coming years.

"By and large, anyone in apparel will tell you that you get the best product most reliably for the least amount of money from China," said Bob Zane, the vice president for sourcing of Liz Claiborne, a fashion conglomerate based in New York. "As we approach the future and Chinese manufacturers become more confident that the quota is truly gone, they'll only become more sophisticated and competitive."

Fuan opened in 1988 as the first foray into mainland manufacturing by its Hong Kong- based parent organisation. Now it can make as much as 16 million kilograms of dyed fabric and yarn a year, and its clients include Victoria's Secret, J.C. Penney, Liz Claiborne and Wal-Mart Stores.

With the ending of the global quotas that held back Chinese exports, established manufacturers like Fountain Set are facing a growing number of mainland Chinese competitors.

The Chinese government has invested $21 billion in local textile and apparel manufacturing in the past three years, and about 3,800 textile plants are under construction, A.T. Kearney, the organisations consultancy, said in a report.

To survive and navigate in an increasingly fragmented and changeable consumer market, retailers and manufacturers have had to find more sophisticated ways to retain profit by cutting costs, time and uncertainties.

"There is definite pressure to reduce lead-times," said Harry Lee, managing director of TAL Apparel, a garment giant based in Hong Kong that produces clothes in China and Southeast Asia. "Everyone is trying to push down prices, and everyone realizes they can't push much further, so everyone is looking at inventory to reduce costs."

In recent years, manufacturers based in China have responded to this looming pressure by accelerating their production cycles and taking on the design and logistics roles once assumed by their retail customers. Soon Nam Yip, manager of TAL's garment factory in Dongguan, said that in the past four years it had cut its manufacturing time to 40 days from 120 days.

TAL also electronically monitors the stock of stores like J.C. Penney and ships clothes directly to the stores, by passing middle managers and whole sale warehouses, Yip said. "We in a sense have become the UPS or FedEx for our customers," he said.

Yen said the Fuan mill had computerized orders and testing to cut the lead-time for orders and reduce mistakes. And down the highway, Luen Thai, the apparel group based in Hong Kong, offers customers a one-stop "supply chain city" where they can design garments; choose fabric and trimmings and arrange deliveries.

"These organisations are the future of the organisations," said Zane, who deals with many manufacturers based in China, "in the ideal world we would send them a sketch and check and that's all."

But while China is now the home of increasingly sophisticated textile factories, many of them still have trouble finding all the ingredients they need locally. "Chinese cotton tends to vary in quality making it difficult to ensure that customers' orders are met quickly and consistently," Yen said.

"China is certainly a very big producer of a lot of the ingredients," he said, "but not all of them are of the quality and standard, or may not have the consistency, that is being asked by the foreign brands and retailers."

Source: International Herald Tribune 2 August 2005. Chris Buckley

Ethical concerns

Buying for an organisation that has a good reputation to maintain means considering ethics, for example, organisations have to be aware that being able to buy cheaper goods from the third world could be because child workers are making them under sweatshop conditions. You therefore have to consider what is going on in the supply chain as a whole.

Public sector organisations are also purchasing from low-cost countries:

Case Study: National Offender Management Service (NOMS)

NOMS has spent the past year buying in uniforms directly from China for its 33,000 officers. They are reaping the benefits of a strong, ethical supply chain, significant cost savings and a more streamlined and efficient service. "We know exactly which factory is producing our garments, when they are producing them, and it's clearly auditable."

"It's also produced a massive cost saving and taken 20 per cent off the uniform bill. We could have taken off another 10 per cent but we chose to invest savings in the quality of garments so we have massively improved the quality of shirts and trousers."

It recognised the benefit of cutting out the middle man.

"We are moving up the supply chain and dealing with it directly instead of employing an agent. This has worked exceptionally well. By cutting out the middleman, we can take the benefit of their margins and we have complete control of the supply chain. Dealing directly with a manufacturer as opposed to an agent has been able to deliver quite a lot of innovation".

NOMS warns, however, that global sourcing is difficult and adds a competent global sourcing team is essential to ensure this approach is a success.

Case Study: Royal Mail

The Royal Mail Group has signed a 10-year deal with a single managing agent to provide clothing sourced from China, Pakistan and other low-cost countries for its 160,000 uniformed staff.

The group spends £11.4 million each year on clothing, purchasing over 50 different lines from post office retail staff uniforms and personal protective equipment, to safety and footwear and postmen and women's clothing.

Previously, Royal Mail had 64 contracts let through 30 suppliers that all used sub-contractors in Asia. But it realised that moving to one fully managed service contract enabled clearer visibility and management of the full supply chain, including greater assurance of corporate social responsibility compliance, as well as providing savings benefits.

"We had little visibility of the supply chain; we decided to move to a single managing agent where we could more effectively manage our end-to-end supply chain. We could then deploy our environmental and ethical standards and monitor and manage compliance via our managing agent."

Cost savings were also part of the organisations case. (In excess of 10% savings.) While it may seem that low-cost country sourcing is no different for the public sector, there are some additional considerations. They must meet strict regulations and in some cases, they must adhere to wider government objectives, particularly when it comes to buying services.

Cultural differences are the most significant barriers to successful sourcing from low cost countries.

Senior buyers at a low cost country sourcing conference stated that procurement must form a comprehensive understanding of the countries and suppliers they intend to source from to achieve the benefits of moving supplies to a lower cost region.

Case Study: Georg Fischer Automotive

GFA have found that the culture in China is the complete opposite to that in the West.

For example, when a contract is signed in Europe it signifies the start of a deal, while in China it represents the start of negotiations. Accordingly they advise that all of the people who deal in China need to get into the network and have personal relationships with suppliers to be a success. "You need to spend time in the country."

Building partnerships could also help to avoid some of the more unusual practices experienced. An example given was of a shipment from China the firm was expecting. When it never arrived, they found the supplier had accepted a better deal while the ship was on route and the goods were redirected to another buyer.

Case Study: Bosch

Bosch emphasise the importance of close relationships, highlighting the importance of establishing trust, otherwise it becomes more difficult to achieve competitive prices.

Using an example of their experience sourcing from Eastern Europe, they state that it is important to have a local contact in the country, someone who can "speak the language, understand the culture and has the technical knowledge".

Case Study: Siemens

Siemens has the view that it is naïve to think you can do organisation in countries without understanding the language. For example, they state that when dealing with Eastern European countries, it is insufficient to think that you can get by only in English or German, especially when you are sending requests for quotations. It is very important to have someone who can speak the language.

In addition, it is vital to investigate potential partners thoroughly and use the help of local research institutes and chambers of commerce to gather data.

Case Study: PZ Cussons (International)

PZ Cussons' global laundry category team has recently carried out a truly worldwide sourcing exercise enabling delivery to multiple global locations.

The cross-functional initiative spanning three continents produced some impressive results for PZ Cussons, whose products include soap, toiletries and laundry products. Its global purchasing network was formed in 2004. This was the first move toward a global purchasing strategy involving all procurement teams. But it became clear collaboration with other functions was necessary to deliver organisations expectations. This led to PZ Cussons' first venture into category management on a global scale.

Participants from purchasing and technical functions in the UK, Australia, Nigeria and Poland were involved in reviewing technical and commercial activity in the laundry category. Spend in this category exceeds £43 million. The project included a detailed review of spending on laundry powder materials, recommending a global sourcing plan, finding strategic suppliers, review (and where possible standardise) raw material specifications and develop a cost model to calculate optimum formulation costs. It also aimed to increase technical and commercial knowledge sharing across the group.

The project has resulted in a successful category review, with 93,000 metric tonnes of raw materials now purchased globally. Specifications for raw materials used in laundry products have been harmonised, representing 56 per cent of total volume bought across the project area and £1.5 million of potential savings have been identified through e-sourcing.

They have demonstrated how an aligned network can provide effective communication and teamwork across continents.

The achievements were made "across three continents, three different cultures and in a short space of time and with some impressive financial results."

Research

Global management consultants McKinsey carried out an analysis in 2009 of the sourcing behaviour of 100 organisations worldwide, interviewing decision-makers in the automotive, engineering, consumer goods, chemicals and electronics sectors. The researchers categorised the respondents to the survey according to two criteria: the maturity of their global sourcing development and the sophistication of their approach.

The survey found that global sourcing is still in its infancy. Even the most progressive organisations allocated only 31 per cent of their total spend to global sourcing. At more conservative organisations the figure was less than 10 per cent.

Researchers identified five barriers to effective global sourcing:

1 .The absence of a global procurement strategy.

2. The lack of effective models to allocate responsibility.

3. Insufficient focus on specific regions.

4. A lack of presence on the ground in discussions with potential suppliers.

5. Poor talent management in Low Cost Countries (LCCs).

Source: Wuellenweber, J (2009) Untapped potential Supply Management October.

Case Study: Kimberly-Clark

K-C recommends looking into global sourcing. First you need to establish the degree of buy-in from the organisations teams, particularly their willingness to optimise global benefit rather than expecting that every deal will be the best for their organisations or region. At Kimberly-Clark they have found this has developed over time as confidence in our team has grown, but you need to know the level of buy-in you have before you approach suppliers.

Other good practice was to take time to develop relationships with your colleagues. Trust is essential, whether you are just sharing data or allocating responsibility for global categories or suppliers.

Finally, assess the most effective strategy for each commodity. K-C has a model that helps them to determine whether to buy regionally, establish a collaborative team or appoint a global lead buyer. Some of the factors they consider are the degree of supply base globalization spend level, opportunity for savings, and speed of technical change.

Research

More than a fifth of organisations do not know how much they expect to save from sourcing overseas. And a quarter of organisations are not aware of the savings they actually achieved by buying globally.

A report, Global Sourcing: Shifting Strategies, by PricewaterhouseCoopers (PwC), surveyed 59 retail organisations based in eight countries. Although many organisations were able to track "easier" costs such as logistics, customs fees and currency risks, they struggled to measure the spend for ensuring suppliers compliance with environmental standards and product quality.

The results show that while some organisations have a robust process for reviewing and monitoring the benefits and savings arising from their global sourcing efforts, other organisations are either not aware of the potential benefits or do not have the systems in place to track them.

Despite these problems with measurement, cost was considered to be the primary reason for global sourcing, with 73 per cent of the organisations opting to buy products and raw materials overseas because of cheaper prices.

Quality of goods remained an issue with 90 per cent of organisations saying it topped their list of concerns.

Case Study: FIAT

Fiat has centralised its purchasing operations and is establishing new global sourcing offices.

The purchase of common goods is now sourced centrally to make the best use of its €34 billion (£26.8 billion) purchasing budget, €25 billion (£19.7 billion) of which is spent on commodities.

The firm plans to cut its overheads by sourcing from "best country sourcing". It has already set up a new office in China. It now has 100 staff including buyers, quality engineers and technical experts who work alongside one another.

As part of developing its global reach, a new 50-strong sourcing office has opened in India month, and the firm is planning a similar centre in Russia.

Research: Procurement consultancy Think Global Now.

Buyers should take advantage of their suppliers' global sourcing strategies. Procurement teams should learn what their suppliers are doing to source goods and services globally and try to join in with these initiatives. In doing so, buyers can minimise the risks involved with direct global purchasing and build stronger relationships with their suppliers. Normal buying practices are often neglected in favour of a quick deal with a foreign supplier.

"It's important to remember knowledge is power and understanding suppliers is the key to getting a good deal."

By adopting these measures, buyers could break down their firm's internal "fear factor" of sourcing overseas and make significant savings.

Managing Global Sourcing

As mentioned earlier in this chapter, improved technologies have enabled organisations to expand their markets worldwide. Intensified competition has also compelled organisations to outsource some of their non-core activities to other organisations possessing the required expertise.

Under the waves of globalisation and outsourcing, it is well evidenced that large manufacturing organisations often develop their products in, for example, Europe then manufacture them in Asia (especially in India/China) and then sell worldwide. Products that are developed in the USA are additionally often manufactured in Latin America. This strategy, as shown earlier, in its more advanced form, we referred to as global sourcing or Low Cost Country Sourcing.

Global sourcing structures and processes, including logistics processes, supply chain processes, and inter-organisational information systems, are important to the effectiveness of global sourcing. Supply Chain integration is therefore vital to the success of International/Global sourcing activities with the three dimensions of Supply Chain integration being shown below:

1.   Information Integration; Information sharing, Collaborative planning, Forecasting, Replenishment.
2.   Coordination: Decision delegation, Resource allocation.
3.   Organisational Linkage; Channels of communication, Monitor performance.

Checklist: Managing the Global Sourcing Process

Management Level	Process Flow: Material	Process Flow: Information	Process Flow: Cash
Strategic	Who controls the movement of the goods?	• ICT • Is the global supplier sufficiently staffed?	
Tactical	• What are the MRP Schedules? • What are the procedures at customs? • What is the best transportation mode? • Who should be responsible for transportation?	• How is information transferred between the trading partners? • What is the ICT infrastructure at the global supplier?	What is the payment cycle
Operational	• Packaging and material handling policies? • How are inventories controlled? • How to determine the procurement cycle?	• Are the ICT components adequate to ensure timely information transfer? • Are their ICT personnel sufficiently trained?	How to analyse the impact of the exchange rate?

(After Zeng ,2003)

Case Study: Kimberley- Clark

K-C has a sourcing team with directors who represent all regions (e.g.an office in Shanghai). Therefore, they have in-depth knowledge of what is happening with their suppliers. For the future, they will be looking at the comparative advantages of countries, for different products, to maximise value, not just to minimise costs.

Checklist: Classification of Logistics Costs in the Global Sourcing Process

Logistics Cost Category	Cost item
Transportation	Transport supplier to supplier's country port e.g. Hong Kong
	Main port-to-port freight charges e.g. Hong Kong to Felixstowe
	Handling
	Documentation
	Transport from, for example, Felixstowe to destination
Inventory Holding	Pipeline inventory in transit
	Warehouse handling and storage
	Stock value on hand
Administration	Order processing
	Communication
	Overheads
Customs	Customs clearance
	Brokerage fee
	Duty and taxes
Risk & Damage	Damage/loss/delay
Handling & Packaging	Materials handling e.g. in Hong Kong and in Felixstowe
	In/out handling e.g. in our warehouse
	Packaging materials

(After Zeng 2003)

An all too common poor practice is where people think only about the buying price of the goods and do not consider the landed/delivered, domicile duty paid costs. Let us briefly flag up some of these costs.

Transport Costs

Here, uncertainty or misunderstanding is the perfect environment for costs to grow. They flourish in last minute arrangements, and therefore the solution is a simple one: planning.

At the time of raising the order, it is a good idea to clarify the buyer's and seller's respective responsibilities using the International Chamber of Commerce Incoterms that we covered fully earlier in the book in part 4. As has been said by a large global MNC British American Tobacco (BAT) "it would be difficult to overestimate the importance of Incoterms to purchasers who engage in cross border trade."

It is essential that the buyer and seller know exactly who is taking responsibility for customs clearance, insurance and the logistics of the sale. Incoterms define exactly the duties of the parties, and adherence minimises misunderstanding and therefore risks. "For instance, should a shipment be damaged in transit, Incoterms will dictate whether it is the buyer or the seller who must replace the goods.

One characteristic of international transport is that it needs an extended network of parties, each of which requires payment. A buyer could forget about these costs if seduced by an attractive unit price. Logistics and shipping often appears to be left to the last minute and dealt with as a less important part of the buying process."

There are a multitude of options to ship products across the globe and these are covered fully later in part 8 of this book; meanwhile, briefly, it will depend on a few questions:
- What type of product is it?
- Does it require specific transport?
- What are the goods for and when are they needed?
- Is an item for stock or is the product urgent?

At the time of purchasing, the buyer is usually in a position to answer most of these questions and therefore make a cost effective choice, therefore procurement can be of tremendous value by specifying the right logistics solution for the whole journey.

Case Study: B.A.T

Based in Europe, B.A.T has buyers around the globe. However, they do not have the infrastructure to send people to China to manage contracts and suppliers, and they do not want to set up a organisations unit.

Accordingly, they have appointed a management firm in China to manage supplier development, CSR and similar issues.

Global Procurement Strategy Summary

Many suppliers are actually applying global strategies. This forces purchasing managers to increasingly co-ordinate and centralise their purchasing strategies in order not to weaken their bargaining power. Hence, global standardisation and coordination of procurement should be the logical decision.

Case Study: Alstom Transport

Alstom, manufacturers of railway trains, have been global sourcing and low cost country sourcing (LCCS) for 15 years. Previously every train was customised with local content and local design. Now they try to standardise everything that is hidden from the customer (e.g. AC/door systems) which allows them to have a global supplier delivery to everyone.

Alternatively, on the other hand, procurement managers are regularly confronted with arguments to decentralise and adapt their processes. Different customer preferences, such as culture, country of origin effects, environmental issues, amongst others, do force organisations to comply with their customer's individual demands. Moreover, product related characteristics (such as perishable nature, volume, weight) will often make it simply impossible, or certainly more complex and costly, to buy from foreign suppliers.

Global Sourcing/Low Cost Country Sourcing (LCCS)

There is room for a summary debate as to whether or not International/Global sourcing/ Low Cost Country Sourcing will always represent the lowest total cost of ownership. Any sourcing, local or low cost country sourcing should have the key objective of minimising/optimising total costs of ownership, and the respective advantages and disadvantages are summarised below:

Advantages of L.C.C.S	Disadvantages of L.C.C.S
Lower manufacturing costs	Risks
Larger volumes/margins	Higher shipping costs
High value added	Longer lead-times
	High account management costs
	Relationships are complex to establish and maintain
	Innovation?

Professor Martin Christopher says supply chain managers need to be driven by demand, but to do this; they must be able to move quickly with an agile, or responsive, supply chain.

Christopher sees that supply management is increasingly about relationship management and supplier development, for example:
*   identifying those organisations to collaborate/partner with.
*   those who can enable them to become more responsive.
*   those who they want to become part of their extended enterprises.

Procurement should be looking, according to Christopher, for "that one organisation" that will work most closely with them and reduce the impact of risk in the supply chain.

In the future, Christopher believes, the preferred suppliers will be the ones that have aligned their processes to the buying organisation. "We are competing not through the quality of the product, or even through the price, but through our capabilities, and in particular, our ability to do things in shorter time frames.

"The only way this is going to work is if you have a much higher level of collaborative planning and if you share information things like demand and inventory availability."

Price versus Responsiveness

One major barrier to agility and collaboration is the growing strategy of low cost overseas sourcing. But Christopher believes that this trend cannot sustain itself for much longer.

"I am convinced that off shore sourcing will, in many cases, prove to be a big mistake. Organisations have done it for what they believe to be sound financial reasons, but what they are actually doing is being less responsive."

Costs, he believes, go far beyond just what you pay a supplier. "If there are longer lead-times, you need more inventory to cover yourself during that time."

As a result, an organisation's agility is reduced and there is a cost to not being able to respond quickly to demand.

On top of this, the cost of transporting the goods continues to rise. "The cost of making things has never been as cheap, but the cost of moving things has never been as high and will get higher."

Quite apart from the increase in the price of fuel, Christopher sees prices are set to rise owing to environmental charges and taxes and notes that Dell has moved its manufacturing closer to its main markets. Other organisations, such as the clothing retailer Zara, also now use low cost sources for goods with predictable demand and local sources for producing the more volatile or less predictable products. Finally, Professor Christopher believes that tomorrow's supply chain might actually find a return in some instances to more local sourcing.

Checklist: Best Practice

•   Link supply chain strategy to overall organisations strategy to align supply chain initiatives to organisations objectives.
•   Identify supply chain goals and develop plans to assure every process is individually capable of meeting supply chain goals.
•   Develop systems to listen to signals of market demand and plan accordingly, including changes in ordering patterns and changes in demand due to customer promotions.
•   Manage the sources of supply by developing partnerships with suppliers to reduce the costs of materials and receive materials as needed.
•   Develop customised logistics networks tailored to each customer segment.
•   Develop a supply chain information systems strategy that can support decision-making at all levels of the supply chain and offers a clear view of the flows of products.
•   Adopt cross-functional and cross organisations performance measures that link every aspect of the supply chain and include both service and financial measures.

International Contract Law

"A contract is an agreement between two or more parties which is intended to be enforceable by the law."

To make an enforceable contract, three essential elements must be present and correct:

- capacity (power or authority) to act, for example, to make an offer.
- intention to create legal relations.
- agreement.

In terms of procurement best practice, a sale of goods contract should always contain the following four elements.

1) A full description of the goods being purchased, including packaging requirements.
This helps avoid misunderstandings and if the wrong goods arrive, the seller is in breach of contract and they buyer can reject the goods and sue for any losses.

Under English law, sales of goods contracts are governed by the Sale of Goods Act (SGA) amended by the Supply of Goods and Services Act 1994 (SGSA) and the Unfair Contract Terms Act, which implies obligations on the seller about description, satisfactory quality and fitness for purpose of the goods. However, the SGA will only apply to contracts governed by English Law and its application can be exclude from the contract. It helps buyers to have the SGA terms in the contract.

2) Shipment/Incoterms.
As noted in Part 4 of this book, various Incoterms are available, which allocate the responsibility and cost of arranging transport between the buyer and seller. The usual terms when using sea freight are FOB (free on board) or CIF (cost, insurance, freight). Under an FOB contract, the seller must take the goods to the loading port and pay any taxes or charges incurred before passing over the ships rail when loading onto the ship. The buyer then has to arrange transport, insure the goods and pay any taxes or charges incurred after loading. FOB gives the buyer control over carriage which, for example with time sensitive goods, may be important.

Under a CIF contract, the seller arranges and pays for carriage to the destination port and for the insurance. The buyer only pays taxes and charges incurred after unloading at the destination port. Under a CIF contract the buyer will pay the seller more for goods and will have no control over the carriage and insurance, but then they do avoid having to make these arrangements.

3) Payment terms.
The interests of the buyer and the seller conflict as the buyer wants to pay at the last possible moment, whereas the seller wants to receive payment as soon as possible, ideally

before the goods are sent. Payment mechanisms, such as letters of credit, have been developed to balance the conflicting interests of the buyer and the seller; these being covered earlier in part .

4) Law and jurisdiction.

A contract should include a law and jurisdiction clause stating what law will apply to the contract and where any disputes are to be resolved. Laws vary between countries and the outcome of disputes will differ around the world. Without agreement in the contract, a separate, expensive argument about where and how to resolve a dispute may arise.

Contracts in International Trade

As we have already seen in part 3 of this book, there are many potential sources of risk in international trade, for example:
- Evaluation and selection of sources.
- Logistics process.
- Logistics timescale.
- Political instability.
- Fraud risk.
- Labour problems resulting in delays in delivery or loss of production.
- Cultural differences in commercial and ethical behaviour.
- Extra costs of shipping/packaging.
- Exchange rate risk.
- Managing quality.
- Tariffs or customs duties.
- Differing legal regimes.
- Language difficulties.

A normal organisation's approach is to try and mitigate such risks by ensuring there is an appropriate legal contract structure in place.

Contractual terms and conditions

It is the responsibility of the buying organisation to ensure that the organisation is protected legally – *Caveat Emptor* (let the buyer beware) – being the rule here. Buyers must consider and decide which are the right commercial terms and conditions to apply. These could be bespoke to the organisation or might be based on available international or national standard forms. Examples of these are as follows:

- IMechE/IEE (Institutes of Mechanical Engineers and Electrical Engineers respectively), Model Form General Conditions of Contract MF/2 for Supply of Electrical, Electronic or Mechanical Plant.
- IMechE/IEE Model Form General Conditions of Contract MF/3 for Supply of Electrical and Mechanical Goods.
- CIPS (Chartered Institute of Purchasing and Supply) Model Form of Conditions of Contract, available to members on www.cips.org.uk.

Model forms of contract will allow for basic terms and conditions to form the main frame of all organisation contracts, with specific clauses being added according to the nature of the product or service being purchased.

Unless made explicit through express terms in the agreement, terms will be implied, according to the local legislation that has been developed to deal with commercial disputes in the organisation's environment.

Conditions and warranties will form the basis of the terms, accentuating the importance attached to each of the obligations, which form the agreement.

Clauses can be used to secure against risk, but also as a bargaining tool. The buyer can agree the inclusion or deletion of clauses for small concessions.

The terms and conditions of sale or of contract do set out the obligations and liabilities of the parties; they are a statement of risks. The key risk areas to be dealt with are as follows:

- Price.
- Payment.
- Sefects.
- Completion and delays.
- Standard of care and workmanship liabilities and indemnities.

Essentials of a valid contract

The essential ingredients of a contract, in English law, following from an offer, are as follows:

- Agreement. This is formed when one party has accepted the offer of another.

- Consideration. The agreement is part of a bargain where each side must promise to do or to give something to the other.
- Intention. The parties must intend their agreement to have legal consequences.
- Form. In some cases, certain formalities (in writing) need to be observed.
- Capacity. The parties must be legally capable of entering into a contract.
- Genuineness. The agreement has to be entered into freely and involve a "meeting of minds".
- Legality. The purpose of the agreement must not be illegal or contrary to public policy.

Where a contact has all these requirements, then it is said to be valid. If one party does not live up to the promises then the other party may sue for a breach of contract. Meanwhile, if essential elements are missing, then the contract will be void, voidable or unenforceable:

- Void means the whole contact is null and that at no time has a contract existed.
- Voidable covers contracts founded on misrepresentation and some agreements made by minors. The contract may operate as a valid contract unless and until one of the parties takes steps to avoid it.
- Unenforceable means it is a valid contract but it cannot be enforced in the courts as one party refuses to carry out its terms.

The conditions of the contract will form the main body of a contract and breaching these conditions allows the claimant the right to disown the contact or assert their right to damages. Warranties are terms, but carry less influence as, whilst a breach of warranty allows the claimant rights to claim damages, they cannot disown the contract.

Usually, express terms are formulated to limit responsibility, the amount of damages that may be incurred and any changes in price.

Specific Clauses

There are many specific clauses that may form part of a contract and these can include:

- Addresses: communications must be sent to the address stated.
- Arbitration: how disputes will be settled.
- Assignment: controlling who the work is contracted to.

- Default: non-delivery.
- Entirety: what is not in the contract does not exist.
- Force Majeure: mitigating events out of your control.
- Law: deciding which countries law is used in foreign contracts.
- Liability and Indemnity: protecting against the risk of consequential or indirect loss.
- Notices: what means of communication will be used to pass information.
- Payment: when and how payment is made.
- Sub-contracting: restrictions on sub- contracting.
- Unenforceable: Protecting the whole contract from individual terms, which cannot be enforced.
- Variations: how variations to the contract are approved.

Checklist: Contracts with Customers and Suppliers

Although in law a simple telephone call can constitute a contract, and therefore would be binding, if would be foolish to rely on unrecorded and unsigned agreements, even to vary the terms of a standard contract.

A written contract not only enables you to record what is done for a customer, it also gives the opportunity to state how important matters, will be handled. But a contract can be a millstone if it contravenes one of the many laws on 'unfair' contract terms.

Professional advice should therefore always be sought.

Meanwhile the following questions may help:
- Do you have a contract or written terms of organisations?
- Do you confirm in writing all telephone agreements or changes over the phone to written terms?
- Are you relying on a copy of somebody else's terms? (These might be defective, inappropriate or illegal).
- Do you know who you are really making the agreement with?
- Do you record the registered organisation number of the customer or supplier on your agreements?
- Does your contract exclude liabilities for, say, your own negligence?

- Do you know that you and your customers have rights concerning the acceptance and rejection of bought goods?
- Do you always read your suppliers terms of organisations, including the small, hard to read grey print on the back of their invoices?
- Do you always check out organisations references?
- Do your terms of organisations make it unambiguous what you will do, when it will be done, how you will he paid, and what will happen if there is a dispute?
- It you are buying or selling overseas, have you settled which countries legal system will apply?

Checklists: International Contract Law Key Issues

What does global sourcing mean from a contractual point of view?
- Parties to the contract more likely to be based in different jurisdictions.
- Services/products to be supplied into more than one country.
- Increased impact of unfamiliar laws, regulations and taxes.
- Challenges posed by differences in language and culture.

Why is choice of law to govern the contract so important?
- Nature of laws and extent of rights/obligations can vary.
- Implied terms will vary considerably.
- In EU for example, the rule is to sue in the jurisdiction/country laws of where the "material obligations" were to be performed; this is however going to be complex when products can be sub assembled in one country and then assembled in another.
- Impacts of having to resolve disputes in foreign tribunals.

Other points
- Agree language for contracts, negotiations & communications.
- Ensure any language translation is checked in all documentation and communication.
- Allow for protracted negotiations with international suppliers and do not allow shortage of time to prevent compliance with best practice procurement procedures and processes.

Summary

International procurement has increased in importance exponentially since the 1970/1980s, as it has become a corporate competitive weapon to maintain or gain market share. Organisational and environmental factors have significantly contributed to this change in procurement activities. The most significant factor, however, which has lead to a proliferation in foreign sourcing, has been the reduction of trade barriers throughout the world.

When one considers for example, that 55 – 65 per cent of the average manufacturer's total costs are represented by purchased materials, it is paramount that management considers strategies to minimise these costs. International procurement appears to be the alternative choice. However, the development of international purchasing partnerships is not for everyone, as broadening sourcing horizons is ideally only suited to organisations which have a significant portion of costs committed to purchase materials, complex bills of materials and a large volume of individual parts, and/or an opportunity to expand their market base.

Price, quality and availability are often cited as the primary factors influencing the global sourcing decision. In order for this strategy to succeed, top management support is essential, in concert with the definition of clear goals, establishment of trust and respect, and the use of information technologies to enhance control.

7: Managing Corporate Social Responsibility and Sustainability

Defining Corporate Social Responsibility (CSR)

The classical view by the economist Friedman is that the social responsibility of organisations is to increase its profits, with the ultimate social responsibility considered to be primarily the responsibility of the government.

According to this stakeholder perspective, organisations are not only accountable to the owners of the organisation, but also to the stakeholders. The argument is that stakeholders influence the activities of the organisation and/or are influenced by the activities of the organisation. Organisations are, for example, accountable to politicians who can curb the activities of the organisation by introducing a Bill.

The broadest approach to social responsibility is therefore this societal-based approach in which organisations are considered to be responsible to society in general. The view is that organisations are part of society. They need a "licence to operate" from society and organisations representing this approach are characterized as "good corporate citizens". Carroll (1996) sees the essentials of the three approaches and considers the role of organisations today as a role which includes four dimensions:

1. Economic.
2. Legal.
3. Ethical.
4. Philanthropic.

Carroll focuses on the stakeholders of the organisation; however the problem with this definition is that it is very broad. Social responsibility is a diffuse and almost non-operational concept, unless organisations learn to "unfold stakeholder thinking".

The European Commission also links CSR to the stakeholder approach and has a definition as follows:
"CSR is a concept whereby organisations integrate social and environmental concerns in their organisations operations and in their interactions with their stakeholders on a voluntary basis". (Source: EU Commission, 2001).

This definition is used by leading organisations in Europe and is considered as the basis of the European CSR policy.

One of the most referred to definitions is by the World Organisations Council for Sustainable Development (WBCSD, 1999) that defines CSR as *"the continuing commitment by organisations to behave ethically and contribute to economic development whilst improving the quality of life of the workforce and their families as well as of the local community and society at large".*

As we have already seen, there are many definitions of Corporate Social Responsibility (CSR).

Another such definition is as follows: *"The firm's consideration of, and response to, issues beyond the narrow economic, technical, and legal requirements of the firm to accomplish social benefits along with the traditional economic gains which the firm seeks."*

The CSR concept is still developing and has not yet reached the maturity stage. It consists of a number of free standing and competing ideas that have not been sufficiently integrated into a broadly accepted and robust theory (Wood, 1991). In particular, there is an absence of consensus regarding the elements underpinning the processes of corporate social responsibility. Therefore, the analysis presented in this section is a work in progress and subject to change as the CSR concept climbs the maturity curve.

Another definition offers the following: *"An ethical organisation is one that is able to reflect appropriately and evaluate its actions in the context of an ethical domain, within the process of organisational decision-making. In attempting to do so, the organisation must grapple with the problem of multiple agency-constituency roles".*

CSR is here concerned with treating the stakeholders of the firm ethically or in a socially responsible manner. Stakeholders exist both within a firm and outside. The aim of social responsibility is to create higher and higher standards of living, while preserving the profitability of the corporation, for its stakeholders both within and outside the corporation.

CSR is pragmatic and acknowledges the importance of economic performance, it recognises that organisations serve a broad range of stakeholders, and it highlights the importance of striking a balance between economic performance, whilst meeting the stakeholder's expectations and responsibility towards society. CSR can therefore only flourish if its protagonists recognise the importance of economic performance.

CSR and Values

The following values underpin the CSR concept:
* Seeks to understand and meet the needs of stakeholders including that of customers, owner, employees, suppliers, and the society at large.
* Integrity of individual and collective action.
* Honour.
* Fairness.
* Respect.
* Participation.
* Individual and collective responsibility to others.

Waddock and Graves' (1997) empirical research showed a positive association between corporate social performance and financial performance. The outcome of studies examining the link between CSR and financial performance is however indeterminate with some other studies identifying a positive link, yet others finding no link and in some cases, a negative link.

Martin-Castilla (2002) argues that CSR serves the long-term interest of the firm by aligning the interest of the firm with that of its stakeholders.

Checklist: Process principles of CSR

CSR Process Principles	Description
No-Harm	This principle draws upon the rights philosophy, by demanding that the firm should not engage in any action that leads to harm.
Transparency	This principle draws on the liberty and informed choice theory. That is full disclosure and provision of information to all parties so that they are able to take decisions that do not compromise their welfare.
Voice	This principle requires that stakeholders' interests are protected through visible and active participation in the decision-making process at all levels.

Equity	This is derived from the theories of rights and justice and its aim is to ensure that there is perceived equity in the actions of organisations.
Benefit	The need to examine the benefits of an action, that is to say, if a certain act is carried out, who wins, who stays the same and who loses from it? What are the gains and losses?
Integrity	This requires integrity of action in all forms.
Liberty	This is based on the liberty theory of ethics by stressing the right of the individual freely to engage in or disengage from transactions with the firm.
Care	This is focusing on protection and promotion of positive rights by the firm.

Source: Table adapted from Ahmed and Machold (2004)

Checklist: Drivers behind Corporate Social Initiatives

• Competitive Advantage.

• Emerging morals and ethics; although some people still believe that an organisation exists solely to maximise shareholder value, many more have come to the conclusion that this should not be at the expense of the environment, community or society in general.

• Thinking in terms of engagement and not speedy solutions; for example, acting with only the shareholders in mind, will create a gap in commitment between employees and investors.

• Understand that society and economics are inextricably linked; just as social situations impact upon the economy, the economy also has an effect on society. This is the view of Mintzberg who vehemently opposes the argument that an organisation exists purely to create profit for its shareholder, he believes that organisations must accept the part they play in society.

Checklist: CSR Critical Success Factors

• Connect with your organisation's core values and competencies.

• Respond to moral pressures; although your response may not be completely to the liking of any pressure groups, it will demonstrate that you are prepared to listen and, in most cases, compromise.

• Measure your success.

Case Study: Top Shop

Top Shop has a buying executive dedicated to sourcing ethical clothing, and has signed a deal to sell Fairtrade cotton lines.

The shift presents buyers with several challenges. They need to develop the core competences of supply chain professionals to include ethical considerations in buying activities. They also need to develop the capacity of the supply base.

Research shows that manufacturers often do not operate to international labour standards, so buyers need to work with suppliers to ensure improvements are made across the board.

Businesses in the Community (BITC)

This was set up by a group of British organisations which had decided to improve the way that organisations affect society. Businesses in the Community (BITC) is an independent charity to inspire, engage, support and challenge organisations to continually improve the impact they have on society. It now has 750 member organisations, including 71 of the FTSE 100, and its combined membership represents 12.4m people in 200 countries.

The creation of their Corporate Responsibility Index began in 1998, when it was decided that organisations needed a way to measure and report on responsible organisations practice. The purpose of the Corporate Responsibility Index is to measure the impact organisations have on the staff they employ and the societies in which they operate and on the environment.

The BITC Index emphasises that corporate responsibility is not just a "feel good" exercise but is of strategic and financial importance to every organisations and that it is vital that the momentum behind CSR is maintained. Organisations that do not keep a grip on working conditions, the activities of their suppliers or pollution are more likely to be prosecuted, shut down by the authorities or boycotted by the public.

Overall, there has been a substantial increase in the number of organisations with policies and targets in the public domain, especially on human rights, and standards in the supply chain and in the workplace.

The organisations in the Corporate Social Responsibility Index are committed to measuring and controlling their social and environmental impact. Organisations that have taken part said it led to organisational advantages, including cost savings, an improved corporate image, better recruitment and greater efficiencies. However, there are still some of Britain's biggest organisations which do not take corporate social responsibility seriously.

Organisations are recognizing that a genuine commitment to responsible organisations can be a source of innovation that produces new opportunities. An example of this is Marks and Spencer, who have made sustainability and corporate citizenship an integral part of the M&S brand as well as a key part of its competitiveness.

Best practice – what buyers can do to improve labour conditions.
- Avoid putting undue pressure on suppliers that might impact on workers; for example, changing an order at the last minute or shortening lead-times that could mean workers are forced to do overtime.
- Think about the effect of the prices you set; insist suppliers comply with the Ethical Trading Initiative (ETI) base code. (This code is considered more fully later).
- Give reasonable time scales for suppliers to address areas of non-compliance and provide support to help them improve, such as education and training.
- Help your major suppliers to share good practice by developing benchmarking groups where they can get together to exchange ideas about how to overcome specific issues in their region or industry.

The Environment and Supply Chain Management

Waste Reduction

It has been estimated that most organisations underestimate the true costs of their waste by a factor of 20. True costs equate to 4% of turnover, of which it is estimated that about 1% could be saved by waste minimisation. "One organisation, specializing in the management of industrial fluids, converted from steel storage to plastic drums. With plastic drums used over and over, the organisation saved approximately $1.8 million annually and significantly reduces the volume of discarded containers."

A 'making waste work' initiative has identified the 'Four Rs' for the reduction of waste. These are:

- Reduce the amount of waste.
- Reuse items i.e. plastic reusable packaging rather than cardboard.
- Recycle items i.e. at recycling depots or recycling organisations.
- Repair items, i.e. increase maintenance and avoid scrapping.

With approximately 50% of turnover as bought-in goods, the Procurement Department is most suitably placed within the organisation to contribute to overall environmental performance. Many larger organisations have already seen financial returns of cost avoidance, cost minimisation and environmental liabilities from waste minimisation. Small and medium sized (SME) organisations are also beginning to change.

Key to the success of a waste minimisation programme is supplier involvement. It means that suppliers are not faced with unreasonable demands and puts a proportion of the innovation in the hands of suppliers who have the greatest technical knowledge of their product. In the case of SME procurement organisations dealing with a larger selling organisation, it also assists in the dissemination of best practice.

The following checklist gives common considerations for procurement and supply chain professional undertaking waste minimisation and pollution control.

Checklist: Procurement/SCM waste minimisation and pollution controls.

- Purchase recycled products as this increases market for recycled products and strengthens the developing infrastructure.
- Purchase recyclable products; products with greater percentage of recyclable materials or more easily recycled materials increase post use recycle value and encourages recycling.
- Purchase from suppliers with preferred environmental status; provides impetus for suppliers to pursue environmental initiatives.
- Purchase products manufactured with renewable resources; minimise depletion of non-renewable natural resources.
- Specify or purchase reusable packaging; reuse on site, at other facilities, or return to the original supplier for reuse.
- Purchase materials that are environmentally benign.

- Purchase products that are manufactured with environmentally superior processes; powder coating versus spray painting reduces air emissions, for example.
- Reduce the number of different or incompatible materials; facilitates recycling, coloured paper reduces value of recycled office paper, labels/stickers that are difficult to remove inhibit recycling.

Case Study: Tesco and CSR

Tesco retailer monitors and assesses overall company performance towards CSR with the following range of KPIs:

- Economic with local sourcing and 7000 local products.
- Environmental:
- Energy efficiency with a year on year % reduction of usage.
- Water consumption.
- Vehicle efficiency.
- Recycling.
- Social, for example, "computers for schools" and an increased value of computers donated.
- Charitable donations at 1%.
- Employee retention and training.
- Supply chain labour standards; e.g. training staff and suppliers (including SA8000).

Case Study: Nissan

Nissan manufacturing UK's environmental journey began several years ago and, initially, was brought into focus by a need to comply with legislation. Achieving this soon brought all functions together, including suppliers, on activities designed to meet requirements but at no on cost.

They set out to look at it from the total organisations need. Foremost was the instruction to meet environmental legislation but at no cost. Achieving this requires savings to be made elsewhere to offset against legislative demands. First, they had to identify and understand all the drivers of the activity. A list was compiled including total detailed costs expended within each category. This involved collaboration with suppliers of components and packaging in order to detail and calculate all costs, including secondary costs.

For example, if they received the components in cardboard box packaging from a supplier and the intention was to delete the cardboard and use a returnable stillage, it took not only the cost of the cardboard versus the cost of the new stillage but included such issues as time saved on decanting the cardboard box to present the components to the assembly line versus the ability to present the new stillage direct to line side.

Also, by working with the supplier of the component, they calculated any benefits in their manufacturing and used those to reduce the piece cost. Also, eliminating decanting operations improved the welfare of employees by reducing heavy lifting operations. This reduces potential for industrial sickness which is a cost to the organisation. A further example is dealing with the safe transportation of airbags. An airbag contains explosives which are subject to handling and transportation legislation.

There are also environmental issues should there be an incident in transit. The initial packaging was aimed at meeting those issues. However, it was expensive and created waste from the protection involved.

The new method for delivery was developed jointly with the supplier and the benefits seen were:
- Elimination of supplier packaging (environmental waste).
- Reduction of disposable packaging (wastes).
- Improved compliance with legislation on transportation of hazardous goods (environmental issues).
- Elimination of decanting operations (safety and cost).
- Prevention of dust ingress (quality improvement).
- Reduced handling requirements (safety, employee welfare).

They have also worked on other issues with suppliers, such as recycling (for example, of plastic fuel tanks); reduction of process waste; paint technology and elimination of environmentally unsound materials. All achieved reduced costs.

The environment was seen as being best dealt with not as a specialised activity, but as a natural part of organisations. It is not an obstacle to performance but an important driver in obtaining organisations advantages. The public does not buy items solely because they are green; they buy them because they are better quality and lower cost as well as green.

Nissan's Waste Strategy
- Conform with all government and European legislation.
- Adopt proactive introduction of strategies to conform with future legal requirements.
- Introduce and maintain cost reduction exercises aimed at achieving waste elimination and improving effective waste management.
- Monitor and control current day to day waste stream activities.
- Adopt a programme of continuous improvement.

Environmental evaluation criteria

What are the likely criteria to be applied in assessing a supplier's environmental performance? There are four main headings which provide a high level view in relation to environmental issues; these are as follows:

1) Regulatory compliance.
This will encompass the various legislative and regulatory issues. Some will be mandatory conditions for supplier approval. Other criteria under this heading, though not mandatory, may nonetheless have a high weighting, both within this high level category and for the overall evaluation.

For mandatory criteria, it is likely that buying organisations would withhold approval/negotiation until such time as the supplier did fulfil the mandatory conditions.

2) Environmental effects and performance measures.
This second category covers the various effects and performance measures, such as eco-toxicological information, volatile organic compounds records, etc.

3) Existing environmental management procedures.
The third category heading covers the existing management procedures relating to the

existing set of products and processes. This will involve environmental effects register maintenance, energy conservation policy, etc.

All the above headings will relate to specific products or sets of products and bout in materials and components relating to the transformation processes involved in the organisations covered.

4) Commitment to management and process improvement.
The final category covers the commitment to continuous improvement in both management and transformation processes. These will apply to the supply organisation irrespective of the various product and materials which are supplied.

CSR and the Supply Chain

Of all the challenges facing organisations, the difficulty of establishing and maintaining responsible organisations all the way down the supply chain is exacting and complex. Ensuring that perhaps thousands of suppliers comply with your corporate responsibility codes is hard enough; in an ever more globalised economy the difficulty is compounded by differences in culture and language.

Best practice: Retail Supply Chain

Supermarket chain Waitrose (part of the John Lewis Partnership) sells 18,000 different products, sourced from 1,500 suppliers in more than 60 countries, all of which must sign up to the ethical and environmental requirements of its Responsible Sourcing Principles.

Waitrose says, *"It's all very well having best practices but you must also ensure your suppliers interpret them in a consistent fashion. It's very easy for different cultures in different countries to interpret things in different ways. Even for something as straightforward as stipulating that workers must not be exposed to hazardous conditions."*

Establishing workable codes of conduct and a streamlined compliance process only go so far in fostering more responsible organisations from your supply chain. However, giving incentives to suppliers is becoming as important as setting out clear rules.

"There should be a carrot as well as a stick. Achieving better compliance should not just be about enforcement, it should also be about working with suppliers to improve working conditions and fostering long-term relationships."

The payback for Waitrose is abundantly clear, *"Where there are good labour standards, there is better productivity and better quality."*

"If you are buying in China, but don't understand the working conditions there, you are not a responsible organisations."

Meanwhile B&Q has noted: *"If you look after your people, you get better productivity. If you are managing the work with your suppliers well, you get better quality products.*

"We do it first and foremost because it's the right thing to do, but the organisations benefits are also clear."

Closed Loop Supply Chains

Think of a typical existing manufacturing supply chain. The products are conveyed from suppliers to original equipment manufacturers (OEMs) and then on, via various other intermediaries, to the end user, who finally disposes of it.

This concept is changing and those of us involved in supply management arena are witnessing the dawn of the "closed loop supply chain".

The most obvious example of the closed loop model is the disposable camera. A customer buys the camera, which can only be used once, with a film already inside. The customer returns the camera for developing; the manufacturer retrieves the camera and then either services it and repackages it for further use or disassembles if for reusable components. Today, makers of products like printers and refrigerators are arranging their supply chains in similar ways, coming full circle to gain economic and ecological benefits. Undoubtedly, these benefits and pressures have been the main forces behind the closed loop shift.

In 2003, the EU's Waste Electrical and Electronic Equipment (WEEE) Directive came into effect in the UK. The directive aims to reduce waste by promoting reuse, recycling and other means by which products can be salvaged to minimise the impact on the environment. Private householders are to be able to return waste goods without charge and manufacturers must meet collection and recycling targets. Producer responsibility is backed up by measures such as disposal bans, increased disposal tariffs, restrictions on waste transportation, emission control and waste prevention.

This has dramatically altered the traditional linear supply chain model where suppliers would sell their products to customers and it would be up to shoppers to dispose of their refrigerator, oven or printer at the municipal dump.

WEEE changes all this, and manufacturers are now seeing a new end to the supply chain as they take back products at the end of their lives. This presents not only a logistical problem in clearing the equipment away, but also a cost.

It also offers manufacturers an opportunity to recycle the parts they produced for the earlier product. By incorporating the recovered parts into the supply chain, they are "closing the loop" and bringing the product full circle.

To make this process work, advances in design are needed to make the product "reusable" and because products will be used again rather than created from scratch, then factory emissions and energy consumption will be cut. Supply chain costs are directly linked to its processes and operating a closed loop model contributes towards cheaper processes.

But for any closed loop supply chain to be successful, manufacturers must look at how they manage the entire life cycle of a product. Organisations must evaluate the environmental burden associated with a product, process or activity. Legislation such as the WEEE directive will mean that manufacturers have to look closely at forward and reverse supply chain processes to minimise environmental impact, energy use and wastage.

The benefits of a closed loop supply chain in terms of both economic gain to the organisation and a positive impact on the environment are clear and when changing any established supply model, there are a number of issues that need to be resolved, as discovered by Xerox.

Case Study: Xerox

Xerox identified a number of barriers to implementation to extending the return and recycling process. These included:

- Customer related issues such as the acceptance of recycled products, and the need for simplicity in the returns process.
- Product related concerns, for example, product design, access to technology and the labour intensive nature of the return and recycling process.
- Internal factors, such as the allocation of costs and financial benefits.
- External factors, such as meeting legal obligations regarding disposal and the public image of the recycling industry in general.
- A consultation period with suppliers is important to get the best value from the relationship.

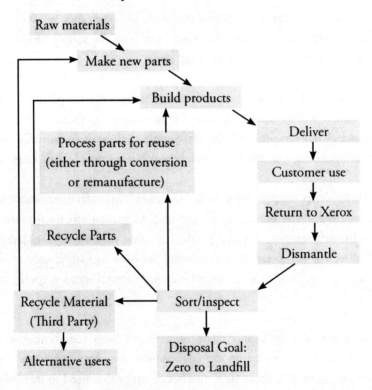

Xerox now reuses 70-90 per cent by weight of machine components, while meeting performance specifications for equipment with all new parts.

Closed loop supply chains are more economical than a linear structure for OEMs and a centralised supply chain outperforms a decentralised network in cost efficiency, although waste and energy savings were not so different.

Green Supply Chains

Role of the Procurement Manager

Procurement managers are entrusted with the task of procuring a wide variety of raw materials, components, consumables and packaging materials that are required to run the industrial enterprise and produce finished goods to satisfy market demand. They have a vital role to play in giving their organisation the competitive edge in the market place by adopting environmentally sound policies and practices. Purchase decisions, besides other considerations, must also be environmentally sound and every link in the supply chain tuned to this philosophy.

They must impress upon their managements that in the present climate of market driven private enterprises, where there is consumer driven competition with an increasing public "green" awareness, then a proactive approach to the environmental issues is beneficial. Adoption and use of environmentally sound technologies and the manufacture of eco friendly products will lead to overall reductions in cost. With increasing public awareness consumers may even be willing to pay a little extra for green or eco friendly products.

Life Cycle Analysis (LCA)

For a proper appreciation of the ecological soundness of a purchase decision and its likely impact on environment an in depth study and analysis of the complete life cycle of the product needs to be carried out. This concept, called the "cradle to grave" approach, must examine the cumulative impact on the environment that the product generates, right from the stage of extraction of its raw material up to its final disposal after completion of economic life cycle. The cradle to grave analysis will study and assess the environmental impact of:
- The raw materials used.
- Manufacturing/production methods/processes employed.
- Energy consumed.
- Modes and quantum of transportation used.
- Pollutants and wastes generated by the manufacturing process.

- Type of packing used, scope of its reuse/recycling.
- Final disposal of the product after expiry of its useful economic life.

To be able to carry out the life cycle analysis the procurement manager must study and understand the entire manufacturing cycle and discuss the subject with the manufacturer and/or supplier of the raw material/component.

The supplier of the component must be taken into confidence and the objectives of the exercise explained. It needs to be conveyed to the supplier that the proposed study will be equally beneficial to them and will in no way affect their organisations prospects. On the contrary, it will help suppliers to improve quality and consumer acceptance of products and reduce overall cost by minimising energy consumption, reducing waste and generation of pollutants and reuse/recycling of hitherto discarded products.

With the introduction of initiatives like partnership sourcing and a reduction in the supplier base, it should be possible to have a proper interaction with the suppliers to obtain the requisite details for life cycle analysis.

Checklist: Important Elements for LCA

The following are the important elements that need to be considered in life cycle analysis and details gathered about them from the supplier or other source of information.

- Raw materials: What are the raw materials used in the manufacture of the product and is their consumption optimal? Is the raw materials derived from a renewable or a non-renewable resource and how can its impact on environment be minimised? Use of raw materials such as lead, mercury, and nickel, found to be carcinogenic, must be avoided where possible.
- Energy consumption: Is the manufacturing process energy efficient? Presently most of the energy is produced from non-renewable resources. It is therefore imperative that use of energy is optimised and non-renewable resource conserved.
- Manufacturing process: Is the process of manufacture efficient in use of raw material/energy/labour and does it employ environmentally sound technology? Does it creates excessive pollution and generates toxic wastes?

Manufacturing technologies have been a major source of environmental degradation. Manufacturing processes using potentially harmful ingredients such as cyanides, chlorine and asbestos need to be avoided. It is better to use clean technologies to reduce pollution rather than using cleaning technologies, to remove pollutants which have already been generated. Use of clean technology will prove to be cost effective besides being environmentally friendly. Another important point to be examined is whether the technology employed permits use of recycled raw materials.

This is an important consideration as it will reduce the need for virgin raw materials and lead to cost reduction and other benefits.

- Waste reduction: Waste during manufacture is very costly and must therefore be eliminated or minimised. It not only represents poor quality but is also a source of employee demoralization.
- Reuse/recycling of by products of production process: Are the wastes and by-products of production processes recycled or reused so as to recover material and energy, thereby minimising downstream pollution? Reuse of reclaimed water, oils and lubricants etc. can lead to considerable savings and also reduce environmental contamination.
- Packaging: Primary and protective packing contributes substantially towards total cost and their disposal presents problems. Use of reusable or recyclable packing needs to be encouraged. With the advent of partnership sourcing and limited supplier bases, the use of reusable and returnable packing can be expanded, resulting in cost reduction and minimising the need for disposal of packing materials. As far as possible, use of recyclable and or bio-degradable packing needs encouragement to reduce the mountains of packaging rubbish.
- Final disposal: Recycling and disposal of the product at the end of its useful economic life is the last stage in the cradle to grave approach. Can the product be recycled for use as raw material? If not, is it bio-degradable? Will its disposal by dumping pollute the environment? All these aspects need careful evaluation as there is an emerging concept that producers are liable for final disposal of their products even after they have been transferred to others. Such concerns arise from the difficulties experienced in disposal of products such as nuclear wastes, used auto tyres and certain on recyclable plastics which can not be easily disposed of in an eco friendly manner.

The result

Having carefully examined the important parameters, based on the data obtained from the manufacturer and/or supplier, the parameters which have a predominant environmental impact can be identified. The importance and role of these can then be discussed with the supplier to enable him to incorporate the necessary changes in the raw material, manufacturing process, packing to make the final product more environmentally friendly.

The procurement manager will have to act as a guide and facilitator to enable the manufacturer to incorporate various changes and derive full benefits from the life cycle analysis.

More on Green Supply Chains is found in **Green Supply Chains: An Action Manifesto** by Stuart Emmett and Vivek Sood (2010).

Case Study: TR Fastenings

TR Fastenings invest a lot of time in investigating and visiting existing and potential suppliers.

Whether they are in the UK, Europe or Asia, the same criteria are applied:
- Do they provide fair conditions for workers?
- Do they protect the environment?
- Do they exhibit reasonable, ethical corporate behaviour?

TR has a regulatory framework which is easy to understand and which conveys the standards which the company require.

In several instances where the above have not been adequate but the companies are interested in improving, TR has agreed a contract at a price slightly higher than the norm, in order to allow the companies to fund the necessary improvements.

In this way, TR sees that they can meet their CSR obligations and remain competitive, and they get a committed supplier who will work well with TR and look after their employees.

Long Range Planning for CSR in Global Supply Chains

Introduction

CSR in a general sense reflects obligations to society and stakeholders within societies impacted by the firm. To illustrate the increasing importance of CSR with respect to supply chain management, consider the case of Wal-Mart and the Kathie Lee Gifford line of women's clothing.

Despite the fact that items with the Kathie Lee Gifford brand carried a "Made in the USA" label, news reports started appearing in 1996 suggesting that the garments were actually being produced in Honduran sweatshops. This news about its suppliers damaged the Wal-Mart brand name and tarnished its reputation. The Wal-Mart case is not an isolated one.

However, recently, Wal-Mart has been aggressively pursuing a variety of environmental strategies that have profoundly impacted its highly integrated global supply chain. The organisation will invest $500 million in sustainability projects, which already involve its vehicle fleet, energy usage, packaging, agri-organisations, organic clothes and food, and eco stores themselves. The trend towards embracing CSR has become so significant that Hau Lee, a global authority on supply chain management (SCM), claims that socially responsible supply chains are, indeed, a new paradigm.

"…implementing CSR initiatives within supply chains effectively (involves) ensuring supplier compliance."

Many issues are involved in implementing CSR initiatives within supply chains effectively, not least of which is ensuring supplier compliance. Recently, organisations have come under pressure to raise the level of supplier monitoring as a means of increasing such supplier compliance. For instance, the International Labour Organization (ILO) initiated the Better Factories Program to raise working conditions in Cambodia's garment factories.

Relying on unannounced visits to factories, it monitors a 500-item check list, notes progress made in remedying problems and reports its findings publicly. Its success is attributed to the fact that all factories are involved and share a similar set of objectives, it is transparent and credible to foreign buyers, and meets the needs of the workers.

High levels of monitoring may also carry unintended consequences relating to managing the exchange relationships that make up a supply chain.

Research suggests perceived fairness can improve commitment and trust within buyer-supplier exchange relationships, which have been repeatedly shown as important to achieving the level of interaction and knowledge exchange necessary for high performing supply chain relationships.

CSR and Global Supply Chains

Several factors drive organisations to accept responsibility for managing supplier CSR, including customer and stakeholder expectations and the potential threat of legal liability.

Organisations primarily use three instruments in implementing socially responsible behaviour among their subcontractors:

1) Social labelling informs the public of the firm's compliance to an established set of criteria, and tends to be more effective in certain situations than in others. Labelling seems to work more efficiently in export markets involving the retail trade, and is often associated with niche products aimed at affluent consumers who are not price sensitive and are willing to trade price for support of the espoused social issue. For instance, Starbucks might label its coffee as being grown by producers who received a premium price because Starbucks negotiated directly with the source. That premium is then passed onto the consumer.

2) Socially responsible investing arises when financial decisions are based on achieving a socially desirable end and acceptable economic returns. For instance, large state pension funds in the USA, such as in California, have for a number of years invested in organisations that align with the fund's position on certain social issues. American universities also have directed investments in their endowment portfolios to support certain social programs and avoided investing in organisations that espouse views contrary to the school's moral conscience. However, in practice, very few funds own enough shares to affect the stock prices of nonconforming organisations.

3) Codes of conduct are applied to corporate policies and actions rather than to goods, and imply that the firm observes and/or enforces the policy advocated. For instance, Levi

Strauss' 1992 code stipulates that it will seek to do business with partners that do not use child or forced labour, do not discriminate, and do not use corporal punishment.

Case Study: Cisco

Cisco began the process of addressing both human rights and environmental issue in 2004. They adopted a code for suppliers that outlined standards to ensure safe working conditions, where workers are treated with dignity and respect and manufacturing processes are in conformance with stated environmental considerations. The code also includes the expectation of full compliance with host country's laws and regulations, as we as compliance with internally accepted standards.

External Standards and Codes

Social Accountability standard 8000 (SA8000)

This international standard specifies requirements for social accountability to enable a company to:

1. Develop, maintain and enforce policies and procedures in order to mange those issues which it can control or influence.

2. Demonstrate to interested parties that policies, procedures and practices are in conformity with the requirements of this standard.

3. The requirements of this standard shall apply universally with regard to geographic location, industry sector and company size.

The company shall also respect the principles of the following international instruments such as:
- Universal Declaration of Human Rights.
- The United Nations Convention on the Rights of the Child.

In summary, the Social Accountability Requirements cover:
- Child labour.
- Forced labour.
- Health and safety.

- Freedom of Association & Right to collective bargaining.
- Discrimination.
- Disciplinary practices.
- Working hours.
- Compensation.
- Management systems.
- Control of suppliers:
  - "the company shall establish and maintain appropriate procedures to evaluate and select suppliers based on their ability to meet the requirements of this standard".
  - "the company shall maintain reasonable evidence that the requirements of this standard are being met by suppliers and subcontractors."

Other social accountability standards and codes of practice are the Ethical Trading Initiative, Fairtrade, International Labour Organisation conventions and the ISO14000 series.

These are explained below:

The Ethical Trading Initiative (ETI)

The Ethical Trading Initiative (ETI) is an alliance of companies, trade unions, development and campaigning groups, which works to improve the lives of workers in global supply chains.

Ethical Trading Initiative base code includes:
- Employment is freely chosen.
- Freedom to join unions.
- Safe clear conditions.
- No child labour.
- Living wages to be paid.
- Fair working hours.
- No discrimination.
- No harsh or inhumane treatment.

Case study: Marks & Spencer

Marks & Spencer is going down the ETI route. It is taking part in the ETI's Purchasing Practices project, which encourages the training of buying teams to increase their awareness of how their buying practices affect suppliers and their employees.

Fairtrade

Fairtrade is a system monitored and operated by the Fairtrade Labelling Organisation, which sets working and social standards that must be complied with before companies are awarded a Fairtrade mark. It aims to change the way we trade, creating fairer working conditions, greater opportunities in the market place and social development for producer partners.

The sourcing principles from Fair Trade are as follows
- Engage with stakeholders.
- Understand the supplier country context.
- Transparent communication.
- Price to cover cost of labour and capital employed.
- Develop partnering relationships.
- Integrate social objectives with other buying functions.

Case Study: Dell considers linking buyers to new standards

Computer firm Dell is considering measuring its buyers' performance by linking it to new supplier labour and environmental standards set by the electronics industry.

Dell agreed to adopt a common set of supplier assessment standards from the Electronics Industry Code of Conduct, which aims to improve workers' rights and sustainability.

The firm will use a single auditor and create a database to share and track supplier information.

International Labour Organisation (ILO)

Adopted in 1998, the ILO Declaration on Fundamental Principles and Rights at Work is an expression of commitment by governments, employers' and workers' organisations to uphold basic human values that are vital to our social and economic lives.

The Declaration covers four areas:
- Freedom of association and the right to collective bargaining.
- The elimination of forced and compulsory labour.
- The abolition of child labour.
- The elimination of discrimination in the workplace.

Some aspects to be considered are as follows:
- Application of the above principles. Excessively high monitoring levels can lead to buyer/supplier conflict, militating against the trust and commitment integral to successful performance.
- Looking Internally. Suppliers will not view a buying firm as applying CSR consistently if it asks seller organisations to follow a course of action it is unwilling to undertake itself.
- Defining your code of conduct. A firm cannot manage its supply chain partners if it has not articulated precisely what its intentions are, what it is doing itself and what it expects from its suppliers and its suppliers' suppliers. The codes represent the efforts of each organisation to put into writing a statement or set of expectations regarding supplier corporate social responsibility.

There can be no ambiguity as to what the goals are, the penalties for those who violate the letter and spirit of the code, and resources available to help suppliers (current or potential) become and remain compliant. Accuracy of information is essential as are consistency in criteria used in selecting and evaluating suppliers, as well as the need for objective (i.e. unbiased) application of the criteria.

Any action that encourages involvement or participation in supply chain issues will go a long way to building commitment and a common CSR vision.

To complete the circle, a corporate policy of statement of the buying organisation's commitment in the form of a corporate social responsibility report should be developed and endorsed. Organisations such as Disney, Gap and McDonald's Corporation publish CSR reports that illustrate their commitment to their codes of conduct, and also highlight the benefits they derive from their efforts. More importantly, they measure the effectiveness of those efforts, and embrace those supply chain partners whose behaviours epitomize CSR.

Environmental Management System (EMS)

An Environmental Management System (EMS) is:

"A method of controlling and regulating the organisation's environmental concerns".

The International Standards Organisation, ISO 14001: Environmental Management System standard states:

"The EMS includes organisational structure, planning activities, responsibilities, procedures, processes and resources for developing, achieving, reviewing and maintaining the environmental policy".

ISO 14001 is an Environmental System Standard and when adopted by an organisation can be assessed by an independent third party who will check conformity to the standard. If the organisation achieves certification the EMS has been independently verified and attained a recognised level of environmental Management.

Checklist: Benefits of an EMS

- Avoiding fines and prosecutions.
- Reduced operating costs.
- Reduced wastes.
- Compliance with environmental legislation.
- Reduced insurance premium.
- Increased public/customer relations.
- Satisfying stakeholder demands.
- Integration of improvement efforts.

ISO 14001 sets out five principles for a successful EMS
1)   Commitment and policy.

2)   Planning.
3)   Implementation.
4)   Measurement and evaluation.
5)   Review and improvement.

Senior management of an organisation must review the effectiveness of the EMS and whether action is required to take into account, for example:.
*   Changing environmental legislation.
*   Modified customer expectations.
*   Stakeholder pressures.
*   Failure to achieve objectives or targets.
*   Required changes to operations.
*   The results and recommendations of audits.

Organisations are required to review where their performance is in relation to best practice. The following outlines The Initial Environmental Review (ER):

The ER helps the environmental team:
*   Compile a register of significant environmental aspects and impact (Cause & Effect).
*   Prepare an environmental policy.
*   Develop objectives and targets.

An ER typically covers:
*   The significance of the above.
*   Quantifies emissions, discharges, wastes, energy usage.
*   Identifies cost saving opportunities.
*   Identifies the "must dos" for legislation and regulation (law).
*   Provides an overview of site activities.
*   Reviews current environmental system documentation.

The above can lead to the development/refinement of an Environmental Policy which should state:
*   A commitment to compliance with environmental legislation.
*   A commitment to continual improvement.
*   A commitment to preventing pollution, and it must be:
*   Written and communicated.

- Specific to the organisation.
- Signed and approved by the person with the highest authority and responsibility for the site.
- A controlled document.

8: Managing Third/Fourth Party Logistics (3PL/4PL)

Strategic aspects of Transport

Transport management is often thought of as being just an operational day-to-day job. However, it should also be involved in the longer strategic aspects of an organisation. Transport has a critical part to play in global supply chain management and it can only play this part, if it is, involved in the strategic aspects of the organisations. This will involve being aware of the expected development of the organisations in terms of the future:

- Production.
- Product.
- Suppliers.
- Customers.
- All the associated product volumes and throughputs.

Then, transport management is able to more fully proactively assess situations and make important contributions to the decision-making process.

Transport has changed its perspectives in recent years and the following diagrams illustrates the evolution in freight transport:

Pre-1980	1980-2000	Post-2000
Physical Transportation	**Evolution of Logistics**	**Supply Chain Management**
Regulated market	Deregulated market	Global market
Cost-based pricing	Price-based costing	Financial re-engineering
Low cost of capital	Awareness of high inventory cost	Total cost of sales
Inventory carried	Lower stocks/make to order production	Total inventory reduced

Inflation and deregulation	Globalisation and Re-engineering

The essential features of transport are as follows:

Movement
It provides for the movement between the suppliers and customers. This movement can be for raw materials, sub-assemblies/work in progress, or for the finished goods.

Distance
It can take place over shorter distances on a national basis, or can be involved over longer distances and on a global basis.

Cost
Transport costs increase with distance and are affected by the size of load. On a unit basis (for example, per tonne), the cost per unit decreases when using larger transport vehicles, as economy is directly proportional to the size of the load.

Speed
Time is often critical in the managing of global supply chains. Generally the faster the method of transport, the more expensive are the transport costs. Transport cost must however be looked at holistically across the supply chain. This can mean perhaps, paying more for the transport element, for a saving in the overall supply chain cost; for example, high stock holding costs may be cancelled, because the speed of transport enables the goods to be received quicker and stockholding levels are then reduced.

Accessibility
The transport system should be convenient for those who use it to send and receive goods. The system should also enable ease of loading and unloading so that the transport vehicle is not kept waiting. All types of transport vehicles (trucks, planes, ships) do incur high fixed costs, so all delays are expensive. Reducing the standing time during the loading/unloading of transport vehicles makes great improvements in transport productivity and is a reason behind many transport and goods handling developments.

Reliability
To manage supply chains effectively, then the reliability is an important aspect. Without this reliability, uncertainty results, meaning knock-on effects to other activities can occur. For example, late arrival off raw materials can mean the production stage is affected, meaning in future a decision that stocks is carried to cover against supply variability and unreliability.

Transport Methods/Modes

In selecting the method of transport to use, various criteria are involved and these include the following:

- Relative cost of different transport methods.
- Past experience, especially on reliability factors.
- Frequency, this can be for either the collection times and/or the dispatch times to the destination. For example, a collection maybe made on a daily basis, but the goods are held by the transport organisation before being dispatched on a weekly basis.
- Forced routing for example, the transport decision may have been made by the customer who buys on ex-works Incoterms (international trade). The customer would then determine the way transport should be organised.
- Operational factors, for example:
  - customer locations.
  - delivery point requirements.
  - size of orders.
  - service level required.
  - product characteristics such as size/weight/value/fragility/hazard.
- Strategic factors, for example:
  - Manufacturing locations, where are goods produced?
  - Warehousing locations, where are goods stored?
  - Marketing/Customer, where are products sold?
  - Financial situation, what can we afford, do we buy, rent, lease, contract the transport?

There are various methods of transport available to use. These range from Road, Rail, Air, or Sea based transport methods and each of these methods of transport has their own particular advantages and disadvantages.

The Main Modes of Transport

The mode decision can be thought of as a hierarchy, as shown below. This hierarchy also summarises some of the varied terms and the "jargon" used with different modes. Assuming a decision has been made to use a scheduled service, the following decisions are involved:

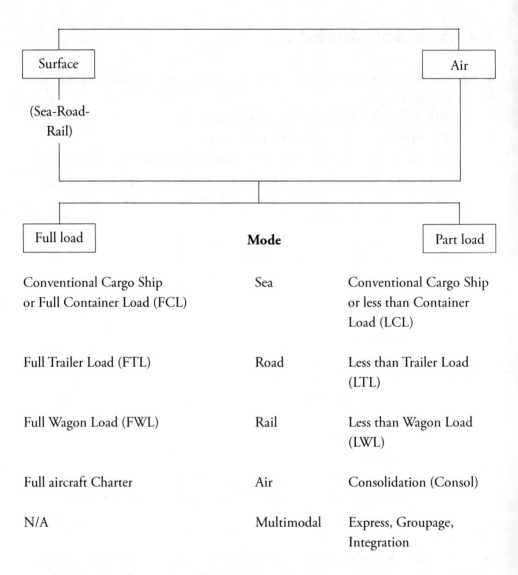

Full load	Mode	Part load
Conventional Cargo Ship or Full Container Load (FCL)	Sea	Conventional Cargo Ship or less than Container Load (LCL)
Full Trailer Load (FTL)	Road	Less than Trailer Load (LTL)
Full Wagon Load (FWL)	Rail	Less than Wagon Load (LWL)
Full aircraft Charter	Air	Consolidation (Consol)
N/A	Multimodal	Express, Groupage, Integration

For global trades then we are effectively considering sea and air, as road and rail are generally going to be national methods, except of course in Europe and parts of Asia and North America. However, in this book we shall only be considering sea, air and intermodal transport - those readers interested in the other modes of transport are referred to **Excellence in Freight Transport** (Stuart Emmett, 2009).

Sea Transport

The UK as an island has a tradition for seaborne trade and has the ports, docks, and infrastructure to accommodate a very large volume of trade. The UK registered fleet has however, declined substantially since the 1980s due the differences in taxation levels by registering ships in more taxation friendly countries and now has only around 1% of the worlds registered fleet. Seaborne transport has the advantage of being relatively inexpensive in relation to bulk loads. However, it is a slow form of delivery between port terminals and most of the goods moved also have to be collected at the port terminal and then delivered to the customers.

Sea is normally chosen because of cost and it moves up to 95% by weight and 60% by value of all world international trade cargo. Examples of such cargo are general consumer goods, automotive vehicles, chemicals, iron and steel, ores, oil, and other bulk products and any product that is not time sensitive and where demand can be forecast in advance, to allow for the relatively slow transit time. Whilst it is therefore the slowest mode of transport, sea transport benefits from economies of scale as very large volumes of cargo are moved by the one freight carrying unit, i.e. the ship or vessel. Vessels up to 550,000 tonnes are found carrying bulk cargo and, since the 1960s, container services dominate general cargo shipping and scheduled services operate between all world main trade centres. These regular liner ocean services are relatively frequent and reliable in operation.

Advantages of sea transport
* Reliable transit between terminals with regular frequent time tabled service frequencies between all major trading countries.
* Suitable for transporting bulky goods.
* Cheap.
* The main mode used for organisations which trade globally.

Disadvantages of sea transport
* Slow form of transport, although potential developments of "Fast Ship" 1400 TEU vessels using gas turbines/water jet propulsion could mean halving the transit times against current more conventionally powered and designed vessels. Originally scheduled for 2006 and currently scheduled to be operational in 2011, it advertises a five-day, port-to-port time-definite express freight service between Europe and the US, and is forecast to enable door-to-door services comparable to standard airfreight, at half the price. The website www.fastshipatlantic.com will carry updates.
* Insurance costs for transporting goods by sea are higher than those for air transport, as the goods spend longer in transit.

- More packing is needed than when using air freight.

Containerisation

A subset of sea transport involves containerisation. This involves the movement of cargo where, instead of packages being handled individually at each stage of their journey, they are stowed in a large container, which is then transported as a single unit to the overseas destination. This reduces the ship turnaround time in ports and improves the cargo security.

Containerisation is dominant on sea trades and the inland transport of shipping lines containers is also a common feature on UK roads. Containers are usually built to International Standards Organisation (ISO) specifications. Originally built to imperial external measurements of 20/30/40 ft length by 8 ft width and height, these 1960s original dimension have been subsequently increased.

For example, up to 8ft 6 inches height is now very common worldwide, with a 9ft 6 inch height on some trades. On length, some 45 foot containers are used on European trades and on the width, also in Europe it is not uncommon to find a width of 2.5 metres (8.202 ft).

The following features of containerisation can therefore be noted:
- The containers are of standard sizes with corner twist locks to facilitate universal worldwide handling.
- Special cellular ships are provided to accommodate the containers.
- There are also special types of crane and other handling equipment to load/ unload the containers.
- Ideally road or rail trailers are used that have twist locks that fasten and engage the container to the carrying trailers/bodies.

There are several types of container in use. In particular, the following ones should be noted:
- General purpose. This is the standard type of container, which is used for most types of cargo. It is fully enclosed, with doors at one end for access.
- Reefer. A refrigerated container, for perishable cargoes (such as food, pharmaceuticals etc.) that have to be transported at low and constant temperatures.

- Open top. Designed for cargoes, which are over height, and so the cargo cannot be loaded into a general-purpose container through the end doors.
- Flat rack. This consists of a base with panelled-in ends, and is used for oversize pieces, which cannot be stowed in any other type of container.
- Open sided. Used when it is more practicable to load the container from the side rather than the ends.
- Half height. Suitable for dense cargoes, such as lead, where the weight is high in relation to the volume. As there are design weight limitations for each container, a considerable amount of space would be wasted if such cargoes were stowed in full size containers.
- There are also special types of container for the conveyance of bulk commodities such as liquids, grain, etc.

Two basic types of container Sea/Ocean Services are provided:
- FCL (Full Container Load). This is suitable for the shipper who has sufficient cargo to fill a complete container, or who prefers to load the container themselves. The container will be loaded at the shipper's premises, and after the shipper has stowed and sealed it, they will hand the container over to the carrier. On arrival at the port destination the consignees can arrange for the container to be delivered to their premises and unpack it themselves.

- LCL (Less than Container Load). This service is most suitable for a shipper who does not have sufficient cargo to fill a complete container. They will arrange for the cargo to be delivered to the carrier, who will stow it into a container together with the cargo of other shippers. On arrival at the carrier's depot, the carrier will unpack the container and the relevant consignees will collect the cargo from the depot/warehouse.

The following four terms are used on container transport:
- FCL/FCL: The container is packed by the shipper to be unpacked by the consignee.
- FCL/LCL: The container is packed by the shipper and will be unpacked by the carrier.
- LCL/FCL: The container is packed by the carrier and will be unpacked by the consignee.
- LCL/LCL: The container is both packed and unpacked by the carrier.

Advantages of containerisation

- The main feature of containerisation is that it can provide a door-to-door service, with no intermediate handling en route of the goods packed inside.
- This, in turn, results in lower risk of pilferage, which can mean lower insurance premiums for FCL/FCL freight.
- In the case of FCL consignments, less packing is required, and often the goods can be stowed unpacked in the container itself.
- Containerisation can enable faster transit times, and allows the carriers to provide through documentation and rates to and from inland origins/ destinations.
- From the ship owner's point of view, it is possible to rationalise the fleet and the ports of call, with the cargo being 'fed' by smaller vessels between the main ports of call and the smaller out ports. Ship turnaround time is also minimised, for example it is estimated a 40,000 tonne container ship can discharge or load in 750 working hours whereas a conventional cargo ship would require 24,000 working hours. Another telling statistic is from the first large UK container vessel in 1969. In its first year's operation between the UK/Australia, it spent 82% of the year at sea with 18% spent in port; this compared to a modern conventional ship on the same trade, of 59% at sea and 41 % in port.

Disadvantages of containerisation

- Not all cargo can be containerised and exceptionally large and heavy pieces can only be dispatched by the traditional break-bulk methods.
- Some kinds of cargo cannot be stowed together in the same containers, a problem, which applies particularly to certain types of dangerous cargo.
- From the ship owning carrier's point of view, containerisation is capital-intensive and needs high levels of investment and management in the container fleet and in using specialised port terminal facilities.

Typical Container Weight/Dimensions in metres

Length	Internal width	Height	Cubic Meters	Tonnes
20 foot external =5.89 metres internal	2.34	2.4	33.00	28.2
40 foot external =12.00 metres internal	2.34	2.4	67.00	28.8

Note: Door openings reduce slightly the width and height.

Note: Tonne capacity is the design build specification. The effective payload will usually be reduced by national vehicle weight legislation.

The flexibility of the inter-modal container enables easy transhipment, not only between primary and secondary feeder vessels, but also between ship and land modes of transport. Container ships, also known as lift on-lift off [LOLO] vessels, are complimented on ocean liner routes by other general cargo vessels.

Whilst some conventional ships remain (these move cargo from land into the ships holds using conventional shore cranes or cranes on the vessels themselves), the growth of Roll on, Roll off [RORO] vessels is noticeable, especially on shorter sea and inter-European trade routes, although some do operate on longer routes. Roll on, roll off vessels on the shorter haul routes generally carry between 50 up to a maximum of 210 x 12/15 metre trailers. These RORO vessels allow for a speedy transfer shore/ship of wheeled freight, for example, road trailers, with Dover being the main UK RORO port, handling around 2.4 million units per annum, around 33% of the total UK RORO traffic of 7.2 million units, with Grimsby/Immingham and Liverpool being the second and third placed RORO ports respectively.

Container ships on longer haul routes generally carry between 3000 to 4000 x 20 ft containers (or 3/4000 TEU - twenty foot equivalent units). Medium sized (Panamax) vessels go up to a maximum of 4200 TEU so they can fit through the Panama Canal that has a maximum width of 32 metres and a draught of 12 metres. With the Canal expansion expected to be finished in 2014, then the new Panamax II standard will effectively enable 12,000 TEU vessels.

Larger so called, Post Panama vessels (these cannot fit the Panama Canal) of 8000TEU and over, are being regularly used on Asia/Europe services operating via the Suez Canal. A new container ship size, reflecting the Malacca straights (near Singapore), gives rise to the Malaccamax vessel size of dimensions of 470 m in length and 60 m wide with a 20 m draught carrying around 18,000 TEU.

Meanwhile, the current (2009) longest ship and largest freight carrier in the world went into service in 2006 at 397 metre long and carrying up to 15,000 TEU by some classifications (although the organisation concerned, Maersk Line, classifies it as 11,000 TEU). This is one of 8 identical vessels for operation on Asia/European services.

Larger vessels have also pushed developments towards main "mega" ports with subsequent increased transhipping. The UK is somewhat behind in the global container port position with Far Eastern ports dominating. Singapore is the world's busiest with around 28 million TEU per annum, with China and South Korea occupying the world ranking positions of 2 to 5; the largest UK port of Felixstowe being ranked 28th in the world and handling 3.3 million TEU per annum. This is 37% of the UK's 8.9 million TEU container movements per annum, with Southampton the UK's second container port. The UK is somewhat behind other European ports with Rotterdam ranked number 6 in the world, Hamburg 9th, Antwerp 14th and Bremen 20th.

Air transport

Air transport is a global industry and is very often regarded as an important strategic part and a "figurehead" of many countries transports services. It operates under strong controls, not only by national government legislation but also through international liaison with IATA (the International Air Transport Association). Governments are often involved as investors, besides being regulators, and from an investment point of view the returns are often below normal commercial organisations criteria meaning in effect, government subsidy can be involved.

Airfreight transport involves the use of both commercial passenger aircraft carrying extra freight and aircraft used entirely for the transport of freight. Improved aircraft technology of wide body aircraft gives an increased availability for "under passenger" space capacity in the lower/under decks. Specialist services have also developed with all cargo aircraft and convertible combined passenger/cargo configurations. The largest freight cargo aircraft (the Russian built AN 225) carries 254 tonnes, 1130 cubic metres, or space for 25 twenty-foot containers with the smaller AN 124 carrying 120 tonnes, 750 cubic metres or space for 12 twenty foot containers.

Air transport is very expensive, but it is also the quickest method of transport over long distances. It is usually used where the goods involved are small, light and expensive, so that the cost of transport is only a fraction of the total cost of the item itself. Cargo that is regularly carried by air freight includes pharmaceuticals, high tech products, spare parts, documents and fashion goods. These have characteristics of having a high value with possible time sensitivity therefore needing a quick response and a high value to density ratio; indeed air carries around 40% of world trade in value terms but less than 5% by weight.

Air transport is often chosen because of the speed needed for freight, such as perishables, fashion goods and emergency supplies. For certain types of freight and volumes, air can also give an overall cost effective solution to global supply chain operations. This will usually mean considerations beyond the basic airfreight cost; for example, financial issues such as the cost of money tied up in stocks, the time to market etc.

Advantages of air transport
- Air transport is very reliable.
- It is the speediest form of transport available (between airport terminals).
- Can be used where surface transport is not viable or easily possible, for example, helicopters flying over jungles, high mountain ranges etc.
- Low security risk (between airport terminals) and reduced risk of damage or pilferage; therefore insurance costs are low.
- Less packaging is required.

Disadvantages of air transport
- It is the most expensive method of transport on a cost per mile basis, especially in comparison with road and rail costs.
- Aircraft may be delayed/diverted because of weather conditions preventing landing/takeoffs. The mode is the most susceptible to weather delays.
- There are limits to the amount of heavy and large freight that a plane can carry.
- It is necessary to transport the goods from the factory to the airport and this increases the transport costs, especially if the factory is a long distance from the airport.

- Ground handling at airports can be slow.
- Ground security pilferage risks as airfreight handles high valued cargo.

Airfreight has its own type of containerisation but these containers are made of a much lighter construction than the sea transport ISO containers. The airfreight containers are of three types; air cargo pallets, lower deck containers and box type containers and all tend to go under the name of "Unit Load Devices" (ULDs). Like the shipping ISO containers, ULDs can be loaned to shippers/consignee's for loading/unloading. As will be seen below, ULDs have unusual sizes, as these have to be compatible with aircraft types/stowage arrangements and are designed to make the best use of the aircraft cube space.

The air cargo ULD pallet is designed mainly for terminal-to-terminal use with the conveyor systems in both terminals and in aircraft; the pallet being fitted with lashing points for securing the pallet to the aircraft deck. Cargo is normally secured to the metal pallet by cargo nets, which are then tightened by tensioned straps. Contoured semi-structural covers called "igloos"; "hula-huts" or "cocoons" can be used with pallets to provide cargo protection and also to keep cargo within the appropriate dimensions for loading onto an aircraft.

Lower deck (LD) containers are mainly for terminal-to-terminal use and fit in the lower/ under decks of high capacity passenger aircraft like the A330, A340, A380 , B747, B767, B777 and MD11. They are fully structured and completely enclosed with doors made from metal, fabric or a combination. LD containers can be closed and sealed and a common use is for passenger's luggage. They lock directly into aircraft restraint systems.

Box type ULD containers were developed in standard sizes to facilitate fixed freight charges and to be used on a door-to-door basis. They can be purchased by users or loaned from an airline. They must be constructed to IATA specifications from wood, plastic, plywood, fibreboard, metal or combinations of these. Contoured box containers ("igloos") are also handled and loaded in the same way as pallet ULD igloos.

Typical ULD Weight/Dimensions

Type	Height	Length	Width	Weight	Cubic feet
LD1	64"	61.5"	64"	1588 kilos	60
LD8	64"	125"	60"	2449 kilos	254

Intermodal Transport

Intermodal transport is characterised by two basic elements:

- The use of more than one mode of transport for the various component legs of a journey from origin to destination.
- Goods remain in the same load-carrying unit (container, trailer or swap body), throughout the journey with the transfers of the unit between the modes, taking place in terminals or ports.

Whilst we have looked at the relative advantages and disadvantages of the various methods of transport, intermodal transport is the combination of different methods. For example, transport across and beyond national boundaries with a movement from China to Europe, which could involve road transport, sea transport, rail transport, and road transport. The following diagram illustrates this:

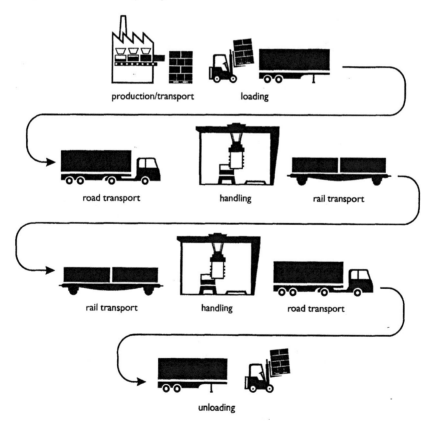

Inter-modal Container transport
(Reproduced with permission from Cheltenham Tutorial College)

Intermodal transport successively uses different methods of transport, and is capable of giving a door/door service between senders and receivers. The receiver, then finally, unloads the freight from the freight container - the consignment being "untouched/handled" since the loading by the sender.

Other combinations of modes include only the use of rail/road transport. This method is receiving strong support in the EU as it is seen as an environmental transport method. It remains to be seen how far these services will remain commercial and required to be competitive with other modes, or whether, legislation will "force" their use. In these mode combinations, the complete tractor/trailer or wagon/drawbar road vehicles or just the road vehicle trailer or a swap body from a road vehicle, are loaded onto rail transport. The following diagram shows these three types.

A – Truck and Trailer; tractor and semi-trailer (complete combinations)

The driver steers his vehicle forward over a ramp
on to a very low special wagon

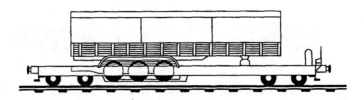

B – Semi-Trailer

Transhipment using (gantry) cranes or by driving
backwards over a ramp on to the wagons

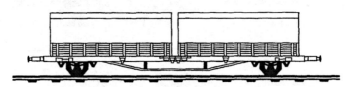

C – Swop-Bodies

(Length of 6m, 7m, 8m or 12m)
Transhipment by (gantry) cranes

Piggyback system

(Reproduced with permission from Cheltenham Tutorial College)

This piggyback system and is more widely used in Europe where the distance freight is moved is greater. Additionally it can also compensate for any travel time restrictions placed on road journeys; for example, during weekends/public holidays in France and the bans on road transit through Switzerland.

Advantages of Intermodal transport
- On long journeys, lower costs can be found by combining modes.
- Potentially can be faster that using just one mode, for example, by using road/sea/air combinations instead of just sea.
- Reduces road congestion, for example, when rail combinations are used in the UK.
- Lower environmental effects than when just using road transport.

Disadvantages of Intermodal transport
- Not widely available for many applications/trades.
- Needs specialised equipments e.g. trailers.
- Non-co-ordinated information/transfers between modes/different operators involved.
- Needs specialised terminals for the interchange to take place between modes.
- Road legs are still needed for the start and destination journeys.

Other Modes

Parcels/Post Office Transport

The cost is low with varied speed of service levels available. Reliability is varied, as this is dependent on the specific national origin/destination office or the other postal authorities for international traffics, and on any available track/trace systems in the national postal authorities. There are capacities issues with post as there are size restrictions. This is mainly 15 kilos, with some countries having a limit of 10 kilos.

Couriers/Express Transport

Courier transport is "hand-held" and express transport is for up to 30 kg packages. Both offer flexible door-to-door services with medium to high cost levels. Speed is fast with guaranteed timed services available. Reliability is good as operators often use mainly dedicated "own" networks and with courier, then one person hand delivers the package(s).

Forwarders/Agents for Transport

A forwarding agent is an intermediary and effectively a middleman who buys freight on behalf of their principal. They are experts who should continually monitor what the best deal is and then give impartial advice.

A forwarder, a subtle change in name, is a freight specialist/operator of services using their own or hired equipment. They are specific route specialists and service operators in their own right. As such, they cannot be expected to give impartial advice. Both forwarding agents and forwarders however will often give useful advice on customs and prepare documentation.

The distinction between forwarders and forwarding agents is often blurred but the difference is fundamental when making a selection; forwarding agents should be impartial, whereas forwarders can prefer to use only their own services.

Forwarders and agents can vary in size:

Base	Size	Facilities
Local agent	1-2 offices	Offices only
National forwarder	Major ports and inland towns	Possibly with road vehicles and warehouses
International forwarder	World wide	Possibly with owned ships and aircraft

Forwarders can have a strong and a dominant role. For example with airfreight, over 90% of freight is handled by forwarders/agents, and 70% of this freight is handled by forwarder consolidations. In sea freight, the percentages are less.

Switching transport modes

Users of transport services may be prompted to search for new modes of transport by the following:
- Improvement in customer satisfaction in terms of time, method of materials handling, degree of security.
- Deterioration of service provided by the existing mode.

- Reduced costs.
- Reduced transit time.
- Changing needs of the organisation and/or the customer.
- Development of new products which require different modes of transport.

Information concerning modes of transport

During the process of selecting modes of transport, the user has to examine a number of considerations before making an effective decision. The sources of information available are as follows:

- Past experience of the user. They will have dealt with a number of organisations and modes and will likely have a high degree of 'market' knowledge to refer to in the decision-making process.
- Marketing/commercial departments of the transport organisations.
- Trade directories and route maps.
- Trade magazines and journals.
- Specialist consultants who will advise on the various modes of transport and the relative advantages and disadvantages of each.
- Other transport managers. If the transport or fleet manager is a member of the Chartered Institute of Logistics and Transport, then information from fellow professionals is available.

The Third Party marketplace & Outsourcing transport

Users are often confused by who they should deal with. Whilst names are important in defining what people do, too often different names are given to the same things and often confusion results. The following therefore attempts to give a view on what the varied name definitions are for Third Party Logistics Service Provider organisations (3PLSP). A few words of explanation first: Fixed terms arrangements in the following definitions means a dedicated provision of services for a specified timed/term contract; Ad Hoc arrangements mean common user/shared provision as required/on demand. Clearly, however, a contract negotiation could also take place for the provision of common user/shared services provision.

Contract Distribution/Logistics

This is a fixed term agreement for provision of dedicated vehicles and/or warehouse resources. It is usually offered by large organisations with access to capital to support such operations which will also offer a high range of services, usually on a national/domestic basis, but which can be extended internationally.

Haulage Organisations/Warehouse Organisations

These offer fixed or ad hoc arrangements for dedicated, but usually common user/consolidated services. The organisations are usually medium to smaller sized operating nationally or regionally, with (sometimes) access to a network of other regional organisations. They offer personal services mainly on a national/domestic basis.

Integrators

Fixed or ad hoc on demand arrangements, using multimodal transport. Often these organisations are multinational organisations operating worldwide.

Express Organisations

Fixed or ad hoc on demand arrangements for local/national express next day deliveries, will usually be a large organisation with an owned network, or smaller organisations with access to a network with other organisations and often on a franchised basis.

Forwarding agents, Forwarders and 4PL

These mainly offer ad hoc on demand arrangements: perhaps they are a traditional shipping and forwarding agent with maybe some transport and warehousing resource. Forwarders usually are smaller and local organisations although there a few large organisations which operate with owned facilities on a more global basis. In the UK, there are around 3000 forwarders, with fewer than a hundred organisations employing over one hundred people.

Traditionally, a freight forwarding agent acts as an agent on behalf of a shipper. They will do anything, anytime, for anyone, to any place in the world, by any means of transport, for a profit. They are perhaps the original 4PL (fourth party logistics provider), a term coined in the late 1990s by Anderson Consulting who defined this as: "a 4PL is a supply chain manager which can combine its own resources, capacities and technologies with those of other service providers to offer organisations, complete solutions."

However some forwarding agents do also act as principles themselves and are the actual service operators or forwarders. In this role for example, the forwarder "buys in bulk" from the freight services carrier/operator on a FTL, FCL, or ULD basis. Then they sell on a groupage/LCL/consolidated/service, which will operate on a terminal-to-terminal basis with additional optional services being provided such as collection/delivery, documentation.

FIATA is the International Federation of Freight Forwarders Associations (www.fiata. com) and CLECAT, the European Association for Forwarding, Transport, Logistics and Customs Services, in 2004, adopted the following official description of freight forwarding and logistics services:

"Freight Forwarding and Logistic Services means services of any kind relating to the carriage (performed by single mode or multimodal transport means), consolidation, storage, handling, packing or distribution of the Goods as well as ancillary and advisory services in connection therewith, including but not limited to customs and fiscal matters, declaring the Goods for official purposes, procuring insurance of the Goods and collecting or procuring payment or documents relating to the Goods. Freight Forwarding Services also include logistical services with modem information and communication technology in connection with the carriage, handling or storage of the Goods, and de facto total supply chain management. These services can be tailored to meet the flexible application of the services provided".

Forwarders are involved in numerous activities such as the following:
- selection of the carrier/operator/service provider.
- organising/supervising the movement by carriage (performed by single mode or multimodal transport means), consolidation, storage, handling, distribution.
- providing documentation and insurance.
- ensuring compliance with regulations (customs, banking, consular etc.).
- advising on packing, warehousing, supply chain management etc.
- ancillary and advisory services including but not limited to:
  - customs and fiscal matters.
  - declaring the goods for official purposes.
  - procuring insurance of the goods.
  - collecting or procuring payment or documents relating to the goods.
  - logistical services with modem information and communication

technology in connection with the carriage, handling or storage of the goods, and de facto total supply chain management.

Shipping Lines & Airlines

Basic terminal-to-terminal providers, who may have expanded into offering door-to-door land based services. Fixed or ad hoc arrangements.

Postal Organisations

Formally these were state-owned, nationally-based organisations with access to other postal authorities' networks. Since privatisation, many have bought into privately-owned contract distribution/integrators/forwarding organisations. Mainly thought of as being available on ad hoc, on demand arrangements, however fixed term contracts are an important part of their organisations.

Parcel organisations

Mainly ad hoc on demand arrangements for non-time sensitive consignments. Similar sized organisations as for Express organisations.

Couriers

Fixed or Ad hoc on demand arrangements for hand carried/small packages requiring urgent time delivery.

Other views

Another view of the 3PL provider market is from an IBM report ("Building value in logistics outsourcing", IBM 2006) that sees the following types of players:
- Foundation providers; mainly national providers of transport services.
- Core service providers; concentrate on specifics and commodity buying, "famous for few things".
- Extended service providers; as core but with a wider range of services, "deliver what they advertise".
- Lead logistics providers; more global with "mass customization" of service offerings.

- Synchronised providers; offering total supply chain management with standard offerings/"plug and play".

The IBM report notes that customers require greater reliability with less cost consistently. IBM also see that to give the full value of trade-offs from outsourcing, 3PLs must broaden their span, for example, away from a transactional, piecemeal and narrow focus towards a more collaborative, larger and wider scope. The report notes that whilst some 3PLs have responded with greater integration and higher performance, conformance is needed and that many 3PLs are found to be lacking as they tend to over promise and under deliver.

The UK Third Party Sector

In global supply chains, the supply chain player's will be using largely third party contractors to supply their transport and warehousing services. The following ideal framework can be seen on the UK third party organisation structures and types:

Feature	Integrators /couriers e.g. DHL	Contract logistics e.g. Wincanton	Forwarders/ 4PLs e.g. Panalpina	Single Mode operator e.g. A Haulier Limited
Assets	Heavy ownership of assets	Managed but not always owned	Asset light	Owned or leased/rented
Basic organisations driver	Volume through the network	Long-term stable customers	Trading	Personal service
Branding	Important	Not important	Some importance	Possible
Customers	Anyone, from one off to long-term contract	Long-term and contractual	Local and possibly Global	Local
Product/ service offering	Network Coverage, offer a range of services	Specialised including warehousing	Anything at all, with "extras" such as packing	Full loads and possibly some part loads

Modes used	Road/Air with some rail	Mainly road based	All modes, especially sea and air	Road only

Using Third Parties

Outsourcing not only applies to transport, or warehousing or distribution. It is often a strategic direction that most organisations take. The following "secrets" were identified by "Supply Management" (29 June 2000):

- Concentrate of what do well and allow specialists in other areas to handle the non-core services.
- Adapt to new ideas and developments, as, what was acceptable in the past, may not be so in the future.
- Choose a provider who understands all your needs.
- It is crucial to fully know your current costs/service level.
- Ensure outsourcing delivers, planned benefits such as cost/service/time targets.
- Acknowledge that information equals power in areas such as service level requirements.
- Develop a strategic partnership with the provider, based on mutual trust.
- Start with a phase controlled service with monitored cost/service levels at all stages.
- Develop the right organisation culture which supports outsourcing.
- Monitor the outsource function with performance measurement regularly.

The following questions also provide a view on whether to use using third parties for distribution:

- Is distribution non-core activity? Whatever the answer, Management control must remain a core activity, as should, customer contact.
- Can we release some capital? The 3PL industries have reported low ROCE ratios, typically 10 per cent, probably well below that expected by many other organisations/sectors.
- Will we retain some operations in house? It may be useful to do this for cost comparisons and service benchmarking.
- Will we retain Management expertise? This is important to do; organisations should never fully sub-contract control.
- What increased monitoring will be needed? This should be the same as is

currently done, but there is often a need to especially watch closely the customer service standards.

- What are the risks of committing to one contractor? Flexibility in the contract maybe possible, alternatively multi sourcing could be the answer.
- Will flexibility be increased? It should be flexible as in theory, as the third party operator can maybe divert non-specialised resources elsewhere, as after all, transport/distribution is their core organisations.
- Will costs be reduced, whilst service increased? This is the ideal.
- How will we account for future changes? Presumably the same as without the contractor; but contract term and 'get outs' is the issue to be considered here.
- Are there any Transport of Undertaking Protection of Employees legislation (TUPE) implications? There probably will not be if there are less than 5 people, or, some direct control is retained of say routing, or, if relocated. There probably will be if the assets or, the whole organisations are being transferred.

Information needed

When considering using third party suppliers of transport (or distribution and warehousing also), the following questions will need detailed answers. Giving third parties inadequate information can mean inadequate responses and if for example, comparisons are being looked for, in order to benchmark against incumbent operators, then a distorted picture will surely be found when giving out poor information. Meanwhile the incumbent operator will have knowledge of all the key parameters/details, and is in a favourable position. Key information must also be made known to the alternative suppliers that are being sought. It is surprising that so often, this is just not correctly undertaken, maybe reflecting that the organisation is no longer fully aware of what is involved or that they are "only go through the motions" of re-tendering and have no real intention to change.

Checklist: Information needed by a 3PL

Product Format
- What are the product sizes/shapes?
- What is the weight?
- What is the value?
- What is the packaging?

- How is product identified?
- Is there any fragility?
- Is there any perishables?
- Any hazards involved?
- Any special handling needed?

Throughputs

- What is the frequency? E.g. daily, weekly?
- What is the seasonality? E.g. over the year, in the month, during the week, during the day?
- What are the usual patterns/requirements?
- How often does the "usual" change?

Collection/Delivery Points

- Where are the geographical locations?
- What are the "features:
- Limited access?
- Limited "windows"?
- Loading docks?
- Side loading?
- Height?
- Day/night working?

Organisation Policy

- What service level is required?
- What is the "returns" policy?
- What is the order size policy?

Infrastructure/Environment

- What are the road congestion places?
- How can these be avoided?
- Any legal restrictions that may affect us?
- Any specific climatic conditions?

Financial Issues

- Is capital released?

- Is off balance sheet finance needed?
- What is the asset utilisation?
- Are there any economies of scale?
- What are the planned and the known costs.
- Has a cost comparison, involving Total Acquisition Cost been used?

Operational Issues

- What is the flexibility in ' spreading' peaks/troughs; in delivery times; in future changes.
- Will we get response to special requests?
- What are the management role changes on existing management?
- How will we keep control (management control MUST remain a core activity).

Strategic Issues

- After the decision, what is the ability to change?
- Have we got "all eggs in the one basket?"
- What is the ability brings it back in house?
- Are we able to use another third party?
- What are the full internal implications?
- Have we spread the risk?
- What will be our customer reactions (customer contact must remain a core activity)?
- Have we completed a fair and complete comparison?
- Will the change assist in any internal change/new strategies/expansion?

Some of the reported advantages and disadvantages from using third party contractors are summarised below. It should be noted that these have come from specific examples of outsourcing transport. They do therefore show a wide range of opinion and varied views; for example, innovation is seen as both "more" (an advantage) and as "none," (a disadvantage).

Advantages

Cost factor advantages

- Less capital on the balance sheet.

- Costs now fully on the profit and loss statement.
- Less depreciation risk.
- More economies of scale.
- Less administration.
- Increase organisations rations e.g. ROCE.
- Cash return for sold off assets.
- Tax advantages if leasing.
- Planned and more fixed cost levels.

Service factor advantages
- Flexibility against future legislation changes.
- Flexibility for sickness, holidays.
- Less risk of IR disruptions.
- Less employment risk.
- Improved service levels.
- More professionalism and expertise.
- More innovation and new thinking.

Disadvantages
Cost factor disadvantages
- Less cost control as costs "fixed".
- More hidden costs for unforeseen "extras".
- Long-term contracts.
- Paying a contractor a profit.

Service factor disadvantages
- Less direct control on service.
- Less feedback from drivers on customers.
- Less response to request.
- No innovation.

Clearly these types of listings also have much to say about how outsourcing is not only approached, but also about how the work was previously conducted by the organisations involved. No "one size fits all" and again varied views are reflected; let the buyer beware!

Selecting Third Parties

Users will generally look for the following three characteristics from third party organisations:

- Cost/price/rates.
- Speed in transit.
- Reliability.

The order and priority of this top three will usually vary dependant on organisation's requirements and its specific offerings in a marketplace. Many different surveys are undertaken in the UK, on principally domestic transport and distribution services, and a summary of these surveys follows:

Important Factors in deciding which 3P to use:
- Service   98%
- Quality of People   94%
- Cost   90%

Important Factors that 3P see they have:
- Quality of Service   100%
- Reputation   100%
- Experience   60%

Why selected a particular 3P operator?
- Cost   58%
- Service   34%
- Reputation   20%

The benefits obtained:
- Lower Cost.
- Focus on Core activity.
- More flexibility.
- Higher efficiency.
- Improved Service.

Implementation fears:
- Fall in Service   30%

-	Lack of Control	26%
-	Higher Costs	14%
-	Staff will not approve	12%

Implementation "reality"

| - | No Problems | 40% |
| - | Had Problems | 60% |

Implementation problems reported were:

- 35% from IT issues
- 22% people issues ('hide', 'fear', changed)
- 11% Service levels were not what expected
- 10% More resource/costs involved
- 8% Initial data found to be suspect
- 14% other reasons were culture clash, no clear agreements before started no planning or thought to implications.

On a European basis (in UK, Benelux, France, Germany, Italy, and Spain), a survey of 700 senior managers/users in the hi-tech, automotive, consumer goods, pharmaceutical and retail sectors revealed the following opinions:

"Not a problem":

- Lack of geographical coverage.
- Specific industry knowledge.
- Limited service range.

"Weak performance in":

- Price.
- Tailored solutions.
- Reliability (their most important requirement).
- Customer service.

"Will lose organisation's business if":

- Inferior value for money.
- Lack of reliability.
- Inferior service quality.

"Satisfied with":

• Expertise.

• Size.

• Geographical coverage.

Sector variables:

• Hi- tech outsources the most with retail the lowest.

• Hi-tech and pharmaceuticals use fewer providers than consumer goods who fragment across several providers.

• Germany outsources the most with Italy the least.

(Source: SHD May 2004: Datamonitor "European Logistics Provider End User Survey").

The following survey also illustrates that different views actually exist when choosing third parties, as each party has different views of what the most important criteria are:

	The Buyers Say % Most Important	The 3PLs Say % Most Important
Quality Service	47%	27%
Lowest Price	19%	26%
Sector expertise	15%	25%
Others: Size/Scope	3%	9%
Geographic experience	6%	6%
Reputation/references.	10%	5%

(Source: 6th Eyefortransport European 3PL Summit)

Once again, this survey illustrates the view of service over price. Additionally the survey looked at the reasons for non-renewal of contracts and found that the 3PL's view was 56% on price, whereas the Client's perspective was 55% on poor service.

Case Study: ITTs: Five things to remember

The Invitation to Tender (ITT) is a critical document is the process of outsourcing. A good ITT means a good contract and likewise a bad ITT means a bad contract

1. Make your ITT easy to understand.

An ITT is a formal document, but that's no excuse for making it difficult to understand. You can't expect a good response from your suppliers if they can't work out what you want. So write one-page introduction that explains what the ITT is all about, and put the important things such as the date of response and the name of the person to contact in there in bold letters.

2. Decide what sort of ITT you want and stick to it.

You can write your ITT in two ways. It can be 'input-based', that is, you tell the contractor what to do. Think off this as giving someone a recipe for your favourite meal. Or it can be 'output-based', that is, you tell them what results you want. That's like telling someone what your favourite meal is but letting them decide how to make it. Decide which approach you're going to use, and then stick to it. You can't do both. It would be like giving someone a recipe for apple pie and then complaining it wasn't what you wanted.

3. Stick to what's relevant.

When you're writing your ITT, remember what its purpose is. Its job is to allow your potential contractors to work out what resources your contract needs. No more and no less. So you do need things such as measurements of activity, service levels, what management information you want, and your forecasts for the organisations and so on. What you don't need are your mission statement, organisation charts for remote parts of the organisations, your standard organisation publicity and so forth.

4. Tell your contractors how to structure their response.

If you don't define this, you can be sure that they'll all submit their quote in different ways. And then you won't be able to work out which supplier is giving you the best deal, which pretty much defeats the object of issuing the ITT in the first place.

5. Don't get bogged down in the legal stuff.

ITTs mean contracts, and contracts mean lawyers and everything that goes with that. However, the place for this is in your contractual negotiations not your ITT. You only need to put legal details in if they're going to affect how the contractor deals with your organisations. Here are a couple of examples. Your contractor will want to know what length of contract and notice period you're planning. This will affect how they purchase their resources, and over what period they write them off. They won't be interested in the details of your dispute resolution procedures. That's something you can leave for your contract negotiations.

Source: Supply Chain Organisations April 2005

An interesting 3PL selection method is shown in the following case study:

Case Study: Toyota USA & Freight Provider Selection

A Description of TOYOTA-NAPO

NAPO-North American Parts Operation is responsible for receiving and shipping $2 billion worth of service parts and accessories globally. The Toyota Way can be called a mindset and an attitude. Toyota says, "it is the way we approach our work and our relationships with others". The Toyota Way is based upon two pillars:
- Continuous Improvement.
- Respect for People.

Each pillar has five (5) major principals:
- Challenge.
- Kaizen.
- Genchi Genbutsu (Go look, go see).
- Teamwork.
- Respect.

NAPO Mission Statement

"To provide our customers with the right parts at the right time in the right place at the lowest cost". Toyota felt compelled to translate this message into one that would be applicable to their carriers. The translation would allow them to effectively convey the right message to their carrier partners, thereby connecting all of the parties, at least, philosophically.

"At NAPO, we wanted our mission statement to convey the following: the Toyota philosophy; the objectives that NAPO strives to achieve; and to lay the foundation for the expectations that will be placed on the carriers."

Carrier Relationships with Toyota

Relationships are based on three (3) principals:
- Mutual Trust.
- Respect.
- Work together to reduce waste.

Toyota only seeks new carriers when:
- A new facility or new geographical responsibility is required.
- A new program such as returnable program is required.
- The existing Carrier is closing down.
- The organisations objectives change and a carrier is unable to accommodate new requirements.
- Carrier is no longer able to do an effective job and countermeasures have not been successful.

When looking for replacements, the NAPO bid process is initially issued only to those carriers who are current partners, or, if the transportation requires a niche or specialized carrier, then they may bid the organisations to new carriers.

How Does NAPO Select New Carriers?

By incorporating all of the principals addressed above, Toyota's selection criteria are presented in a manner that tests the viability of their philosophy and principals:
- Can the partners build a successful relationship?
- Will the Toyota Way be realized?
- Will the partnership withstand the long term, 5, 10, or 15 years?
- What are the organisations drivers?

- What is the legislative environment?
- What issues or challenges may be on the horizon?

What does it mean to be a Toyota NAPO Carrier?

Toyota has established a set of guidelines that will help the partnership prosper. Through this process the parties reaffirm their principles by employing the following techniques:

- Continuously seek improvement.
- Can we move this part better?
- Faster?
- Cheaper?
- Most importantly: All three constraints are balanced equally.
- Toyota will not compromise:
- We will not give up quality to save a buck.
- Do not carry more inventory if it does not make financial sense.
- Genchi Genbutsu.
- Who better to tell how we can improve than those actually doing the work! Ask your partners, what can we do to be a better shipper? And listen!
- Teamwork.
- We took for "partners" to achieve Respect, not "vendors & carriers".

Toyota-NAPO has established and maintains a process that defines the organization and its philosophy in ways that foster the development of strong logistics partnerships.

Source: after www.transportgistics.com

Developing the relationship with third parties

Effective working relationships need to exist in day/day contacts and during monthly/quarterly/annual reviews; such meetings often requiring more of the "soft" skills rather than the hard skills of management.

The key to successful long-term relationships between an organisation and the carrier/forwarder is that both parties should feel they are obtaining a positive benefit. They need to have mutual goodwill and the feeling of being "in this together". This involves "a shared destiny" approach of going for the same goals, the same added value and mutual long-term survival and profitability.

People relationships need to be right in both of the organisations with compatible cultures. Positive benefits will only be achieved if there is a long-term relationship between the Organisation and Contractor based upon trust and understanding at all management levels, but particularly from the top. Any type of relationship depends upon trust and understanding. This needs to be at all levels and particularly from the top.

To help on this, a statement of principle can be agreed between parties. This for example, could include an agreement on the following:
- The relationship will be ethical and progressive.
- Both parties will endeavour to deliver benefits and adopt a continuous improvement philosophy.
- Both parties will commit to achieving mutual trust and understanding and an open sharing of ideas.

The first key sign that a relationship is breaking down is when people fail to talk to each on a regular basis. It should be remembered that issues could usually be resolved by:
- Talking ("It's good to talk").
- Not wanting to prove who is right.
- Seeing the other person's viewpoint.
- Not dragging up past matters previously resolved.
- Openly sharing the benefits of the relationship.

It not handled in this way, then the first key sign of potential breakdown in relationships is when the senior management of either the Organisation or the Contractor fail to talk to each other on a regular basis, leading to a meeting where the Organisation has a list of minor grievances gathered over time and the Contractor requires an increase in fee to cover unexpected costs. The first sign of unresolved conflict may lead to a breakdown in the relationship if it is not resolved rapidly by senior management.

A large number of minor grievances incurred by either party may also lead to the organisation evaluating their position and seeking alternatives.

In the final analysis, a large number of unresolved minor grievances may eventually lead to a re-evaluation by either party. A final resort will be to consult the original contract to determine the term of the Agreement and the conditions that apply for termination.

Meanwhile the following have been proposed as Strategies for 3PLs to ensure they have successful relationships:

- Develop long-term partnership relationships with customers in which both parties' challenge each other to establish supply chain advantages.
- Offer cost-effective methods of doing organisations by stressing productivity and efficiency goals through technological change and work flow redesign.
- Provide value-added service to customers in terms of individual attention, positive communications and caring/courteous service.
- Formal commitments to continuous improvement processes are critical to the encouragement and streamlining of rational changes.
- Provide two-way mobile data communication systems to customers that ensure availability of real-time information on all orders or loads to customers.
- Offer specialised services as well as information systems and logistics consulting for customers. This should encompass a thorough examination of customer needs as well as tailoring carrier offerings (placing the right people, equipment, processes and systems to specific customer accounts).

Source: International Journal of Logistics Research and Applications. Volume 3, no. 3.

Case Study: Pitfalls of a 3/4PL haul

With the road ahead looking increasingly rocky for the 3PL/4PL, Logistics Organisations looks at how to best navigate the difficult legal terrain often facing these hardy and adaptable service providers. Putting forward the case for the defence is Jeremy Clarke, the Head of LLC Law Solicitors (www.LLCLaw. Co.uk), a UK based law firm dedicated to logistics and specialists in 3PL/4PL contract logistics.

Some five years ago supply chain consultants focussed their research on developing an all-encapsulating supply chain solution which swiftly became known as 4PL. The objective behind that short acronym was a solution which would allow logistics operations to overcome very real physical limitations and be more effectively managed for the future.

To understand the catalyst for this development you need to consider the changing market for production and product flows at the time. The '80s and '90s saw outsourcing of conventional supply chain services mature into a new multi-billion Euro market comprised of larger asset intensive providers like Hays, Wincanton, Exel and Christian Salvesen.

A demanding market

The consequence was double digit growth as organisations increasingly outsourced their conventional transport and warehousing operations to the third party providers of logistics services (3PL). Simultaneously, the horizons for the sales and marketing arms of all producers were fast expanding in the fight for market share and increased volume, lower unit costs and increased profitability. The intense competition for the sale of consumer and industrial products meant that more than ever all potential cost savings and efficiencies had to be realised.

Unquestionably the strategic importance of both 3PL and in-house logistics had risen in the '80s. The early '90s saw a wide gap evolving between the end-customers' realisation of the operational demands inherent in their global and trans-national operations, and the ability of 3PLs to provide management of worldwide operations seamlessly.

So having matured only recently, by the mid to late '90s, conventional 3PL services appeared unable to meet the challenge of their customer's cross-continent and increasingly just-in-time production (JIT) flows. As such the industry came under intense scrutiny with commentators focussing on the industry's palpable failure to meet its customers' needs.

By the late '90s an integrated vision of logistics suggested that global production, distribution and sale would necessitate a new breed of truly global 'single source' 3PL operators. Such a vision anticipated massive investments in country-wide offices, assets and IT systems spread across continents under the umbrella of a single organisation. This vision was never realised, in part because of the fragmented nature of local and national distribution, the associated costs and because, fortunately, an alternative evolved to save the day.

That alternative was the concept of the 4PL, the term originally coined by Andersen Consulting (formerly Accenture, now IBM Consulting). At its simplest, the model provided for an additional and higher layer of logistics management.

Crucially, 4PLs would operate at a holistic level, using IT to gain access to and to disseminate all the product sourcing, distribution and end-customer data required to properly manage a fully integrated network of conventional service providers. Such conventional services would for the most part be physically performed on the ground by the traditional 3PLs.

Proper management

Organisations like Lex Auto Logistics include as part of their 4PL service offering the acquisition of its customers' inventories which sit on Lex's balance sheet enabling it to properly manage and reduce its customers' inventories. In the extreme, a 4PL working alongside a network of 3PLs can perform or at least manage all of manufacturing organisation's non- core activities outside of sales and marketing.

The potential growth still has a long way to go but sits comfortably with the other value adding activities (postponed manufacture etc.) which the 3PLs are keen to develop. The positive effects of this transformation have been at least twofold. 4PLs have been able to provide the essential ingredient for an end-to-end solution and the cement required to network globally disparate operators in a way that was unthinkable in the '90s. Secondly, 3PLs entering the 4PL market have been able to move away from the low margin commodity pricing increasingly associated with transport and non value-adding warehousing, focusing instead on more profitable 4PL services.

Let's collaborate

This development and the degree of collaboration required to make 4PL as a concept work was and will continue to be in large part made possible by the simultaneously advances taking place in mobile technology, web-enabled and browser-based IT solutions and the synchronisation and integration of such applications into manufacturers ERP systems. This has provided, in theory, almost limitless visibility across global supply chains.

Being IT driven, operators have been able to set-up dedicated 4PL operations up as separate and independent organisations, like 3T Logistics in the UK. However, in the case of TDG, this included forming a separate 'Scio' organisations in partnership with Cap Gemini Ernest and Young with whom TDG has sought to develop a consultancy style offering with the ultimate aim of providing a more intelligent solution. However, the state of current technology, its costs and the inherent risk of obsolesce are still a limiting factor for some 4 PL's future development.

Take control

However, 4PLs are continuing to be set-up despite the lull which followed their modelling in the 90s. Tesco has forged ahead with its factory gate pricing arrangements by which it has taken over control of inbound supplies to its RDCs.

Last year GIST set up a 4PL with the High Street retailer New Look involving over 280 suppliers in over 30 countries. UPS has for several years made a conscious effort to build-up its 4PL applications organisations in the form of UPS Worldwide Logistics and which, for a number of years, was the fastest growing part of its organisations. UPS has for several years made a conscious effort to build-up its 4PL applications organisations in the form of UPS Worldwide Logistics and which, for a number of years, was the fastest growing part of its organisations.

The introduction of the 4PL function results in day-to day responsibility for interfacing with and managing product flows being transferred from the manufacturer to its chosen 4PL service provider. As a result, the multiple interfaces that must necessarily exist between suppliers, supplier's transport organisations, manufacturer, manufacturer's transport organisations, manufacturer's RDC and ultimately to end customer are now primarily routed through the 4PL.

This simplified scenario should, in the global context, be extended in the reader's eye to cover containerised and conventional shipments, air freight movements, factory gate pricing initiatives etc which result in a vastly more complex matrix of contact points and resulting management problems.

Perhaps unsurprisingly, the new breed of 4PL service providers have to make use of conventional 3PL contact structures in order to meet the requirements of 4PL arrangements. At best this has resulted in confusion and at worst a failed solution.

When properly constructed, 4PL arrangements are likely to include any or all of the following over and above the sister 3PL arrangements which will continue both up and down stream:

- Gain-sharing financial incentives: With the focus on 4PL's delivering measurable cost savings and service level improvements, the financial structures must incorporate workable mechanisms for establishing the original or base-line costs and the means by which these will be assessed against future costs so that any actual cost savings can be shared in an agreed ratio between the 4PL and its customer.

The broader picture

- Agency Functions: As noted above, in relation to the selection, negotiation and contracting of 3 PL services, the 4PL does not replace conventional 3PL services, but rather over-lays such services. Those arrangements will continue to exist. However, with its broader experience of 3PLs generally (including comparative cost and service level data) and a holistic overview of the specific operations in question, the 4PL should leverage efficiency and reduce costs acting for and on behalf of the manufacturing principle.

The parameters of the 4PLs agency appointment need to be clearly set out and all too often this important structural point is omitted completely. In particular pro-forma 3PL contracts should be prepared for use by the 4PL which in turn need then only revert to its customer to agreed material changes to the same.

Where a 4PL is held-out as part of the manufacturer's own operation (undisclosed agency), the specific safeguards should be put in place regarding intellectual property, use of organisation letterheads e-mail formats and similar with an exclusion of any rights in respect of the same, especially post termination.

- Independence and Arms Length Conduct: Given that 4PLs may well purchase 3PL services from within their own organisation the assessment and charging mechanisms by which the 4PL makes its decisions have got to be open book, arms length and designed so as to realise an improvement over related market prices.

- Service Levels, Liquidated Damages & Key Performance Measures: These require much more careful consideration and drafting for 4PL arrangements, especially since many operational issues which must be addressed will inevitably be being considered for the first time. The KPIs for the 4PL will focus in part on achieving the cost savings referred to above, but also on enforcing, back-to-back, the 3PLs service levels for which it is responsible for managing.

- Format and regularity of Reporting: With the strategic importance of the operations managed by the 4PL greater care and attention should be focussed on the data received by the 4PL's customer to ensure that the end-to-end supply chain is clearly being properly managed. The reporting will not only address the 4PL's compliance with its specific service levels, but also include exception reports in relation to the 3PLs' performance.

- In plants and related Security Issues: Given the matrix of interfaces between both the data held on the Relevant ERP system and physical flow of products and operators responsible for transporting or storing the same, the 4PL will frequently wish to have a presence on its customer's site(s). As such, care needs to be taken to ensure compliance with security, health and safety and the customer's general codes of conduct and procedural requirements when on site.

Make it clear

- Use of and Access to Customer's ERP system: The level of required access for employees of the 4PL in the new operating environment far exceeds that which would have been provided under earlier 3PL arrangements. Clear procedures must be set out in relation to authority to access, security, and the avoidance of alterations to the system and/or the introduction of viruses. Additional development and or enhancement may be required to all or a part of the IT system, and responsibility for and rights to such work should be clarified and expressly provided for. The market for the required integrating software is now mature, with organisations like CAPS Logistics and Descartes (used by GIST - formerly BOC) actively building market share. The issue of IT is critical to the success of any 4PL solution and the process of transitioning to and integrating the 4PL solution with the rest of the ERP will need careful management.

- Contract Monitoring: This particular area of the contract takes on a whole new dimension where the 4PL's responsibilities extend either up or downstream of conventional manufacturing logistics. If something goes wrong in such an environment, the escalation procedures need to be in place to ensure that the customer of the 4PL can immediately have a say in any decision which may impact adversely on its organisation.
- Employees: Frequently the outsourcing of 4PL functions will result in a transfer of the customer's staff to the 4PL (albeit that some strategically important ones may remain).
- Termination & Disputes: Additional issues may need to be addressed in relation to change of control (should the 4PL sell out) and exiting the sites and returning key data post the termination of the contract. Mechanisms for resolving otherwise contentious financial disputes should be built-in to resolve so as to avoid unnecessary litigation.

The Future

In a sense, there is nothing new behind the concept of 4PL arrangements. Management, supervision and planning have always taken place albeit internally and perhaps inefficiently. However, with the growing sophistication of supply chains such functions are increasingly outsourced to expert 4PL service organisations or at the very least separate, identifiable units within the customer's organisation.

The nature of such integration services are clearly here for the long term. However, there are additional costs involved and, as such, 4PLs may not be appropriate for all products across all supply chains — it certainly is not the case that one size fits all. For the time being at least 4PL arrangements appear to be working well for high value, short life products with high price depreciation. But as the scope of 4PL services becomes better known and more common place costs will fall, and 4PL will expand its reach.

At that time the activities and services associated with 4PL functions will increasingly be considered as standard components (at their more basic level) in the package of basic outsourced logistics services across all 'product lines and equivalent to the basic 3PL services of today. As such, we can say that the 4PL concept is not a redundant dinosaur and will be with us for the long term.

www.LLCLaw.Co.uk (Source: Logistics Organisations February 2003)

The Supply Chain and Transport costs

With a whole, complete and holistic supply chain view, all the relevant processes must be looked at. Then, what might seem to be the best from one single individual basis may not, in fact, be the best when viewed from a total supply chain perspective. This will thus involve "trading off" processes and functions to find the right balance in the overall supply chain. The concept of Total Acquisition Cost (TAC) from purchasing is one way to examine trade-offs in the supply chain. Cost is seen not just as the price paid for something, but as the whole cost of a purchase.

The essential components of TAC are as follows:
- The price paid for the goods, say on an ex-works basis.
- The costs of quality, for example, defects, errors causing inspection/re-working costs.
- The delivery costs, for example, the transport charges.
- The performance costs, for example, reliability, KPI measures .
- The lead-time costs, for example, money investment, delivery frequency issues.
- The packaging costs, for example re-packs.

- The warehousing costs, for example, break bulk handling storage.
- The stock/inventory costs, for example, for raw material, work in progress, finished goods.
- The costs for a new supplier, for example, start up costs, negotiations.
- The administration cost, for example, ordering, payments.

The price paid may well be the largest item but all other costs will have many variations. If these costs were equal or of little significance, then the price paid would be the determining factor. Rarely however, are all the other costs equal. So with TAC, the principle is that all relevant costs have to be allowed for. For example, transport varies by mode and within modes; variations can be related to performance, transit lead-times, and packaging and stock/inventory costs, so all the variations would need to be examined.

Air versus Sea T.A.C. example:
- If Value Ex-works is £15,000.
- If delivery costs via sea to CIF is £ 4,600, and via Air to CIF is £8,800.
- Then Value CIF via sea = £19,600 and via Air = £23,800.
- (Note: The difference between transport costs is 1.913 times, nearly 2 times).
- If the stock/inventory costs are accounted for, then, if Annual stock turnover via Sea is 2 times per annum and via Air is 5 times per annum, the Stock on Hand via Sea is 180 days pa and via Air 72 days pa.
- If the Cost of Holding Stock is 20 per cent of the value, then the cost via Sea = £1,960 and via Air = £952.
- Then the total cost via Sea = £21,560 and via Air = £24,752
  (Note: The difference is 1.148 times)

Clearly this quick example does not consider variations such as lead-time, order size, frequency of ordering etc., but it does illustrate that transport cost is only one part of the analysis.

Freight Rate Structures

We will now look at how international transport freight rates are calculated and charged. First, some important principles can be established from the following figures (table overleaf):

Ship Charter Rates

TEU/DWT	$ per day Index	Cost Index per TEU day
350/5500	100	100
550/8000	55	90
1000/14000	175	61
1700/22500	240	49

These examples show simply, that whilst the cost to operate smaller ships will be cheaper (as shown by the figures for ship charters); when the carrying capacity is considered, the cost per unit carried (per TEU) falls dramatically. This simply demonstrates the economies of scale that are found in transport.

There are other anomalies with freight charges; simply, distance is not always a good indicator of the rate charged, as a longest distance may have a comparatively lower rate. This can be due to many factors such as traffic imbalances on a round trip basis, the ratio of time spent moving/not moving (e.g. a ships unloading time in port, a road truck waiting to be unloaded), the competition in the market, the port charges paid by a shipping organisation, etc.

The following comparisons show this very clearly for indexed sea freight rates for one TEU from North Europe to destinations in the Middle East/Indian sub continent and the Far East. The ports have been ranked from shorter to longer distance from North Europe:

Dubai	100
Mumbai	125
Colombo	111
Singapore	78
Shanghai	78

It can be seen it is actually cheaper to ship a TEU to the Far East than to the Middle East/Indian sub-continent. Of course such figures are valid only at a specific time as the causal variations will change at a non-constant rate.

Variations found in Freight Charges

Freight charges can be complex in their application, not only can the bases used for charging vary between modes, but also often within the modes themselves. Additionally, international freight rates are often expressed in US Dollars with variable surcharges applied, all of which can create a varied cost base and one that can change on a daily basis.

The following two basic rating principals are found across all freight modes with some examples indicated. We shall explain these examples shortly:

1) Rating by the Unit of Charging:
- Weight factor (W)   e.g. per kilo and per 1000 kilos
- Measurement factor (M)   e.g. per 1CBM and per 3 CBM
- Value factor per W/M   e.g. up to $1000 value per W/M ,then $90 per W/M
- Value factor percentage   e.g. 3% of FOB Value

2) Rating by the Type of Goods:
- Commodity factor   e.g. Woollen rags $50 W/M
       e.g. Combed wool $80 W/M
- Freight All Kinds (FAK)   e.g. 50 pence per kilo
- Per Piece/unit   e.g. $2000 per 20 ft container
       e.g. £15 per metre on the vehicle length

Where more than one variable exists in the rate structure, then, usually, the one that produces the higher revenue is the one applied. For example, a rate of $100 W/M for cargo of 2000 kilos/4CBM is charged as 4CBM @ $100 giving a $400 charge (and not 2000 kilos @ $100).

As with many rules, however, they exist to be broken. For example, air freight rates do allow for adjustments to be made to give whichever brings the lower revenue (we shall refer to this later).

As general principles, ratings are applied as follows (table overleaf):

Mode	W/M Rule	Value Rates	Commodity Rates	FAK Rates
Sea	1000 kilos 1CBM	some	some	ylrian
Air	1000 kilos 6 or 7 CBM	some	some	mainly
Road	1000 kilos 3 CBM	no	no	yes
Rail	N/A	no	no	yes

Finally, in addition to freight rate application variations, other variables that are found are as a result of trade imbalances causing freight price variations, frequency service level variables, service supplier variables and liability. We shall now examine all these variations in freight charges by looking at each mode.

Basic Ocean Liner (Deep Sea) Rates

The majority of these are expressed as per freight ton or per ton W/M. For sea freight, this means the charge is per 1000 kilos or per 1 cubic metre, whichever is the greater. This W/M breakpoint is low, so the majority of freight is effectively volume measurement rated.

Some freight tariffs are published (but often not widely so) and the tariffs also include standard rules on applications. The majority of freight was traditionally rated by the Commodity and meant many hundreds of different base rates; the principle with commodity rates being one that says that a ton of gold can stand a higher rate than a ton of scrap iron. Increasingly however, basic FAK rates (Freight of All Kinds) are found with around fifteen different base rates. For example:

For packages each under 500 kilos/1CBM:

a) *Value not exceeding $1000 W/M*
Consignments up to 5 tons $100 W/M
Consignments 5 - 10 tons $90 W/M

b) *Value exceeding $1000 W/M*
Consignments up to 5 tons $130 W/M
Consignments 5 - 10 tons $120 W/M

Container Rates

Whilst the basic ocean leg maybe rated as above, the tariffs are usually structured to reflect the through movement.

For example on UK Imports:
* Foreign collection haulage on a box basis or weight basis.
* Foreign terminal charge on a box or weight basis.
* Basic freight charge on the basis as above.
* UK terminal charge on a box or weight basis.
* UK delivery haulage on a box or weight basis.
* For a full container load (FCL) the freight tariff incorporates safeguards for shipping lines against the under utilisation of the container capacity.

Basic Short Sea Routes

For Europe, another variable situation is found. Whilst FAK rates are more common for the few remaining conventional services; for LO/LO or RO/RO services the FCL or FTL movements are charged for the sea leg of the movement per box or per metre respectively. For example, £1500 per 20-ft container, £35 per metre for a 13 metre trailer. For part loads, LCL or LTL movements, then an FAK rating dominates with the weight or measurement factor applied based on 1000 kilos/3CBM (and this usually expressed per 100 kilos/0.3 CBM).

Surcharges

These are a feature especially of ocean (deep sea) services. Typically, they involve upward and downward adjustments for currency and bunkers. The currency adjustment factor (CAF) is justified on the basis that revenue is needed in one currency, typically US Dollars, but that expenses are paid in a local currency. As exchange rates vary, then the CAF accounts for these. The Bunker Adjustment Factor (BAF) is related to the cost of purchasing fuel oil. This is a critical cost for all transport modes and as the price of oil changes then the BAF make an appropriate adjustment.

Other surcharges can also be found:

- Congestion Tariffs are built up by calculating a normal turnaround time at port terminals. The standing cost of a ship is high (like for all transport vehicles), so if congestion is occurring regularly at specific ports then the tariffs will include a surcharge to cover for the extra costs involved in serving the port.
- War risk. This reflects the increase in insurance premiums when vessels are operating in dangerous parts of the world.

The existence of surcharges complicates the freight rate calculations. For example, 40-ft container rate is $5000.00, with surcharges of BAF 10%, CAF Minus 5%, Congestion $100 per 40 ft container.

The calculation is:

Base Rate	= $5000
BAF 10% of $5000	= $500+
CAF -5% of $5000	= $250-
Congestion	= $100+
Surcharge subtotal	= $350
Total payable	= $5350

The End of European Shipping Conferences

Most ocean trade routes serving Europe used to have a "conference", indeed some trades that do not serve Europe still do. A conference is effectively a cartel of major shipping lines who have established a common freight rate tariff in return for established regular and scheduled services, irrespective of the shipping line operating.

To maintain shipper loyalty to the conference, shippers signed an agreement to restrict their shipments to conference operators. For this loyalty, the conference gave a discount to the published tariff; for example, a 9.5% immediate rebate. If shippers decided not to sign, then a deferred rebate was payable, 6 or 12 months after the shipment. Some conferences however choose more simply perhaps, to give a lower basic rate to signatories.

This was up to a 30% discount available for regular large volume movements. Those shipping lines not in a conference were known as "non-conference lines" or "independents". Whilst they did not always offer such regular and frequent services as conference lines, they offered cheaper freight rate.

However, such conference cartel practices were ruled by the EU as anti trust competitive practices and were abandoned formally from the 17th October 2008. This means that it is unlawful for shipping organisations to jointly fix freight rates or any additional charges such as BAF, CAF on a collective basis.

The impact is of this radical change will remain uncertain for some years. The ban also applying to sharing information and will therefore take a degree of management culture and mind set changes that take some time. Meanwhile, the EU expectation is for rates to fall and service levels to be maintained. It remains to be seen if this EU pro customer friendly practice will spread to the non-European trades.

Air Freight Rates

Airline rates also have a weight/measurement ratio, called "chargeable kilos" or "volumetric units".

Generally the ratio is 1000 kilos/6CBM - usually expressed per kilo/6000 cubic centimetres; although for some areas the ratio still remains at the former ratio of 1000/7CBM (or per kilo/7000 cubic centimetres). The airlines have attempted in recent years to lower the ratio to 1000 kilos/5CBM, but this was resisted by trade and lobby groups.

Within this W/M structure, airline rates are categorised as follows:
*   General cargo rates (GC).
*   Specific commodity rates (SC).
*   Classification rates.
*   FAK rates.
*   Containerised rates (ULD).

General Cargo Rates apply for most freight. Typical weight breakpoints are:
*   Minimum flat charge (M).
*   Normal rates (N) up to 45 kilos or up to 100 kilos.
*   Quantity rates (Q) over 45 kilos or 100/199 kilos etc.

It is allowed to over-declare the weight to achieve the cheaper higher weight band rate, for example where the GC Tariff is:

- M £70.00 in full.
- N £6.00 per kilo.
- Q100 £2.50 per kilo.
- Q200 £1.60 per kilo.

160 kilos @ £2.50 = £400. But this can be rated as 200 kilos @ £1.60 = £320.00 payable.

Specific Commodity Rates offer substantial discounts to the general cargo rates. SC rates apply for large quantities of specific and named commodities moving between specific airports. For example, Kiwi fruit - Auckland/London.

Classification Rates apply to only a few cargoes. These are discounted or surcharged SC rates. For example, gold is surcharged, newspapers are discounted.

FAK Rates have been introduced onto major trade routes, like the transatlantic, where they replace the GC/SC rates. Effectively then, the SC rates are abolished and a lower GC rate structure applies.

Containerised Rates apply for ULDs. The rate is a flat FAK charge per unit regardless of weight, providing the maximum weight allowed per ULD is not exceeded. The ULD rate is usually a flat minimum rate above which a rate per kilo then applies. These rates are therefore charged per container/ULD without reference to the commodity loaded therein.

Integrators rates

Integrators use rail, road, air or sea modes offering a door/door service.

Rates are FAK and are commercially decided between customers and the integrator. The usual way is a flat rate plus a rate per kilo.

The services are fast, often marketed under words like "express." Service levels of 24-48 hours are available to major worldwide destinations for up to 30 kilo consignments.

Determining Rates with Forwarders/Agents services

Knowledge of both the operational costs and knowledge of how an operation is performing are critical aspects to be understood in the management of freight transport. Before improvements can be made it is necessary to know what the current levels are for efficient and effective operations. Then commercial decisions/negotiation applies.

Assuming a forwarder is operating a groupage consolidation service of their own, the following examples will give some indications of how they calculate the freight charges.

Example: Deep Sea LCL
- FAK charge terminal/terminal = $2500 per TEU of 20 tonnes/20 cbm.
- At 60 % utilisation = 12 tons w/m payload
- Base Rate therefore is $208.33 w/m
- Charge rate plus 10% profit = $229 w/m FAK

For Forwarding Agents, if they are contractually acting as an agent to principals, and charge @ cost/as paid, plus an agency fee (usually negotiable up to 5 % of the outlay on the freight cost only), then it is fair to ask for evidence of the costs paid on behalf of the principals; for example by providing a copy the shipping lines, airlines or the forwarders freight invoice(s). Clearly here, the principal is exactly that and is using the services of an agent who is legally obliged to evidence the charges incurred in carrying out their duty as an agent.

Costing/recovery of freight charges by suppliers/shippers/senders

Suppliers and shippers often strangely handle the method by which freight costs are incorporated into the overall cost/charges that are made to customers. Whilst we referred earlier in this chapter to the concept of Total Acquisition Cost (TAC), which emphasised that freight and transport costs are only part of the equation, the examining and impact of freight cost must be correctly assessed.

We looked earlier at the variations that are found in transport rate charge structures; meanwhile some points to be considered when costing/recovering the freight charges are as follows:

- Average freight costing: A highly dangerous method; the range that is involved in calculating the average is always useful to look at. Too often, however, when average costing is used, the range is large and the average costing is then less than helpful. Average forms of costing can mean that say smaller delivered quantities are being subsidised by full load movements. If the larger full load movements volumes decrease, then the smaller movements are exposed to higher costs, for example. Such forms of cross-subsidising need to be a conscious and closely monitored decision.

- Percentage of product value: Here for example, a year's total freight costs are divided into the year's total ex-works sales price, to give an average freight cost figure. A dangerous practice, unless perhaps we are dealing with high valued products like diamonds where the percentage cost is miniscule. Whilst this method is commonly used to assist in establishing say delivered prices from a known ex-works prices, the reality of this figure needs to be monitored against the actual costs incurred. It is very rarely found that the product value will equate directly to freight costs incurred as simply freight costs are based more on the weight and the volume and there is rarely a co-relation between these factors and a product value.

Trade imbalances can affect freight charges

Movement of goods are driven and determined by market forces. Transport is the economists' classic derived demand. So with no economic activity there is no transport service. From the viewpoint of the provider of the transport service (the shipping line, the airline, the road hauler, the rail operator), they will wish to maximise the utilisation of the equipment; (the vessel, the aeroplane, the tractors/trailers etc.). If they are successful at this on a round trip basis there and back, then they can offer competitive rates and make more profit.

This balance, however, between economic activity and freight tonnages moved can be a delicate one.

On an international basis, more freight moves from the Far East into Europe, and in the late 2000s, for every TEU sent full from Europe to Far East, then around 2.5TEUs come back full. For example on Transatlantic trades, the pattern is reversed as more TEUs are sent from Europe, and around 30 % more are sent to the USA full than come back full. Clearly this has implications for the shipping lines and means empty containers have to be positioned; accordingly "swapping" an empty TEU for a full TEU freight rates means a marginal rate is available. As examples, rates from Europe to the Far East have been around 50% cheaper than the rate from the Far East and from the US to Europe have been around 40% cheaper than the rate to the US from Europe.

Meanwhile, to illustrate the dramatic changers that can occur on freight rates; the Far East European trade is one of the most competitive and busiest in the world and in 2008 due to reducing traffic levels, this meant that operator's became engaged in a price fight for a larger piece of a smaller cake. The rates therefore fell between May 2008 to September 2008, from USD900 to USD350 per TEU; truly unbelievable figures. (Source: International Freighting Weekly dated 6 October 2008.)

All these trade imbalances in a market economy will affect freight rates and for example with airfreight, the specific commodity rates for a specific route give an indication of how this industry has adjusted freight rates to encourage freight traffic.

Case Study: Add Value with 3PL

Warehousing and distribution is complex and tightly regulated and there is a need to streamline processes, maximise IT capabilities and take cost out.

For organisations selecting a 3PL service provider, the starting point for getting maximum value out of the tendering process is to be clear about your objectives. If your existing arrangements are working well for you, but you are obliged to review costs regularly, or you wish to benchmark your service, the best option may be to find a formula which is the least time-consuming and stick to it.

If your existing 3PL service provider is failing you in some way, or your organisations is changing, it is worth setting up a dedicated team to carry out a thorough review of the options available from different suppliers. This will provide you with 'must-have' information in a readily comparable format and a proportion to allow suppliers to really demonstrate and discuss with you how they could do things differently.

For best results, you should encourage innovation and creativity. Take the time to find out about the different service providers' cultures, their values, management retention record, contract renewal rates and training stance so that you can make an informed judgement about whether they could work alongside your organisation and meet changing demands over time. In the long-term this will be a more cost-effective option. There is little to be gained on either side by a request for an "all singing, all dancing proposal" in an unrealistically short timescale and you may miss out on valuable insights if you keep your tendering process within too narrow confines.

You needn't necessarily limit yourself to 3PL specialists in your field when considering who to include on the tender list. Experts in logistics may have knowledge and skills from other industries which can be transferred to yours to provide mutual benefit. It is more important that you find a organisation you can work comfortably with.

Good working relationships and streamlined joint procedures need to be developed over time. There are great benefits to be gained by working in partnership rather than in a culture of 'keeping your service provider on his toes'. Sharing technology, accurate demand forecasting and successful just-in-time delivery, with windows of a few hours rather than a few days, all require open channels of communication and a culture of co-operation between organisations. The right 'chemistry' between staff, trust and cultural affinity are important ingredients in achieving the best solutions.

As trade becomes increasingly global, the logistics market is growing at three times the rate of Gross Domestic Product. This is within the constraints of continual downward pressure on costs, industry consolidation (fewer buyers, ever-changing requirements) and a tendency for purchasers to opt for short term contracts. Service providers are looking to add value to your organisations and avoid becoming over commoditised. Investment in the necessary systems to offer the best solutions is best done in partnership with committed end users.

Of course working in partnership requires buy-in throughout the organisation, not just commitment from the procurement team. There will almost certainly be implications relating to culture, strategies for growth, organisational structure, investment in technology and training requirements. There will be a need to understand the need for change and to embrace it on an ongoing basis on both sides to ensure that the relationship remains valuable to both parties.

Key Performance Indicators should be agreed by both parties and used positively to spot trends and develop the service throughout the life of the contract. Enabling a culture of ongoing change management requires joint responsibility, access to decision-makers on both sides; a hands-on style, excellent communication links and a flexible commercial relationship.

If you invest time over cash, people and paper in the process, it is certainly possible to achieve a 'win- win' position and add genuine value to your warehousing and distribution operations through your tender process.

Source: SHD July 2004, 'Taking the Medicine' by Mark Wallace, NYK Logistics.

International Transport Liability Conventions

Whilst we covered insurance provision earlier in part 4, it is important to realise that the different transport modes have variable liability provision. It is a reality that most users are not aware of these different carrier liability regimes.

With international transport, conflicts between differing legal systems can arise. To standardise this conventions have developed. This means that all parties involved - shippers, operators, consignees - are represented at an international convention. A set of rules is worked at this convention and then agreed between the parties, after which they go back to their home country where they attempt to persuade authorities and governments to enact the rules into domestic law. Once this has been done by many countries, then conflicts of law are prevented.

There are five basic conventions which cover international transport, as follows:
- Sea; The Hague/Visby Rules, replaced by the Hamburg Rules.
- Air; The Warsaw Rules, replaced by the Montreal Rules.
- Road; CMR Rules (The Carriage of Merchandise by Road Hauliers).
- Rail; CIM Rules and the COTIF convention (Organisation for International Carriage by Railway).
- Multimodal; ICC298 The International Chamber of Commerce Uniform Rules for Combined Transport Documents.

The following table gives a comparison between those conventions:

Mode	Liability	Limits	Documents used	Time Limit to claim
Sea	Liable if no due diligence, goods not loaded properly, handled or stowed. Not liable if errors in navigation, fires, perils and some other factors.	666.67 SDR units per package, or 2.0. SDR units per kilo; whichever is the greater (Hague/Visby) 835 SDR Units per package or 2.5 units a kilo; whichever is the greater (Hamburg)	Bill of lading	Normally one year
Air	Liable if loss or damage or delay. Not liable if the carrier took necessary measures or due to fault of claimant	250 gold francs per kilos (Warsaw) 17 SDR units per kilo (Montreal)	Air way bill	Two years
Road	Liable if loss or damage or delays. Not liable if faults of claimant, inherent vice or circumstances beyond carriers control.	8.33 SDR units per kilo. (The average value of cargo is approx.1600 Euros per 1000 kilos according to EU sources on road freight).	CMR consignment note	Normally one year
Rail	As road	7 SDR units per kilo	CIM consignment note	Normally one year
Multi-modal	Liable for lass or delay	30 gold francs per kilo	Combined Transport Document	9 months

These different liabilities are what the international carriers maintain. Users will need to be aware of these differences so they can take informed decisions on arranging appropriate insurance covers. Meanwhile for pure domestic transport, liability will be subject to the standard terms and conditions of the carrier used, or subject to agreed terms and conditions between users and carriers.

Packing & Security

The prime function of packing is to ensure product protection. The two basic types of packaging are as follows:

1) Outers
- Fibreboard boxes/cartons.
- Nailed/screwed wood boxes/crates.
- Steel or fibre drums/kegs.
- Wooden barrels/casks/kegs.
- Fibre/fabric bales/trusses.

2) Unit Loads
- Wood or plastic pallets/skids.
- Plastic slips.

The packaging outer should be clearly marked to enable identification, taking care however not to advertise the contents to potential thieves. Effective marking ensures safe arrival at the correct destination, a speedy identification, compliance with regulations (for example, hazardous cargo), damage prevention and compliance with any customer requirements, for example:

Checklist: Standard Shipping Package Outer Markings

Line 1	Initials or abbreviated name		
Line 2	Reference number		
Line 3	Destination		
Line 4	Package Numbers		
Example:	SAE		ABCD
	1234		0161
	LAGOS		MANCHESTER
	1/25-25/25		1/16-16/16

It is useful to follow a procedure for packing using the following stages and considers especially, packing for the toughest leg. The author has many unfortunate experiences of receiving LCL cargo in Nigeria that was already received badly damaged in the container, simply because it had been packed for a short domestic journey in the country of shipment, and it too often seemed packed for a journey in the back of someone's car! The following flow chart will help to ensure correct packing is undertaken.

Checklist: Packing Flow Chart

1. Study the product, the journey, the transport mode. Pack for the "toughest" leg.
2. Select the most suitable external packing outer.
3. Stow goods well, inside the packing outer.
4. Small packages should be consolidated into one load.
5. Consider any effects of co-loading or stacking with other products during the transit.
6. Secure, strap, band all packages.
7. Select an effective marking/labelling scheme.

Once goods are packed and are ready to be loaded, then the following procedures can be followed during loading:

Checklist: Loading Container Units/Trailers

- Inspect interior for damage, water-tightness, cleanliness and adequate fittings, fastenings/lashing points.
- Inspect exterior for dents/tears and the doors/openings for secure locking and sealing.
- Observe safe working loads(SWL) of all equipment, including any weight limitations of the unit/trailer.
- Observe any special cargo regulations for example, hazardous cargo, temperature controlled freight.
- Have all cargo and stowage materials ready before loading.
- Put heavy times at the bottom and lighter ones on the top.
- Distribute the weight evenly.
- Arrange a compact stow.
- Stow tightly to prevent movements whilst ensuring ease of unloading at

the destination (such as forklift openings facing doors, stowing in the reverse order for the desired discharge, etc.).
- Avoid mixing incompatible cargo.
- Keep the stow with the unit/trailer dimensions.
- Secure and tighten any load restraining equipment.
- Close and lock/seal.

Security and minimising loss

Particular modes of transport have specific security requirements. Airfreight requires regular (or so called "known") customers to give written certificates confirming they have packed and prepared air cargo to an acceptable specification. For some shippers, this known customer will be their freight forwarder, who in turn will have arranged appropriate cover from their shipper client.

"Unknown" cargo will be subject to security process, before it can be loaded by a listed agent and again, this could be the freight forwarder, a freight handling agent or by the airline themselves. The inspection process will involve a hand search or x-ray. Listed agents can also inspect and examine "known" premises to enable verification and the training of individual personnel.

On the physical loss of product on international trades, insurance experts advise that loss is due to the following factors:
- Fortuitous loss 20%, for example Acts of God, crashing, fires, collisions.
- Preventable loss 80% for example:
  - Theft is 40%
  - Handling damage is 30%
  - Water damage is 10%

Almost 50% of preventable losses are attributable to theft and pilferage therefore the wise shipper will take the following simple precautions:
- Use only new, well-constructed packing for products. Early deterioration or collapse of flimsy or previously used cartons, boxes or bags invites pilferage through exposure of the contents.
- Use of uniquely patterned gummed tapes will make possible the quick detection of tampering.

- Corrugated fasteners will add to the security of wooden boxes.
- Shrink wrapping, strapping and banding will further contribute to package security.
- Don't advertise product to thieves and pilferers.
- Descriptive labelling, illustrations or prominent display of trademarks and well-known organisation names on any type of cargo simplifies the pilferer's task, so the use of coded markings, and changing the codes frequently is advisable.
- The ultimate retail customer/consumer will very rarely see the shipping package and therefore any 'en route' advertising certainly does not impress him.
- Use cautionary markings both in English and the language of the country of destination.
- Use of international handling symbols provides added effectiveness because handlers who lack the ability to read can readily understand graphic illustrations.
- Clear, concise and complete delivery and handling instructions should appear on at least three surfaces of the exterior package.
- Limiting marks to only one or two surfaces invites rolling, tumbling, and flipping of the packages in the search for marks and delivery information.
- Bright colour coding of sides or corners of items in the same shipment facilitates identification and minimises the parcels straying.
- Utilise various-sized boxes, crates and pallets to consolidate small multiple or non-uniform parcels into single load units.
- Unitising and palletising as well as use of ISO containers will help keep cargo together and also make it inconvenient to thieves and pilferers.
- Process documents and customs papers expeditiously to avoid unnecessary delay in pick-up or delivery.
- Insist on prompt pick-up and delivery. The longer cargo rests on piers/dock areas, in terminals or in truck bodies, the more it is exposed to loss by theft and pilferage.
- Make immediate reports of losses or non-delivery to law enforcement agencies, carriers and the insurer.
- The quicker you act, the greater the probability of recovery.

Cargo handling in the various air and seaports of the world ranges from highly professional to totally unskilled levels. Rough seas, turbulent air, heavy traffic and substandard roads subject cargo to every imaginable kind of motion and impact. Remember to pack for the toughest leg of the journey! The following are points to be remembered:

- Wise selection of packing depends on the nature of the cargo.
- Items which completely fill the box or carton and contribute to the strength of the package are normally the easiest and most economical to package.
- Articles which do not completely fill the selected container must be cushioned, braced, fastened or blocked to prevent damage to the article itself or destruction of the container.
- The capacity of the box, bag or carton should not be exceeded.
- Any inner bracing or blocking must distribute the contents' weight over interior surfaces, rather than concentrate it on one or two critical points.

Unitised, palletised or assembling cargo into the largest practical unit consistent with handling, weight, and dimension requirements, will assist greatly the handling. A unitised load of 50 cartons adequately wrapped, strapped and provided with a pallet or skid base will have a much greater survival factor than 50 cartons which must be handled individually. Unitised cargo invites the use of mechanical handling equipment, which substantially reduces exposure to the inherently rougher loading techniques.

Water Damage, rain, high humidity, condensation and seawater (separately or in combination) can reduce otherwise stable cargo into a ruin of soggy, stained, mildewed, and rusty merchandise. A rain-swept Customs compound, an open truck on an airport apron in a torrential downpour, the insidious dripping of condensation from the chilled interior of a ship's hold, or sweat forming on the cargo itself, are all common hazards.

Each different commodity has its own unique characteristics which react differently when exposed to water. It should be noted that containerisation does not guarantee protection against moisture. As containers age, "leakers" become more commonplace. Containerised or trailer cargo must be packed to the same degree of water protection as with most general cargo. The following are some guidelines to follow:

- Cargo should be protected from water damage from external sources such as rain, seawater, high humidity and ship's sweat by adequate preparation and packing.
- Apply preservatives, corrosion inhibitors or waterproof wrapping directly to the item.
- Provide waterproof or vapour-proof barrier liners in individual packages.

- Use of desiccants (moisture absorbent materials) in conjunction with vapour-proof barrier liners and wraps is particularly effective in protecting moisture sensitive items.
- Shield cargo on the top and the sides by use of waterproof shrouds.
- Crates and other large containers should have drain holes in the bottom to preclude collection of water within the packing. This is of particular importance where the cargo itself is subject to formation of condensation (cargo sweat).
- Indelible inks, paint, and water repellent labels should be used to preclude obliteration of marks, shipping instructions and handling symbols.

9: Managing Performance Improvements in Global Supply Chains

Performance Improvements

Throughout this book we have considered many improvements, and it has often been noted that a manager has two jobs; the job they currently do and the job of improving and changing the way things are currently done around their job.

Improving performance is therefore a fundamental aspect of management and should be a continuous process.

A set of rules for performance improvement according to Balle (1997) are as follows:
- Start close to the customer.
- Look at the lead-times.
- Simplify, simplify, simplify.
- Keep processes independent.
- Process redesign teams are temporary.
- Build a cross-functional organisation.
- Keep a team focus.
- Top management commitment is vital.

This approach is a useful overview for improving supply chain performance and, as we shall see later, success will come more from people/culture change aspects than from the use of technical solutions alone. Meanwhile, a useful starting point is process mapping.

Supply Chain Process Mapping

This analyses a supply chain by breaking it down into the component parts/processes and providing a structure for data. It acts as a lens through which to view the process and to focus the efforts on making improvement.

When evaluating any business processes, it is usual to find that they do not actually and fully work the way which management thinks they do. Mapping will therefore also show how the informal system will be different from the formal, designed system. It therefore enables a better understanding, and will generally involve questioning those who actually work with the process. It will therefore show "how it actually works". (We cover the "how-to" of supply chain mapping below).

Optimising dependant processes

This approach looks more at processes that are dependant upon each other and therefore has excellent parallels with the supply chain. An overview on the approach in Balle (1997) follows:

1.   Determine the Output
- Start at the customer end and establish what they do with your output.
- Never ever forget that the next link in the chain is always the customer (whether internal or externally located).

2.   Sketch the Process
- Walk through the process, collecting forms, paperwork etc.
- Challenge each paper process.

3.   Map the process
- Establish the inputs and the outputs.
- Draw the customer process.
- Draw in the feedback loops.
- Determine the lead-times.
- Time the operations.

4.   Redesign the process
- Look for bottlenecks.
- Remove them one by one, thereby reducing lead-time.
- Concentrate on what adds value and reduces waste.
- Watch for the improvement killers, such as its not possible; it's not our job; it should not be like this; the answer is obvious; I am already doing it; I will do it tomorrow etc.
- Eliminate processes and think parallel.
- Split processes.
- Remove unnecessary steps.

5.   Test and Refine
- Check, check and test.
- Recognise limiting and restraining factors.
- Expect unexpected reactions to change.
- Polish the redesign.

6.   Implement and standardise
- Determine: Action/Owner/Deadline/Check up date/Comments.
- Develop best practice checklists.
- Ensure that customer needs have been met.

Using Questions

As Peter Drucker has noted, "the problem with Western managers is the emphasis is in finding the right answer rather that asking the right question." Asking the right question first will assist in getting the right answer.

Clearly the above methods use questions extensively, and many more follow. These questions can be used to ensure effective performance improvements are made. They are very wide ranging and can be applied and used in many and varied ways.

Checklist: Questions to ask

Cost Reduction
- What does it cost to operate the process?
- Which steps cost the most?
- Why is this?
- Which steps add value?
- Which steps do not add value?
- What are the causes of costs in this process?

Lead-time reduction
- Which steps consume the most time?
- Why is this?
- Which steps add value?
- Which steps do not add value?
- Which steps are redundant?

- Which steps cause bottlenecks?
- Which steps add complexity?
- Which steps result in delays?
- Which steps result in storage?
- Which steps result in unnecessary movement?

Quality Improvement
- Why do we get defects/variations?
- Is this due to common or special causes?
- What has to be managed to have the desired effect?
- How should the process be changed to reduce or eliminate defects/variations?
- Is there a culture of continuous improvement?

Measurement systems
- What, from the customer expectations, are the requirements for inputs and outputs in the process?
- What should be the measured to ensure the requirements are met?
- Do the current measures assess what is important to the customers?
- What happens to the measurement data currently collected?
- Why is one measure preferable to another?
- Does the process performance data, compare to the customer expectations and perceptions?

Management
- Who is accountable for the horizontal Cross-functional end to end process performance?
- How can the company be re-structured to manage processes, in addition to the functions?
- How does what we do, look and appear to the customer?
- What are the best in class indicators available?
- What is the root causes of superior performance?
- Why is the process configured to run this way?
- How can the process be performed differently?
- How can we make the process more effective, efficient and flexible?
- How can we add value while reducing cost?

- What will the jobs in the new process consist of?
- How can we better motivate job performers?
- Is every manager dedicated to creating an environment in which every employee is motivated and happy?

Customer service aspects

- How well do we deliver what we promise?
- How often do we do things right the first time?
- How often do we do things right on time?
- How quickly do we respond to requests for service?
- How accessible are we when customers need to contact us?
- How helpful and polite are we?
- How well do we speak the customer's language?
- How hard do you think we work at keeping customers a satisfied client?
- How much confidence do customers have in our products or services?
- How well do we understand and try to meet customers special needs and requests?
- Overall, how would customers rate the appearance of our facilities, products and people?
- How willing would customers be to recommend us?
- How willing would customers be to buy from us again?

Strategic aspects on inventory

- Why do you have inventory?
- What drives the present level of inventory?
- How are inventory levels set?
- How current is the decision on the inventory levels?
- How often are inventory decisions reviewed?
- What direction is inventory being driven, and why is it?
- What are the actual service requirements of customers?
- How do the direction and/or change in inventory compare with the direction and/or change in sales?
- How much of the inventory reflects safety stock?
- Who is responsible for setting and for managing inventory levels?
- Are they the same person/department or not?
- How are excess inventories, and the cost of, reflected in management responsibilities?

- How is the alternative, inventory stock outs, and the cost of, reflected in management responsibilities?
- How are ICT system algorithms and underlying assumptions reviewed?
- Is customer input used?

Demand and forecast aspects of inventory
- How variable is demand?
- How is forecasting done?
- Is forecast accuracy regularly measured?
- How accurate is it, at the item/SKU level?
- How timely is it prepared and submitted?
- How does purchasing and manufacturing handle the forecast inaccuracies?
- Do they overbuy or overbuild to compensate for doubts about the forecast?
- Is inventory forecast to the distribution centre level so the right inventory at the right quantity is carried at each facility?
- Or, is the forecast at a macro level with no direction on what inventory, how much inventory and where inventory should be positioned?

Lead-time and methods aspects of inventory
- How variable is supplier lead-times?
- How are the total lead-times, including in transit stock lead-times and internationally sourced items, incorporated in the system?
- How accurate are the free stock inventories that are used in the resulting production planning and sourcing?
- How is supplier reliability and lead-times reflected in inventory planning and management?
- Are additional inventories factored in to buffer for each of these issues?
- How these aspects are factored into supplier selection decisions?
- Does purchasing have purchase order visibility with suppliers to control ordered items at the SKU level?
- Do suppliers understand and collaborate with the inventory philosophy and approach?
- Do purchased products flow to keep inventory in the supply chain or are they irregular, aggregated?
- How are transportation reliability and transit times reflected in inventory planning and management?

- Are additional inventories factored in to buffer for each of these issues?

Warehousing aspects of inventory
- Where is inventory stored and why?
- How many distribution centres are used and why? (Each distribution centre means additional safety stock will be carried)
- Are they in the right locations?
- How much obsolete/dead, old promotions and very slow-moving dead inventory is there?
- What is the storage cost for such "dead" inventory?
- Is inventory often transferred between distribution centres to provide inventory to fill orders? (That is inefficient use of transportation, not good customer service and resulting from wrong forecasting allocation).

Procurement Process
- What are the annual spend and requirements of the purchasing portfolios?
- Is there a programme to reduce the procurement lead-times?
- Is component variety limited by looking closely at users specifications (avoiding brand names), and duplicated purchasing?
- What are the supplier assessment methods and supplier management policies?
- What codification is used?
- Is end to end product evaluation used by applying the total costs of ownership (TCO)?
- What programme is there to develop relationships with users/customers and with external suppliers?
- Have buyers changed from being reactive order placers to be proactive commodity managers?
- Should you outsource or manage procurement yourself?
- Is there a programme to reduce the supplier base to a small number of qualified suppliers fully integrated into the business?
- Are alternative suppliers approached?
- Are quotations obtained from a number of sources?
- Are all purchase requisitions/purchase orders properly authorised?
- Does a policy exist for inviting bids/estimates/tenders?

- Are safeguards in existence to prevent the procurement of excessive quantities?
- Is the procurement department given a sound forecast of materials and other requirements in good time to enable them to be bought on favourable terms?
- What are the ordering costs against stock-holding costs?
- Do buyers have the authority to speculate in commodity markets?
- What are the cost implications of overdue deliveries?
- Is sufficient information available by specific cost element to know the reasonableness of the price quoted?
- Is the price reasonable in terms of competition?
- What is the supplier's current financial position as shown in their most recent balance sheet?
- What are the supplier's current and projected levels of business?
- Are price breakdowns by cost element on fixed price contracts furnished?
- Will designated individuals in the supplier's organisation be specified from whom the buyer can obtain relevant information and data?
- Are there any special handling, packaging or shipping requirements that may delay delivery?
- Are spares allowed for in the supplier's plans and schedules?

Global Sourcing
- Do we have the knowledge of culture, organisations differences?
- Do we have the freight and import knowledge?
- Have we the necessary expertise?
- Should we source direct or use an agent?
- Will we get reliable supplier lead-times?
- Will we need to "cushion" for supply lead-time?
- What is the countries infrastructure?
- What is the countries political stability?
- What are the countries organisations methods?
- Will we be able to specify clearly what we want?
- What about fluctuating currency?
- What payments terms will be used?
- What Incoterms should be used?
- What are the impacts to varied landed costs?
- Can we fully implement our SCM methods with suppliers?

- Are there any local import requirements that apply, such as licences, quotas?

Warehousing

- Are the warehouses viewed as a critical step in the material flow cycle?
- Is there a high regard for the customer?
- Do we know the customer requirements?
- Do we consistently meet these requirements?
- Are warehouse standards established?
- Is performance measured against these standards?
- Are timely actions taken to overcome any deviations?
- Are systems and procedures put into effect that will allow proactive planning of operations as opposed to reactively responding to external circumstances?
- Have we examined the trend towards larger, centralised warehouses instead of smaller, decentralised warehouses?
- Do we make use of third party public warehouses to handle peaks will be in commonplace?
- Do we appreciate that the reduction of lead-times, shorter products lives, and increased inventory turnover will result in an increase in the pace of the warehouse?
- Do we appreciate that different SKUs and additional special customer requirements will result in an increase in the variety of tasks performed in the warehouse?
- Are all warehouse systems, equipment and people flexible?
- What do we minimise uncertainty?
- Are all activities within the warehouse (receiving, storing, picking and delivery) integrated within the overall material flow cycle?
- Is cycle counting used to manage inventory accuracy with accuracy above 95 per cent?
- Is space used efficiently and effectively?
- Is quality housekeeping a priority and a source of employee pride?
- Is the critically of order picking understood?
- Are procedures and layouts designed to maximise picking efficiency and effectiveness?
- Are suppliers, customers, and the functions within the warehouse integrated into a single service-providing facility?

- Are automatic identification systems the norm for data acquisition and transfer?
- Do we use real time, paperless control systems throughout the warehouse?

People and performance

The above discussion has shown that there are many approaches to performance improvement. The use of models is useful in as much as they can be usefully applied to a specific purpose. Additionally various aspects from different models can be used, with there being no "one size fits all" model. Ultimately however, all performance improvement will involve people and a specific case study in improving people (and therefore performance) follows:

Case Study: Land Rover and people improvements in production operations

This well-known vehicle manufacturer had falling productivity and rising costs. This forced an examination of work methods.

The methods used were:
- Labour was organised into teams who were given responsibility and training in improvement methodology.
- "Work with People" was used as a theme to break down adversary relationships.
- "Everyone has two jobs-their own, and improvement of their work" was another theme introduced.
- The production line was viewed as a series of supplier/customer relationships.
- 2 hours a week was allocated to discussion groups - either internal or with external suppliers.
- Clocking in was abandoned and uniforms introduced.

Tangible results were reported as:
- Inventory fell from £23 million to £8.6 million in two years.
- Output rose by 28 per cent in two years.

Source: Director Magazine January 1994

An approach to involve people and recognise improvement is called performance management and this is defined as "Getting results by getting the best from people and helping people achieve their potential". An extremely brief overview on how optimising performance needs to impact on people, is seen below:

Leading
- Listening to others, to understand them.
- Empowering others, by giving responsibility, trust, training and support.
- Adapting to changing situations.
- Delivering high quality results with clear goals linked to end results.
- Self understanding; the more you understand yourself and your impact on others, then the easier it is to manage yourself and adapt your style to bring out the best in others.

Coaching, delegating, motivating
- Coaching is listening, questioning and giving feedback.
- Delegating is analysing a task, analysing a person, agree a monitoring system, setting the climate and reviewing progress.
- Motivating involves understanding people and recognising what motivates them at different times and at different life stages.

Appraising
- Performance development reviews formally, e.g. once per year, but also, continually by "Leaders" and "Coaches."

Teaming
- Team roles vary and each person has their own strengths. Teams are made effective by building on individual strengths that work towards a common goal.

As mentioned, the above is only a brief coverage of the critical aspect of people in improving performance. This has however been more fully covered in **Improving Performance Management Toolkits** by Stuart Emmett (2007):

- Systems Thinking Toolkit.
- Motivation Toolkit.
- Learning Toolkit.
- Customer Service Toolkit .
- Team Toolkit.
- Developing People Toolkit.
- Communication Toolkit.

...and the **Human Resources Toolkit** by Richard McNamara (2007).

Finally in this section, the link between making technical improvements and the needed people/culture improvements is made very clear in the following case study:

Case Study: Staples USA Supply Chain Improvements

Staples USA undertook a major three-year supply chain transformation process with goals as follows:
- Reduce inventory by $200 million while supporting double-digit sales growth each year.
- Expand operating margins by over $100 million.
- Contribute directly to sales growth through improved use of limited resources to drive demand.

To achieve these financial goals, they drove improvements in four areas:
- Improved return on resource investment.
- Improved measures of supply chain reliability.
- Increases in effective service.
- Greater coordination among supply chain participants.

Within each of these areas, over the course of three years they had over a hundred individual improvement projects.

While many of the changes made were technical in nature and involved process improvement work, the key that has unlocked dramatic value has been cultural change.

Disciplined management of a transformation from a culture of safety and siloed behaviour to a culture of synchronization based on trust and teamwork has delivered a leaner more efficient and more reliable supply chain.

It has also created a performance improvement culture within Staples that led to more improvements in economic performance and value to customers. Supply chain transformation has helped Staples deliver a combination of wins for shareholders through improved return on net assets and for customers through increased service at lower cost.

Extracted and adapted from source: Paul J. Gaffney, Executive Vice President, Supply Chain, Staples, Inc. 91st Annual International Supply Management Conference May 2006.

Model for Supply Chain Improvements

Throughout this book we have considered many improvements and we hope readers have been able to note and use these as appropriate.

What follows is a guiding framework and a summary of what has been considered thus far. It is not a definite step-by-step process that must be strictly followed. Indeed many of the steps overlap and iteration will be needed. So, please, a "health warning" follows.

It seems many fundamental change initiatives fail in the UK. Look for example at the quality movement. In the 1980s this had a wide audience. By the 1990s however it was rarely heard of, apart from those companies who had succeeded.

Why is this? Many reasons, but one strong reason is our preference for using tools that we believe will instantly fix things. When they don't, then "quality does not work here."

We do seem to want an instant solution that is a prescriptive, "use these, rather than that" and because it worked for company x, then we believe it will work for us. But it's likely "there will be trouble ahead" as rarely will this tool-fixing be effective. Many, for example, are unsuccessful with Toyota Production System (TPS) as they concentrate on the explicit tools and not on the implicit principles; they want the easy tools but not the thinking behind them.

What is first needed, then, is to change the thinking that has brought us to where we are today, so that in moving forward, we can have a better foundation and not just rely on using some "one size fits all" tools. What will also help here is to review the earlier discussion on supply chain re-thinking. After all, "the significant problems we face cannot be solved at the same level of thinking we were at when we created them." (Albert Einstein).

This will then likely involve us in doing thing differently, for example, using supported learning by doing:

- "Discovery by solving problems".
- "Discovery by asking questions".
- Changes are structured as controlled experiments.
- Mistakes are allowed, this demonstrates learning.
- Experiment frequently as possible.
- Managers are enablers, e.g. they coach/mentor, and are not fixers.

We could continue, but the aim here is to guard against seeing the model as a "one size fits all" tool. See it rather as something to guide the thinking; you may wish to consider it to be your own supply chain improvement thinking reference guide.

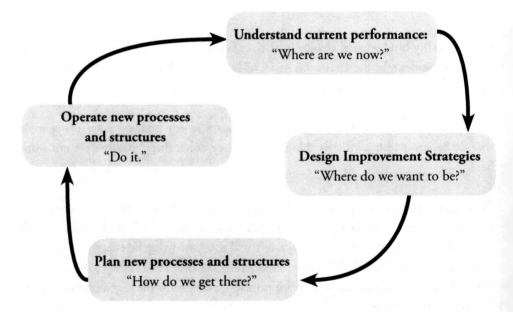

Step 1. Where are we now?
Aim: Describe the current supply chain process that exists, between your suppliers and your customers.

At this stage, do not consider any changes; only a description of how it is now.

How is the supply chain managed?
- Is it linked to and part of the corporate strategy?
- Is it seen as giving added value and competitive advantage to the business?
- What are the Cross-functional organisational structures?
- Will we ensure that information "lubricates" all the processes and the decision taking?
- Are key areas and performance measured?
- Are lead-times checked, reviewed and evaluated, regularly?
- Does "customer first" and "customer satisfaction" underpin all decisions?
- Do we adopt a continuous improvement culture that enables people development and fosters good relationships?
- Are external suppliers viewed as being "integral partners" with collaboration also being found internally in the company?
- Is trade off analysis undertaken?

Map the current process/inputs and outputs
- Draw the customer process; start at the customer end and establish what they do with your output. Never ever forget, that the next link in the chain is the customer. Answer the following questions:
  - who are the customers?
  - what do they need?
  - what is the product-service?
  - what do they expect?
  - does we meet their expectations?
  - what process is involved?
  - what action is needed to improve the process?
- Draw the supply process
  - who are the suppliers and the supplier's suppliers?
  - what do they need?
  - what is the product-service?
  - what do they expect?
  - does we meet their expectations?
  - what process is involved?
  - what action is needed to improve the process?
- Draw in the feedback loops

Some important aspects on how to supply chain process map are as follows:
*   Doing it quickly, is better than doing it slowly.
*   Update regularly and often.
*   Use the right people (for example with the doers and the decision makers).
*   Display the process on cards or post it notes/flip charts.
*   Walk and record the real process.
*   Enlist the help of people closest to the process.
*   Ask questions (see step 5 below).

The following five basic steps may also be used when process mapping:
1.   Define that the supply chain/process to be improved.
2.   Identify the steps by brainstorming.
3.   Display the process in sequence.
4.   Change the map to correspond to the actual physical process.
5.   Evaluate the process by questioning:
     -   What is the purpose of?
     -   Where is it done?
     -   When it is it done?
     -   Who does it?
     -   How is done?
     -   Why is it necessary?
     -   Why is it done then?
     -   Why does the person do it?
     -   Why is it done it this way?
     -   What is the lead-time?

Action time: Supply chain mapping exercise
*   Mentally walk and record the processes.
*   Display these in sequence on the wall.
*   Collect ideas from a discussion.
*   Go through the total supply chain step-by-step.
*   Starting with the first operation, ask:
     -   What is the purpose of this?
     -   Is in this value-added?
     -   Can it be eliminated?
     -   If it cannot be eliminated can it be combined with another?
     -   Is there are any other waste that can be eliminated?
*   Repeat for all operations.

Do we need to make detailed process charts for each activity?

Break down jobs into a visual form using, for example:
- Flow process charts: focuses on distance.
- Multiple activity process charts: focuses on time.
- Operator process charts: focuses an individual's movements.
- Input/process/output diagrams: focuses on the connections.

For each activity (for example, pre-order planning, procurement, suppliers, transit, receiving, warehouse, delivery, payment), provide the following information:
- Activity decision.
- Frequency that activity occurs.
- Who is responsible for that activity.
- Information required to conduct that activity.
- Average activity lead-time.
- Minimum activity lead-time.
- Maximum activity lead-time.
- Cause of activity lead-time variability.
- For the inventory, describe the types/format (RM/WIP/Finished goods) and amounts (value/quantities/days of supply) that are held.
- What KPIs do you use to assess the overall supply chain performance?

Ensure coverage of all the applicable lead-times from the users need to order placement, to being finally, available for issue/use by, customers/consumers.

Step 2: Where do we want to be?
Aim: Design improvement strategies and challenge every detail in the current supply chain

At this stage, consider changes needed to make improvements or to take you towards the vision/future situation required.

Use the mapping exercise to improve by:
- Eliminating steps.
- Performing steps in parallel.
- Re-arranging steps.
- Simplifying steps.

- Use less expensive operations.
- Use consistent operations.
- Eliminating all waste and non value adders such as:
    - Time spent on correction.
    - Over production.
    - Inventory.
    - Waiting.
    - Non-required processing.
    - Non-required movement.

The minimum (but very acceptable result) that can be expected, will be lead-time reductions in the processes.

Study "what can be done better" by challenging every step and asking for each step, in order:
- What and why?
- Where and why?
- When and why?
- Who and why?
- How and why?

Then:
- Check for waste, like any, "make ready" and "put away" steps.
- Which steps are redundant?
- Which steps cause bottlenecks?
- Which steps add complexity?
- Which steps result in delays?
- Which steps result in storage?
- Which steps result in unnecessary movement?
- Jobs that take too much time.
- Jobs where costs are high.
- Jobs that require chasing for materials, tools, supplies.
- Jobs where money can be saved.
- Jobs that can be done quicker.

Management (SCR 1 (Supply Chain Rule 1))
- Who is accountable for the horizontal, cross-functional, end-to-end process performance?

- How can the company be re-structured to manage supply chain processes, in addition to the functions?
- How does what we do, look and appear to the customer?
- What are the best in class indicators available?
- What is the root causes of superior performance?
- How can we better motivate job performers?

Inventory (SCR 2)

Strategic aspects on inventory
- Why do you have inventory?
- What drives the present level of inventory?
- How are inventory levels set?
- How current is the decision on the inventory levels?
- How often are inventory decisions reviewed?
- What direction is inventory being driven, and why is it?
- What are the actual service requirements of customers?
- How do the direction and/or change in inventory compare with the direction and/or change in sales?
- How much of the inventory reflects safety stock?
- Who is responsible for setting and for managing inventory levels?
- Are they the same person/department or not?
- How are excess inventories, and the cost of, reflected in management responsibilities?
- How is the alternative, inventory stock outs, and the cost of, reflected in management responsibilities?
- How are ICT system algorithms and underlying assumptions reviewed?
- Is customer input used?

Lead-time and methods/aspects of inventory
- How variable is supplier lead-times?
- How are the total lead-times, including in transit stock lead-times and internationally sourced items, incorporated in the system?
- How accurate are the free stock inventories that are used in the resulting production planning and sourcing?
- How is supplier reliability and lead-times reflected in inventory planning and management?

- Are additional inventories factored in to buffer for each of these issues?
- How these aspects are factored into supplier selection decisions?
- Does purchasing have purchase order visibility with suppliers to control ordered items at the SKU level?
- Do suppliers understand and collaborate with the inventory philosophy and approach?
- Does purchased product flow to keep inventory in the supply chain or are they irregular, aggregated?
- How are transportation reliability and transit times reflected in inventory planning and management?
- Are additional inventories factored in to buffer for each of these issues?

Warehousing aspects of inventory
- Where is inventory stored and why?
- How many distribution centres are used and why? (Each distribution centre means additional safety stock will be carried)
- Are they in the right locations?
- How much obsolete/dead, old promotions and very slow-moving dead inventory is there?
- What is the storage cost for such "dead" inventory?
- Is inventory often transferred between distribution centres to provide inventory to fill orders? (That is inefficient use of transportation, not good customer service and resulting from wrong forecasting allocation).

Collaboration (SCR 3)

Purchasing

As purchasing is central to dealing with suppliers, then we need to ensure we understand this function. The following questions will help to do this:

General Questions
- What does the Kraljic procurement portfolio tell us?
- Are quotations obtained from a number of sources?
- Are alternative suppliers approached?
- Are all purchase requisitions/purchase orders properly authorised?
- Does a policy exist for inviting bids/estimates/tenders?

- Are safeguards in existence to prevent the purchasing of excessive quantities?
- Is the purchasing department given a sound forecast of materials and other requirements in good time to enable them to be bought on favourable terms?
- Are some components currently being made that could be bought from outside at less cost?
- Ordering costs against stock-holding costs?
- Do buyers have the authority to speculate in commodity markets?

Financial questions
- What are the suppliers financial and credit ratings?
- What credit terms are offered?
- How do these compare with other supplier's credit terms?
- How do they compare with the supplier's cash flow needs?
- What are the cost implications of overdue deliveries?
- Are make or buy studies undertaken?
- Are the prices competitive (given quality levels)?
- What controls do suppliers have over their activities?
- Is standard costing employed?
- Is sufficient information available by specific cost element to know the reasonableness of the price quoted?
- Is the price reasonable in terms of competition?
- What is the supplier's current financial position as shown in the most recent balance sheet?
- What are the suppliers' current and projected levels of business?
- Are there additional sources of capital if they are needed (for the supplier)?
- What type of accounting system is employed
  - Job cost?
  - Standard cost?
  - Other?
- Price breakdowns by cost element on fixed price contracts should be furnished.
- Is there any objection to contracting on other than a fixed price basis?
- Is cost accumulated by lot release, and how is initial production costs estimated?
- Is special tooling being purchased separately?
- Are there any mating/inter-changeability problems?
- Should tooling be coded?

- Have we distinguished between special tooling required for the contract and facility items?
- How are labour costs accounted for?
- Are operations covered by time standards?
- If so, how are they established?
- Are learning curves employed in projecting labour costs? If so, what rate of learning is employed?
- Are supplier's employees unionized? If so, when do union contracts expire?
- Will designated individuals in engineering, production, and finance be specified from whom the buyer can obtain pertinent in formation and data as he requires it?
- Are all necessary activities included?
- Check realistic control points and flow- times have been established.
- Are loads balanced among activities so that production will proceed without delay?
- Are there any special handling, packaging or shipping requirements that may delay delivery?
- Are spares involved, and are they allowed for in the vendor's plans and schedules?
- Are all inspection, test, and engineering requirements fully understood?
- Is the item adequately described on the specification, purchase order etc?
- Are there any special test or quality control requirements the supplier must meet?
- Does the supplier fully understand them, and do they have the time, facilities and know-how to comply?
- Are sources accustomed to manufacturing this item?
- Do they demonstrate ability to meet this schedule?
- Do their past rejection experiences demonstrate ability to meet test and quality requirements?
- Is a performance bond advisable?
- Should the IP rights be obtained to use or acquire tooling, designs, and materials to manufacture the item in case of default?
- Do we undertake TCO (Total Cost of Ownership), TAC (Total Acquisition Cost) and WLC/LCC (Whole Life/Life Cycle Costing)

Answering the above questions will help us to understand our current procurement activity; we can now more fully consider collaboration.

Why consider collaboration?
- Where are we on the Kraljic procurement portfolio?
- Are bought in products/services more than 50% of our turnover?
- Can supplies be a source of competitive advantage?
- What are the real drivers for considering making the change?
- In 3 years, will existing suppliers be able to meet all our requirements?
- Do we need to develop new suppliers?
- Do we need suppliers that are more responsive?
- Are we prepared to be more responsive to our suppliers?
- Are we prepared to treat suppliers as partners?

Lead-time reduction (SCR 4)
- Which steps consume the most time?
- Why is this?
- What actions could you take to improve the lead-times for Supply?
- What actions could you take to improve the lead-times for Customers?
- What actions could your suppliers take to improve the lead-times for Supply?
- What actions could Customers take to improve the lead-times?
- What actions are needed to prevent lead-time variability?
- What are your suggestions to make these actions happen?

Customer Demand (SCR 5)

Establish the Key Components of Customer Service

Market research surveys identify that the top items identified (in order), are usually:
- Time to deliver ("On time").
- Reliability and "constancy" of service.
- Availability of stock ("In Full").
- Advice and communication when non availability.
- Quality of sales representatives/customer service department.
- Product support.

Identify the relative importance of each component
- If On time, is it 2 or 3 or 4 days?
- If In Full, is it 80 or 90 or 100 per cent?

Establish "where are we now" against the importance

- Rate current against competition by market research.

Segment the market

- Do all customers require the same service?
- Which customers are sensitive to what specific service component?

Design the customer service package

- Price brackets related to service levels?
- Promotions

Establish, measure and control

- Ensure measurements are understood by all involved:
    - Order Cycle Time/On time (OT): e.g. Suppliers view maybe, despatch within 24 hours of order receipt but the Customer view is, time order placed to time received.
    - Reliability/Quality: - e.g. how often 'fail', e.g. track/trace facility e.g. damage free, e.g. order convenience, e.g. documentation accuracy.
    - Accuracy/Availability/In full delivery (IF): e.g. Suppliers view maybe is to deliver 100% of what is available but the Customer view is, 100% in full order receipt.

Demand and forecast aspects of inventory

- How variable is demand?
- How is forecasting done?
- Is forecast accuracy regularly measured?
- How accurate is it, at the item/SKU level?
- How timely is it prepared and submitted?
- How does purchasing and manufacturing handle the forecast inaccuracies?
- Do they overbuy or overbuild to compensate for doubts about the forecast?
- Is inventory forecast to the distribution centre level so the right inventory at the right quantity is carried at each facility?
- Or, is the forecast at a macro level with no direction on what inventory, how much inventory and where inventory should be positioned?

Cost Reduction (SCR 6)

- What does it cost to operate the processes?

- Which steps cost the most?
- Why is this?
- Which steps add value?
- Which steps do not add value?
- What are the causes of costs in this process?

Trade-offs (SCR 7)

Quality Improvement
- Why do we get defects/variations?
- Is this due to common or special causes?
- What has to be managed to have the desired effect?
- How should the process be changed to reduce or eliminate defects/variations?

What impact do the current processes have?
- Why is inventory held?
- What are the inventory levels being held, downstream by suppliers and upstream, by customers?
- What adds value?
- What does not add value?
- How can we add value while reducing cost?
- Why is the process configured to run this way?
- How can the process be performed differently?
- How can we make the process more effective, efficient and flexible?
- What will the jobs in the new process consist of?
- Are we sure that we have examined all trade off opportunities for overall supply chain benefit; for example:
  - Within activities/processes.
  - Between processes and functions.
  - Between functions.
  - Between organisations.

Information (SCR 8)

Is ICT being used to enable the:
- Automatic generation of performance monitoring against pre-set key performance indicators.

- Automatic tracking of materials in vehicles, ships, airplanes using global positioning satellites giving constant visibility, improved safety, security and responsive routing and scheduling.
- Automatic decision-making e.g. stock reordering against pre-set levels and quantities.

Is ICT being used to transfer:
- Trade data e.g. quotation, purchase order.
- Technical data e.g. product specifications.
- Query response e.g. order progressing.
- Monetary data e.g. electronic payment of invoice, electronic ticketing.
- Consignment details e.g. manifests and customs details.

Are the following systems being used:
- Enterprise Resource Planning (ERP).
- Automatic Planning & Scheduling (APS).
- Warehouse management systems (WMS).
- Inventory management systems (IMS).
- Bar coding and Radio Frequency Identification (RFID).
- Computer controlled systems for storage and mechanical handling equipment (MHE).
- Computerised routing and scheduling, routing of transport.
- Modelling.
- E-business applications.

Step 3: How do we get there?
Aim: Plan new processes and structures

Redesign the process
- Look for bottlenecks.
- Remove them one by one, thereby reducing lead-time.
- Concentrate on what adds value and reduces waste.
- Watch for the improvement killers = (it's not possible; it's not our job; it should not be like this; the answer is obvious; I am already doing it; I will do it tomorrow).
- Eliminate processes and think parallel.
- Split processes.

- Remove unnecessary steps.

Increase Capacity
- Forecast demand (moving averages, regression models, intuition, expert opinion).
- Plan capacity (level/fixed or chase/variable or a mixture).
- Avoid capacity risks by changing demand and, or the resources.
- Watch for the balance between the too little/too much utilisation.

Work out a better method
- Can we eliminate unnecessary detail? (Watch especially for transport/ movements and storage items).
- Can we combine? (For example, inspect "on the job").
- Can we change the sequence? (For example, eliminate back-tracking).
- Can we change the place?
- Can we change the person?
- Can we improve all the remaining aspects?
- Remember the viewpoint: "If I find a job is done the same way as it was one year ago, then I know very well it is wrong".

Set the right objectives
- Are strategic/functional/team and personal objectives aligned?
- Appropriate S.M.A.R.T objectives?
- Appropriate Q.C.T.D.S.M Objectives?

Measurement systems
- What, from the customer expectations, are the requirements for inputs and outputs in the process?
- What should be the measured to ensure the requirements are met?
- Do the current measures assess what is important to the customers?
- What happens to the measurement data currently collected?
- Why is one measure preferable to another?
- Does the process performance data, compare to the customer expectations and perceptions?

Implement and standardise
- Determine: Action/Owner/Deadline/Check up date/Comments.

- Develop best practice checklists.
- Ensure that customer needs have been met.
- Manage Risks by Appraisal (likelihood, probability, prioritise) and Contingency Planning ("what ifs", establish procedures, test, refine, revise).
- Improve housekeeping (The 5S approach of sort, straighten, scrub, standardise, systemise).
- People make the process work, so use job enrichment and empowerment.

What approach will be used?

- As the changes are likely to be fundamental, what overall type of approach will be needed:
  - High level of urgency, but with low resistance; this will need a more visionary/charismatic approach.
  - Crisis/low resistance; this needs a more visionary/persuasive approach.
  - High urgency/high resistance; this needs a more visionary/coercive approach.
  - Crisis/high resistance; this needs an autocratic, almost dictatorial approach.
- Do those you wish to involve, have the ability to participate?
- Are they motivated to participate?
- Does involvement (or lack of it) fit the cultures of the organisations involved?
- How important is the post-change motivation of your and suppliers' employees?

What are the reasons for resistance?

- What threats are those affected likely to feel?
- Will there be resentment the imposed change?
- Do you understand the emotional aspects of those resisting the change?
- Do you understand the steps involved in people's behaviour during change?
- Have you considered reducing resistance by using:
  - Participation.
  - Communication.
  - Training.

What are the impacts of making the change?

- Have you assessed the implications and effects of the change?

- Have you used force field analysis or other approaches to think through all aspects of the change?
- For the following, have you considered all aspects of the change to the organisations:
  - Tasks.
  - People.
  - Structure.
  - Culture.
  - Goodwill.
  - Information systems.
  - Procurement/buying process.
  - Manufacturing/production process.
  - Distribution process.
  - Marketing process.
  - KPIs and control systems.
  - Reward Systems.
- Have you thought through, which of the above elements have to change and how these may, in turn affect the other elements?

What are the Internal Issues?

- Will you form a multi disciplinary project team, for example: 1 Senior Manager with Purchase – Production – Logistics – Marketing epresentation as well as having the appropriate and similar representation from supplier(s)
- Explore the following:
  - Consider one supply chain, or all of the supply chains?
  - Is the remit agreed and clear?
  - Who is to be involved/consulted?
  - What are the core values of the philosophy?
  - Does this fit with the current company cultures?
  - How will we evaluate suppliers?
  - What resources are needed for this programme?
  - Is a multi functional approach valid?
  - How will effective communications be developed?
  - How will trust be developed?
  - What training is needed for our/suppliers employees?
  - Do we need a "best" supplier award?
  - How will we be consistent in practising the philosophy?

- Format an Action Plan (Written Document).
- Develop a Vision/Mission Statement, ensuring it is:
  - Credible?
  - Challenging?
  - Consistent in all parts?
  - Clear?
  - An integral part of the company cultures?
  - Providing a bridge from the past to the future?
  - Something that all project team members believe in whole-heartedly?
- Quantify Objectives.
- Detail Resources & Responsibilities.
- Implementation Mechanisms.
- Develop a Statement of Principles.
- Agree the start date.
- Project team future.

Get the message across
- Have you determined how to get going?
- How to demonstrate your own belief in the vision?
- How you will use personal contact to communicate the vision?
- Whether to use workshops and conferences?
- How opportunities for two-way communication can be created?
- What communication media will be used to support the messages?
- How can you use everyday meetings to build the vision?
- The use of external public relations.
- How will you seek out and use examples of success?
- Have you thought through the detailed implementation actions to make the change happen, including:
  - Strategies to implement the vision?
  - Short-term plans and budgets to turn strategies into action plans?

Help people through
- How will support be given to those working with you to implement the change?
- Will coaching be provided when it is needed?
- How are key people empowered?
- How will praise and thanks be given when appropriate?

- How will people be helped and assisted after making mistakes and "failing" (which are a natural part of change and of learning)?

Monitor and control the change process
- How will you monitor and control the change process?

Key Issues about Starting Out
- Recognise you are on "A Journey to a Destination" and a process of "Courtship> Engagement > Commitment"
- Ensure internally there is:
  - Understanding.
  - Commitment.
- Recognise that the core concepts are:
  - Suppliers are seen as assets/partners.
  - Internal company processes in "partnership".
  - Long-term & HOT (honest-open-truthful) relationships.
  - Joint views/analysis of TCO (Total Cost of Ownership), TAC (Total Acquisition Cost) and WLC/LCC (Whole Life/Life Cycle Costing).
- Anticipate problems, for example you will need:
  - more time in the early days.
  - management of resources.
  - "will, and all try to succeed".
  - to exchange information.
  - to use open communication.
  - to listen before acting.
  - to receive criticism.
  - to understand people's behaviour.
- Recognise that major barriers are:
  - Trust (Historical mistrust will remain until the "new" trust is formed).
  - Sharing information (Information will be seen as Power).
  - "The most powerful player is seen as wielding the biggest stick".
- Maybe it is better to start out by selecting a supplier/product group that will give an early and visible win/win?

And finally
- Have you thought how you will motivate by giving recognition to those playing a part in the change process?

271

- Are you emotionally prepared to deal with all the unexpected things that will crop up, and all the matters you should have thought of but overlooked?
- And finally, have you:
    - A clear understanding of the change?
    - Evidence to support the need for the change?
    - Assessed the levels of support you are likely to receive from your boss and the top management of the firm?
    - Considered the value of finding a champion for the change from the ranks of top management?
    - Examined ways that you can get key managers on your side through using participation approaches?
    - Understood the dangers that face a specialist unit that is implementing change, but is otherwise isolated from the organisation?
- It is rarely easy changing "the way we have always done things around here", so do not:
    - embark on a programme lightly.
    - abandon it easily.
    - begin unless senior management know what could happen.
    - begin unless senior management supports it fully and openly.
- Ensure that you do:
    - match actions and words.
    - publicise success.
    - anticipate problems.
    - expect eventual success.

Step 4: Doing it
Aim: Operate the new processes and structures

Applying the new methods
- Technical aspects. Does it reduce costs, increase productivity, service and improve quality?
- Human aspects. Remember people resist what they do not understand and people do not like being criticised. So discuss changes with those affected in advance, explain why, and "sell" the change.

Test and Refine
- Check, check and test.
- Recognise limiting and restraining factors.
- Expect unexpected reactions to change.
- Polish the redesign.
- Follow through/review.

Check the customer perception
- How effective have you been?
- How can you tell?
- Ask the customer how you can further improve
- "Walk it through wearing the customers hat".
- Determinants of service are many, like access, aesthetics, attention given, availability, care, cleanliness, comfort, commitment, communication, competence, courtesy, flexibility, friendliness, functionality, integrity, reliability, responsiveness, security.

Continually improve as:
- New customers/products/competitors and rising costs with falling revenues all means change.
- The "big bang" approach is not always needed, and when it is, then, it may be too late!
- Small, continual, incremental approaches work well where there is a culture of continual improvement.

Review the current performance
- Start again "where are we now?"

Finally, the following provides a useful example of many improvements that were made in a global supply chain (table overleaf).

Supply chain operational KPIs	Before	After
Total pipeline lead-time	97 days	62 days
Transportation time	41 days	31 days
Manufacturing lead-time	6 days	3 days
Value Adding time	3 hours	3 hours
Inventory time	50 days	28 days
On-time delivery performance to Singapore warehouse	75%	Warehouse was closed
Number of organisations controlling supply chain operations	7	1
Order processing time within the organisation	Mean was 8 days with range 5-21 days	1.5 days
Demand variability at the factory (i.e. variation around mean weekly demand)	Plus/minus 150%	0%
Annual cost of emergency shipments	£493,000	0
Customer moments of truth		
Average lead-time from OEM placing order to receiving product	22 days	5 days
On-time delivery performance to OEMs	77%	98%
Shipments received by OEMs error free in terms of product quality or paperwork	65%	94%
Delivered cost per 1000 m2	Confidential	Less 15%

Source: An application of value stream management to the improvement of a global supply chain: a case study in the footwear industry by David H Taylor, International Journal of Logistics Research and Applications, Volume 12. Number 1, February 2009.

Bibliography

6th Eyefortransport European 3PL Summit.

7 mistakes with customs entries www.internationaltrade.co.uk.

Arminas, D (2004). "Corporate Social Responsibility - Supply Chain CSR criteria unveiled" in **Supply Management**.

Balle (1997). **The Business Process Re-engineering Toolkit**. Kogan Page.

Bennet, M. (1993). **Development Model of Intercultural Sensitivity**. Yarmouth Intercultural Press.

Birchall. J. (2006). "Corporate Responsibility" in **Financial Times**, February 2006.

Birou, L.M., Fawcett, S.E. (1993). "International purchasing: benefits, requirements, and challenges" in **International Journal of Purchasing and Materials Management**, Spring, pp. 28-37.

Blackburn. A (2004). "Audits ineffective against irresponsible purchasing" in **Supply Management**, July.

Blackburn. A (2004). "CSR Academy is open for business" in **Supply Management**, July.

Boyd. D.E., Spekman, R.E., Kamauff, J.W., and Werhane, P. (2007). **Long Range Planning: CSR in Global Supply Chains: A Procedural Justice Perspective**.

Carroll, A.B. (1991). "The pyramid of Corporate Social responsibilty - towards the moral management of organisational stakeholders" in **Organisations Horizons**, vol 34, pp38-48.

Carroll. A.B (1996). "Defining Corporate Social Responsibility" in **Business and Society Journal**. Blackwell's.

Castka, P., Bamber, C.J., Bamber, D.J. and Sharp, JM. (2004). "TQM and CSR" in **The TQM Magazine**, Volume 16 – Number 3, pp. 216-224. Emerald Group Publishing Ltd.

Chaffin, J. (2009). "WTO sees global increase in world trade" in **Financial Times**, July.

Christopher, quoted in Gilbert, H. (2008). "Straight to the Source" in **Supply Management**, November.

Christopher and Lee. (2004). "Mitigating Supply Chain Risk through Improved Confidence" in **IJ of PD & LM**, Vol 34, No 5, 2004.

CIPS. Exchange UK, Regional Event.

Clarke, E. (2005). "Supply Chain Management: Response Time" in **Supply Management**, September.

Clarke, E. (2007). "Purer Source" in **Supply Management**, January.

Contracting Excellence, IACCM. (October 2008). "East and West Contracting Styles".

Cummack, D. (2008). "Features, A spotless start" in **Supply Management,** October.

Dearing, D. (2004). "Ethical Traders" in **Supply Management,** November.

Ellinor, R. (2009). "Features - Noble deeds" in **Supply Management,** January.

Ellinor, R. (2008). "On the level" in **Supply Management,** November.

Ellinor, R. (2008). "Centralised buying helps Fiat go global" in **Supply Management,** March.

Emmett, S. (2009). **Excellence in Freight Transport**. Cambridge Academic.

Emmett, S. (2005). **The Supply Chain in 90 minutes**. Management Books 2000 Ltd.

Emmett, S. (2007). **Systems Thinking Toolkit**. Management Books 2000 Ltd.

Emmett, S. (2007). **Team Toolkit**. Management Books 2000 Ltd.

Emmett, S. (2007). **Motivation Toolkit**. Management Books 2000 Ltd.

Emmett, S. (2007). **Developing People Toolkit**. Management Books 2000 Ltd.

Emmett, S. (2007). **Learning Toolkit**. Management Books 2000 Ltd.

Emmett, S. (2007). **Communication Toolkit**. Management Books 2000 Ltd.

Emmett, S. (2007). **Customer Service Toolkit**. Management Books 2000 Ltd.

Fagan, M.L. (1991). "A guide to global sourcing" in **The Journal of Organisations Strategy**, March/April, pp.21-6.

Gaffney, P.J. at 91st Annual International Supply Management Conference, May 2006.

Ghobadian, A., Gallear, D. and Hopkins, M. (2007). "TQM and CSR Nexus" in **International Journal of Quality & Reliability Management**, Vol 24, No. 7 2007, pp.704-721.

Gilbert. H .(2006). "Ethical Supply Chains – Sourcing Good CSR" in **Supply Management.**

Gilbert, H. (2008). "Straight to the Source" in **Supply Management**, November.

Gooch, F. (2003). "Socially Responsible International Purchasing: The Why and How" in **Tradecraft Management**, March.

Grant, J. (1997). "Embracing Cultural Differences in the Global Work Place". Organization Development Specialist for Rasmussen & Simonsen International Pte Ltd.

Gray, R. (1996). "No Back-Seat Driving" in **Supply Management**, September.

Grenwood, M. (2005). "The nuts and bolts of CSR" in **Supply Management,** February.

Hemmings, M. (2004). "Closed Loop Supply Chains" in **Supply Management**, February.

Herbig, P. & O'Hara, B.S. (1995). "Broadening horizons: the practice of global relationships in procurement" in **Management Decision**, Vol 33, No 9.

Hurst, R. (2006). "Ethics and the Purchaser" in **Supply Management,** March.

IBM. (2006). Follow the leaders.

IBM. (2006). Building value in logistics outsourcing.

ITT. (2005). "Five things to remember in Supply Chain Organisations" in **International Journal of Logistics Research and Applications**, Volume three, number three.

John, G. (2004). "CSR Roundtable – Beyond the greenwash" in **Supply Management,** July.

Kanter, J. (2008). "Web news - Savings from global sourcing unclear to many organisations" in **Supply Management,** June.

Kanter, J. (2008). "Global Dealings" in **Supply Management,** November.

Kanter, J. (2008). "News, Break cultural barriers, buyers urged" in **Supply Management,** October.

Kauffman, R.G. and Crimi, T.A. (2002). "Building Global Supply Chains: A New Mosaic Comes of Age" at ISM, 87th Annual International Conference Proceedings.

Kohn, L.F. (1993). "Global sourcing: broadening your supply horizons" in **Organisations Forum**, Winter/Spring. Pp.17-19.

Kotabe, M. and Murray, J.Y. (1990). "Process/Product Innovation and International Sourcing" in **Journal of International Organisations Studies**, Vol 21, No 3, pp 383-404.

Lloyd, M. (1994). "How green are my suppliers?" in **Supply Management**, October.

Logistics Organisations. (2003). **Pitfalls of a 3/4PL haul** at www.LLCLaw.Co.uk.

Martin-Castilla, J. I. (2002). "Possible ethical implications in the deployment of EFQM excellence model" in **Journal of Organisations Ethics**, Vol 39 nos 1-2.

McIntosh, A. and Bradley, B. (2006). "Law – Goods Advice" in **Supply Management**, August.

Mehta, S.K. (1994). **Green Supply Chains, Purchasing and Supply Management**.

Meredith-Smith, J. (1993). "A Model for Assessing the Merits of International Purchasing" in **Proceedings of International Symposium on Logistics**, Nottingham, pp 185-190.

Monczka, R.M. and Trent, R.J. (1991). "Global Sourcing: A Development Approach" in **International Journal of Purchasing & Materials Management,** Vol 27, No2.

Mosco, L. (2004). "Lip service won't suffice" in **Supply Management,** September.

Norman, D. (1996). "Window of Opportunity" in **Supply Management**, September.

O'Brien, L. (2000). "Global Sourcing: Reach Out" in **Supply Management,** April.

O'Brien, L. (2005). "Charity case rings an ethical warning" in **Supply Management,** June.

Pettigrew, A. and Jackson, R. (2008). "East Versus West" in **Supply Management**, November.

Price Waterhouse Coopers. (2007). **Procurement Risk report**.

PTRM. (2007). **Global Supply Chain Trends Global Supply Chain Trends 2008-2010**. Price Waterhouse Coopers.

Quintens, L., Pauwels, P. and Matthyssens, P. (2006). "Global Purchasing Strategy; Conceptualisation and Measurement" in **Industrial Marketing Management**, July.

Rajagopal, S. and McDermott, M. (1992). **Internationalisation of the purchasing process: a conceptual view**, at IPSERG Conference.

Riley, H. (2002). "Yes, we have ethical bananas" in **Supply Management**, March.

Ritchie, B. and Brindley, C. (2002). "Reassessing the management of the global supply chain" in **Integrated Manufacturing Systems**, Vol 13, No 2.

Sandilands, J. (1994). "The world is your oyster" in **International Journal of Physical Distribution and Logistics**, Vol 24, No.3, pp. 37-9.

SHD. (December, 2002). Restructuring UK Manufacturing Supply Chains.

SHD. (May, 2004). Datamonitor European Logistics Provider End User Survey.

Snell, P. (2007). "Diageo cures 'audit fatigue" in **Supply Management,** March.

Stone, A. (2007). "Net Closes on Suppliers" in **The Sunday Times**, 6th May.

Strugatch, W. (1992). "Tapping the source" in **World Trade**, January/February, pp.110-13.

Sunday Times, The. (2007). "Organisations That Count", 6th May.

Supply Management. (2000). Lead-times Crunch at B&Q.

Supply Management. (2000).

Supply Management, CSR Section. (2006). Dell considers linking buyers to new standards.

Supply Management. (2007). 20th September.

Supply Management. (2008). Use suppliers' global strategies.

Supply Management. (2008). What next for Low-Cost Country Sourcing?

Supply Management. (2008). Sourcing: global or local?

Taylor D.H. (1993). **International Journal of Logistics Research and Applications**, Volume 12. Number 1, February.

Taylor, I. (2005). "The time for excuses is over" in **Supply Management.**

Treacy, B. (2003). **Contractual issues in International Procurement** at CIPS Regional Members Events, September.

Trompenaars, F. (1993). **Riding the waves of culture**. Nicholas Brearley.

Toyota. **USA & Freight Provider Selection** at www.transportgistics.com.

Truel, C. (2004). "Imports: Duty Calls" in **Supply Management**, October.

van Hoek, R.I. and Mitchell, A.J. (2006). "The Challenge of Internal Misalignment" in **IJLRA**, Vol 9, issue 3, September 2006.

Waddock, S. and Graves, S. (1997). "The corporate social performance -financial performance link" in **Strategic Management Journal**, Vol 18.no 4.

Wallace, M. (July, 2004). "Add Value with 3PL Taking the Medicine" in **SHD**. NYK Logistics.

Wayt, K. (2005). "A World of Difference" in **Supply Management**, June.

Wayt, K. (2005). "International Players" in **Supply Management**, May.

Whitehead, M. (2002). "Corporate Social Responsibility" in **Supply Management,** March.

Wuellenweber, J. (2009). "Untapped potential" in **Supply Management,** October.

Zeng, A.Z. (2003). "Global Sourcing: Process and Design for Efficient Management" in **Supply Chain Management – An International Journal**, Vol8, No.4.

Further information

Institutes

Chartered Institute of Logistics and Transport: www.ciltuk.org.uk.

Chartered Institute of Purchasing and Supply: www.cips.org

Institute of Export: www.export.org.uk

(There are also hundreds of links available from the above sites)

Useful websites

www.berr.gov.uk (this is the former DTI).

www. businesslink.gov.uk.

www.demandsolutions.com.

www. europe.eu.

www. hmrc.gov.uk.

www.sitpro.org.uk.

Index

Lightning Source UK Ltd.
Milton Keynes UK
UKOW04f2353241014

240563UK00001B/7/P